THE ART OF PERSONALITY

THE ART OF PERSONALITY

in

Literature and Psychoanalysis

by

Meg Harris Williams

KARNAC

First published in 2018 by
Karnac Books Ltd

118 Finchley Road, London NW3 5HT

Copyright © 2017 to Meg Harris Williams

The right of Meg Harris Williams to be identified as the author of this work has been asserted in accordance with §§ 77 and 78 of the Copyright Design and Patents Act 1988.

All rights reserved. No part of this publication may be reproduced, stored in a retrieval system, or transmitted, in any form or by any means, electronic, mechanical, photocopying, recording, or otherwise, without the prior written permission of the publisher.

British Library Cataloguing in Publication Data
A C.I.P. for this book is available from the British Library

ISBN 978 1 78220 6194

Edited, designed and produced by The Bourne Studios

Printed in Great Britain

www.karnacbooks.com

CONTENTS

Acknowledgements		vii
About the author		ix
Preface		xi

1   Prometheus and the mythological
consciousness   1

2   Electra complexities across three
dramatists   19

3   Women, gods and witches: Euripides
and the roots of perversity   41

4   Reversing perversion: a musical
resolution to *Wuthering Heights*   65

5   The wound and its transformations:
some stories by Kafka   87

6 The valley and the mountain:
Ibsen's inner landscapes   111

7 Dostoevsky and the education of
a man of faith: *The Brothers
Karamazov*   155

8 The evolution of artistic faith in White's
Riders in the Chariot   187

9 On psychoanalytic autobiography   205

10 The infant and the infinite:
on psychoanalytic faith   223

References   237

Index   247

ACKNOWLEDGEMENTS

Many of the essays in this book were originally presented in the form of talks given to the Psychoanalytic Association of Biella over the past several years, and I would like to warmly thank Selina Marsoni Sella and all the participants of the discussion group.

Versions of some chapters have been previously published in journals or edited volumes and I would like to thank the editors and publishers of the following: "The hieroglyphics of Catherine: Emily Bronte and the musical matrix", in *The Brontes in the World of the Arts*, edited by Sandra Hagan and Juliette Wells (Ashgate, 2008); "The evolution of artistic faith in Patrick White's *Riders in the Chariot* (*Ariel*, 40 [4], 2009; "On psychoanalytic autobiography" (*Psychodynamic Practice*, 18 [4], 2012); "Playing with fire: Prometheus and the mythological consciousness", in *Classical Myth and Psychoanalysis*, edited by Vanda Zajko and Ellen O'Gorman (Oxford University Press, 2013); "The infant and the infinite: on psychoanalytic faith" (*Psychodynamic Practice*, 21 [2], 2015); "The oedipal wound in two stories by Kafka" (*Psychodynamic Practice*, 23 [2], 2017).

ABOUT THE AUTHOR

Meg Harris Williams is a writer and a visual artist. She studied English and Cambridge and Oxford universities. Her writings have been translated into many languages and focus on the relation between psychoanalysis, literature, and aesthetic experience. Her books include *Inspiration in Milton and Keats* (1982), *A Strange Way of Killing: Emily Brontë's* Wuthering Heights (1987), *The Apprehension of Beauty: The Role of Aesthetic Conflict in Development, Art and Violence* (with Donald Meltzer; 1988), *The Chamber of Maiden Thought* (with Margot Waddell; 1991), *Five Tales from Shakespeare* (for children; 1996), *The Vale of Soulmaking: The Post-Kleinian Model of the Mind* (2005), *The Aesthetic Development: The Poetic Spirit of Psychoanalysis* (2010), *Bion's Dream: A Reading of the Autobiographies* (2010), *Hamlet in Analysis: A Trial of Faith* (1997, 2014), and *The Becoming Room: Filming Bion's* A Memoir of the Future (2016). She has also published many articles in psychoanalytic and literary journals.

Meg is a visiting lecturer at the Tavistock Clinic and for AGIP, an Honorary Member of the Psychoanalytic Center of California, and editor of The Harris Meltzer Trust. She teaches and lectures widely in this country and abroad. Websites: www.artlit.info and www.harris-meltzer-trust.org.uk.

PREFACE

In what sense can the shaping of personality be considered an art? Milton wrote that whoever wished to "write well in laudable things ought himself to be a true poem" (Milton, 1958, p. 69). He saw the writer's role or responsibility as that of a teacher in matters both ethical and aesthetic, not by making pronouncements but through example – by aiming to make his own personality a true poem, and so to act as a guide to others in their own personality development. Yet he, and other creative writers, are well aware of the impossibility of perfection, even of perfectly fulfilling one's potential: such an aim can only be a narcissistic delusion, and that is not what is usefully meant by becoming a true poem. Rather, the building of a person, like a poem, happens in stages that have a cumulative aesthetic quality: what is poetic is the exemplification of mental growth itself, just as a play or novel is a container for meanings that have been discovered in the course of its creation, rather than a moral or message.

For this reason the essays in this book concentrate on the aesthetic qualities of the container rather than on the application of psychoanalytic theory. Too great a reliance on theory restricts one's observation of the emotional facts that emerge from the creative work. Nonetheless, inevitably, a psychoanalytic model of mental development supports the significance given to these emotional facts. In the post-Kleinian model, the mind is created by the process of having thoughts, step by step in a logical process of evolution. Gradually, through a succession of minor and major catastrophic changes, in response to some emotional conflict that begins to press on the existing structure of the mind, the personality becomes itself. The first step is to notice and observe the existence of the emotional pressure; the next step is to build a symbol that can contain its attributes and reflect a true or aesthetic picture of its meaning. This is essentially the same model, Platonic in origin, that has evolved and been pursued by poet-philosophers through the ages.

The Aristotelian definition of the tragic hero was of a man who was full of admirable qualities apart from having some particular unfortunate tragic fault that causes his ultimate downfall – generally associated with narcissism or hubris. Another definition or picture of the hero was later given by Keats, who imagined the sense in which we are all heroes, waiting in a dark space that he called the "chamber of maiden thought", then noticing a door standing ajar, which we begin to move towards, impelled perhaps by forces beyond our willpower or desire. Then we are on the threshold of "soul-making". Both Aristotle and Keats are describing what Melanie Klein calls the "epistemophilic instinct", and Bion in his Grid first denominated "Oedipus", to stress the essential moving power of scientific curiosity born from emotional ambivalence – the emotional complexity of LHK (love, hate, and knowledge, held in creative tension).

All creative literature is all about the process of coming to knowledge; and the hero's search for identity is co-extensive with the organic shaping of the play or poem. The representation of a "hero" – a developing mind – rarely belongs to one fictional character but to a wider context; the setting and other aesthetic features are of equal psychological significance. The sense of a complex personality is evoked by the way all the characters interact in context, even though one or two may be the structural focus and we think of them as the hero or heroine. This is most evidently the case in drama, but it applies to other genres as well. The entire spectrum of characters align themselves around the curiosity of the protagonists, mapping out the main developmental conflict. At a certain point which Aristotle called peripateia, and Bion catastrophic change, the mind either seeks refuge in the status quo or claustrum, or it expands to incorporate a new thought – a new vision of the world and itself. The struggle has become symbolised and this process is itself cathartic. For as always in a poetic narrative, we are looking for the deep grammar – the underlying implications of the art-symbol – not simply the overt subject of the narrative (the plot). This entails observing closely the aesthetic structure and characteristics of the narrative, not just recognisable portraits with which we identify most easily. It is the whole art-symbol that represents the inner world, the mind; and unconsciously, we are identifying with the whole.

In the light of this model of working through turbulence, a hero may be defined as a personality that is capable of development. This requires emerging from the narcissistic shell of the moment (for every resting-place can become a restrictive shell) and engaging in catastrophic change. And it is clear from both literature and clinical work that this is something the self is not capable of doing on its own; it is done by internal objects through a container–contained link with the infant or developing self, like that of artist and muse. Hence Bion's stress on links, not just on the qualities of objects. What matters is finding an aesthetic organisation; and the way elements are linked in a work of art mirrors the way that psychic elements are linked in a mind that is attempting to become a true poem.

This book, which includes several essays on the classics, begins with the story of Prometheus and his struggle between creativity and his own omnipotence. Following this is a comparison of the way the three classical dramatists Aeschylus, Sophocles and Euripides, treated the story of Oedipus' sister Electra: a character who in all renditions seems to have more of a pathological Oedipus complex than Oedipus himself. I have previously described how Sophocles' Oedipus trilogy presents an aesthetic picture of the weaning process and of the origins of healthy curiosity, as in Bion's K-link) (Williams, 1994, 2005b). Electra, however, acts out her desire to dispatch the parental usurping couple.

Pursuing the theme of perversity, the next chapter examines two of Euripides' brilliant psychologically intense dramas, *Medea* and *The Bacchae*, in both of which women, while socially inferior, acquire the voice of power and use it as a deadly corrective to the naughty intrusive boys who have political but not psychological dominance. Then the fatalistic perversity which characterises Euripides' investigations is contrasted with Emily Bronte's reformation of the tormented Byronic hero in *Wuthering Heights* – about which I have written in the past (1987), but this essay is concerned specifically with the role of music in achieving an aesthetic resolution to the psychological deadlock.

After this the book explores some stories by Kafka, based on his preoccupation with the existential "wound" of living. Kafka's idiosyncratic self-consciousness highlights how (as is always the case with creative artists) the writer is his own psychoanalyst, and the actual process of writing is his means of self-revelation. The chapter on Ibsen considers the inner landscapes of some of his poetic or symbolic plays, which bring into sharp focus questions about the nature of identity and of truth-seeking, in relation to both the adolescent and the artist. This is followed by Dostoevsky's analysis of three Karamazov "brothers" (parts of the personality) in their educational interweaving of splitting and integration; and then by the modern novelist Patrick White's allegory of riders in a multi-spoked chariot which is both a spiritual and an aesthetic container.

In all these writers the protagonists or parts of the personality are engaged in a quest for understanding of their predicament, sometimes in conscious contact with one another, sometimes simply in unconscious apposition, moving alongside in parallel. There tends to be a focus on the developmental period of adolescence (with echoes of *Hamlet*) and we can frequently glimpse the presence of a prototypal analyst-figure who observes somewhat helplessly the interaction of these various parts of the personality. The narratives have an inevitability characteristic of classical tragedy, in its original meaning of serious drama (not necessarily of disaster); and the goal, whether or not it is achieved, is catastrophic change in the developmental sense.

The book concludes with two general essays summarising themes which have underlain all the works discussed: namely, the nature of artistic faith, and of autobiography. For every author in the process of shaping a fictional narrative is also writing his autobiography – a personal process which nonetheless is sufficiently real to be able to "advise" the reader. It cannot be done without self-analysis; and it cannot be done without the faith in internal objects that enables the author to become a true poem along with the work itself. Not permanently, and not completely, but for the duration of the work, so that – to end with another Aristotelian definition – it might serve as an example for the entertainment and instruction of others.

CHAPTER ONE

Prometheus and the mythological consciousness[1]

This book begins with the story of Prometheus, since of all the Greek myths it is the one whose very subject is the mythmaking or mythological consciousness – the fiery spirit at the roots of man's creativity in art and science, and his struggle with his own omnipotence. Myth of course just means story; and whether or not one can subscribe to the notion of a collective unconscious, the nature of myths as stories about origins is meaningful in the sense of making contact with the roots of our culture, and in a wider more universal sense, with the origins of our nature as human beings and as symbol-creators. According to Susanne Langer (1942), symbol-formation is the "generative idea" of the twentieth century: an idea that informed and linked the different perspectives of aesthetics, psychoanalysis, and philosophy of language.

The role of myth in psychoanalysis

Myths are often seen as adult fairy tales. Myths are "adult" in Langer's view because their theme is tragic, whereas fairy tales

---

1 A version of this chapter was first published as "Playing with fire: the mythological consciousness" in E. O'Gorman & V. Zajko (eds.), *Classical Myth and Psychoanalysis* (Oxford University Press, 2013).

2   THE ART OF PERSONALITY

follow a wish-fulfilment pattern. Yet as Martha Harris has pointed out, fairy tales and other stories are "ways of rephrasing and re-enacting relationships and events in the light of the child's feelings about them", and constitute "a bridge to the acceptance of reality" since they enable things to be seen "from different points of view" (Harris, 2011, p. 80). They enable typical or universal emotional dramas to be observed from a psychic distance. According to the philosopher Ernst Cassirer in his book *Language and Myth*, the nature of myths, like fairy stories, is to capture "forces" or "presences" in a visible shape where they can interact, and make reality "an object for intellectual apprehension" (Cassirer, 1946, p. 8). Language and myth both stem from "the same impulse of symbolic formulation, the same basic mental activity" derived from the self's "encounter with the not-self" which calls forth the "striving for vocal expression" (p. 88). Where logical analysis dissects and connects in an ever-widening web, the mythical consciousness fuses and intensifies in a metaphorical mode, seeing resemblance and identity rather than difference; these forms and forces are "carved out of an undifferentiated whole". Yet such forms have "their own inner lawfulness: do not arise from a caprice of imagination, but move in definite avenues of feeling and creative thought. This intrinsic law is what mythology seeks to establish" (p. 13).

According to the Cassirer–Langer–Wittgenstein tradition, which is the basis for the post-Kleinian aesthetic model in psychoanalysis, the mythological consciousness is what makes thinking possible, and what differentiates man from the other animals. It is the fertile seedbed from which diverse meanings can take shape. As Jung pointed out, myths cannot be invented – they evolve from within a society, and are an aid to the apprehension of reality: just as, according to Donald Meltzer, religions were not invented by adults but arose spontaneously in the minds of children (see below, p. 224). Myths by their very nature have psychological significance, measuring "our forebears' developing capacity to be conscious of themselves", in the words of Roger Money-Kyrle (one of the few Kleinian analysts to pay serious attention to myth); and it was not action, however unpleasant or violent, that disturbed their "peace", but rather this very self-consciousness or growing self-knowledge (Money-Kyrle, 1978, p. 367). According to Money-Kyrle, indeed, myths are at the foundation of concept-building; and that great myth-maker (and myth-denier) Plato himself created not only specific myths but a mythological system of innate ideas "laid up in heaven" which are "the mythical forerunners of Bion's 'Innate Preconceptions'" (p. 418).

Indeed the mythic consciousness sees life as phases, each one a new self with a new name; it is essentially narrative, forming cycles and webs (Langer, 1942, p. 52). It is historical and evolutionary in scope. Langer says all new "generative ideas" have their first shadowy expression in mythological form, and are generally imported into society by poets and artists. This first creates a storm, then the myth settles down into being used, then when its energies are exhausted, gradually paves way for the next idea, which in turn makes its first appearance through a revitalised mythmaking phase of human mentality; although the old myth may become degraded or ossified into dogma and then used to undermine the new one.

There was once a view (espoused by Jung, Abraham, and others) of myth as belonging to the childhood of the race – not in the sense of being invented by children, but as deriving from the time when men were supposedly like children (as in Rousseau's noble savage). Carl Kerenyi wrote of "the primordial child in primordial times" (Jung & Kerenyi, 1951). Karl Abraham (1913) saw myths as "fragments of a people's childlike inner life", containing "the wishes of the childhood of mankind". As an anthropological explanation, this viewpoint has lost favour, since it seems to equate any society that is different from our familiar western civilisation with the "primitive". (The idea of myths or dreams as mere wish-fulfilment has of course also been superseded.) Yet as all these authors agree, the mythic consciousness – like the religious – is an innate feature of human mentality that arises spontaneously in childhood, or at least, in the context of object relations in childhood; and individual development (ontogeny) is seen to follow phylogeny in psychic terms as much as in physical terms. This corresponds with much in Bion's view of mental origins, which he also extends (in his Grid) into the microcosmic mythology of how particular thoughts develop within an individual's mind. Thoughts too have a natural history of their own, and follow a logical development, from beta-elements through sensuous or pictorial form as in myth or dreams, gradually working up to more abstract formulations. Whether poetical or mathematical, these formulations are false and empty if they do not somehow contain their primitive origins and roots inside them. Each step rests logically on the one below it, and is incorporated into the structure of the mind. Moreover these "real" thoughts, however idiosyncratic they may seem, are rarely new, but follow essentially similar patterns of evolution in everybody. The "new idea" is only new *to them*.

Langer also suggests that in any society, myths emerge first in the form of situations, not of animal or human figures alone (as in the Jungian archetypes). Narrative is inherent to myth. This view comes from seeing song-and-dance as the original art forms, parents of all the others – as indeed is well known in the case of ancient Greek drama, which began with a singing and dancing Chorus and gradually acquired speaking actors, first one, then two, then three. The drama of "characters" (parts of the self and of internal objects) emerges from this moving, dancing matrix.

Bion in fact also talks about "the childhood of the race", but it is more that the Child represents the developmental principle, the inner fire that needs to be reignited otherwise the mind becomes a "lumber-room" of ashes (a common metaphor, used by Bion and Jung who both said psychoanalysis should concentrate on stirring the sleeping vitality of the mind – the embers of the mythological consciousness – as in the myth of Prometheus). In the Grid Bion places myths in the same row (C) as dreams. Meltzer disagreed, saying that myths were too infinitely interpretable, whereas dreams were much more condensed and were autonomous, individual symbols with a particular meaning – though not necessarily to be encompassed by a single interpretation (Meltzer & Williams, 1988, p. 229). Presumably Bion was thinking of dreams as personalised myths, like Joseph Campbell (1949). Although he expressed doubts about the usefulness and viability of the Grid itself, he often returned to myths such as those of Palinurus or Oedipus to aid his personal formulations about the journey of knowledge. And as Langer pointed out (1946), the inveterate belief of all mankind in myth should not be excluded from philosophical consideration; the Greek gods are not just colourful characters but "figures of thought"; and the world of gods and heroes echoes (in psychoanalytic terms) that of internal object relations, hence (as Abraham said) is not so different in its psychic mechanisms from that of dreams, given the universality of mental structures.

Cassirer, at the beginning of *Language and Myth*, cites Socrates in the *Phaedrus* saying he couldn't be bothered with the fashionable academic game of interpreting myths about chimaeras, gorgons, Pegasus, and other strange monsters, since he didn't even "know himself": if he didn't know himself, how could he know anything else? Implying however that his own mind was no doubt populated by any number of such monsters, if he should but turn his attention inwards, he continues: "Therefore I think not of them, but of myself – whether I be indeed a creature more complex and monstrous than Typhon, or whether I be a gentler and simpler animal, whose nature contains divine and noble essence" (cited in Cassirer, 1946). Socrates is part teasing, tongue in cheek; it is like

PROMETHEUS AND THE MYTHOLOGICAL CONSCIOUSNESS 5

Plato banishing the artists whilst clothing all his own teachings in the guise of myth and parable. But Socrates' point is the crucial one that mythological figures and narratives are all just a game or diversion unless there is some way they can be understood in terms of advancing self-knowledge.

Freud and Abraham saw myths – and dreams and art – as "symbolic veilings" of repressed infantile sexual fantasies. The philosophical and poetic traditions, however, see symbol-making as an expressive (revelatory) mechanism, not as a secretive one. Is Prometheus' fennel-stalk that bears the gift of fire to mankind hiding a stolen secret, or conveying the vital idea in its symbolic container, from the all-knowing gods to the infant human race? As Coleridge said, an idea can only be conveyed through a symbol. Symbols are containers for a fantasy meaning that cannot be formulated in ordinary verbal discourse, rather than lexical veils intended to disguise a coded meaning.

A myth is a wideflung net; but once the mythical consciousness has found expression in true symbolic form such as theatre or poetry, it loses all vestiges of the "primitive" and becomes extremely sophisticated. To the iconography of archetypes is added the organisational power of composition; as Aristotle declared, plot (*muthos*) is the soul of tragedy: the relational context comes first, the characters crystallise out of it. Meanings become overlayered, rather than variable in their interpretability: they focus in to the depths rather than meander outwards. Indeed the ancient tragedians *were* the mythmakers, rather than vice versa, it has been said (Burian, 1997, p. 184) – and also, perhaps, the first psychoanalysts, just as Freud saw his theory of instinct as a "psychoanalytic myth". And the significance of the theatre space as the World, a playing-space trapped between heaven and earth, was always fully realised, as is impressed on us when we stand in the theatre at Epidaurus and our senses fully breathe in the significance of its setting.

This is where we find Prometheus, the fire-bringer and benefactor of mankind: chained to a cliff somewhere between earth and heaven – the very position adopted by the mediaeval cosmologists to define the essence of humanity in their "chain of being". Prometheus is, as Langer put it, "mankind in a single human figure" – the original man in a way that identifies him with Adam, or Christ the "second Adam", or indeed Satan who (in Milton and the Romantics) is Christ's alter-ego, born of mother Earth yet endowed with immortality. The story is a type of Fall, with Adam-Christ nailed to the Tree of Knowledge; indeed the Romantics, following Goethe, saw Prometheus as the representative of

6   THE ART OF PERSONALITY

humanity's creative powers and of the revolt against social and political constraint. Almost inevitably, psychoanalysts, following Freud, reverse the received ethical ideology and see Prometheus as engaged in a masturbatory or urinatory playing with fire which is secreted in his fennel-stalk penis, in imitation of Zeus' thunderbolt (and the eagle sent to devour his liver, seat of the passions, is interpreted in terms of homo-eroticism). Although Prometheus is not one of Bion's basic myths, it is clear that just as Oedipus gathers together conflicts associated with Bion's K or Klein's epistemophilic instinct, so does Prometheus gather around him conflicts associated with creativity, with the vital spark that motivates and energises the quest for knowledge; and the central conflict is the battle between omnipotence and patience, narcissism and object-dependence.

Prometheus' story is set at a transitional moment for humanity and concerns the dynastic change from Titans to Olympians – from values of power to those of intelligence and order. It is often seen as marking the development from prehistory to history, animal to human, physical to mental powers, and the beginning of the fertile era of multifold myths and stories about the relation between humans, heroes and their gods. Coleridge saw the play as a drama between "law" (Zeus) and "pure reason" (*nous*) (Prometheus), influenced by a cultural switch between the Phoenician and the Hebraic mindsets: between the religions of earth, and religions of the Word (the Logos in the fennel stalk). This is parallel to the dynastic switch from a mythological consciousness to reason and logic. Indeed the story could be said to mark what has been called "the moment of tragedy" itself (Vernant and Vidal-Naquet, 1988): the epitome of the mythmaking consciousness yet also the point at which it is superseded by more discursive modes of philosophy.

Prometheus possesses an evolutionary perspective and his goal is to "establish the right of man to exist and develop" (Vellacott, 1961, p. 9) despite his ignorance, poverty, brief lifespan, etc. According to legend his mother Earth (Gaia) gave him the foresight to see that the values of the future would be founded on mental activity not on physical supremacy:

> Not brute strength
> Not violence but cunning must give victory
> To the rulers of the future. (ll. 210–12)[2]

---

2 Line references to *Prometheus Bound* are to P. Vellacott (ed.), *Aeschylus: Prometheus Bound and Other Plays* (1961).

Prometheus Bound is only one play from a lost trilogy and perhaps the revolution was only partly worked through; indeed it was taken up centuries later by the Romantic poets such as Keats, Shelley and Coleridge who all interested themselves in the complexities of evolution implicit in the ancient tragedians' use of myth. For the Titans are not just brute strength, but also house vital powers that need to be touched and rekindled with each new achievement of mankind, each new idea; thus Prometheus describes his brothers Atlas (holding up the firmament) and Typhon crouching at the roots of the volcano – the place where fire was first found and garnered. Zeus is an offshoot of Prometheus, rather than vice versa: it is as though Prometheus' pride in his own cunning (fire) has given birth to a tyrannical ruler, who nonetheless represents the new dynasty or level of development of the mind. As Bion often puts it: man having once got a mind – which somehow metamorphosed out of his bodily constitution – what on earth is he to do with it?

Mountainous thoughts

The ancient Greeks really invented the dreamplay. Prometheus is bound upon a rock like so many of his later avatars – Milton's Samson, "eyeless in Gaza, at the mill with slaves", Shelley's Prometheus "eyeless in hate", or Shakespeare's Lear who feels he is "bound upon a wheel of fire". His senses and physical powers bound up in this way, the hero is visited by Dreams – characters from his internal world. The Greeks took dreams literally to be visitations from a traveller between worlds. Meanwhile, the protagonist is provided with a Chorus who are generally sympathetic and sensible, and represent the values of the everyday world, yet are powerless to make any changes. They give the hero's struggle a context, and emphasise how he is servant to Necessity and cannot alter his situation in any commonsense way, however well intended.

The play opens therefore with Prometheus being cruelly nailed to the cliff, victim of his own attributes – titanic strength and the fire which Hephaestus uses to temper his metal tools even though it makes him "hate the skill of my own hands". The technology is not matched by mental skills. But like Samson Agonistes or Kent in the stocks his physical imprisonment enforces introspection. Spiked halfway up the rock (the skene at the back of the stage, with the overarching sky), nailed and bound, Prometheus demonstrates with phenomenal visual impact his identification with man

8   THE ART OF PERSONALITY

in what the medievals called the "chain of being" and Hamlet described as "crawling between earth and heaven", infantlike. It is the place where the essence of humanity is located. The "god of mountainous thoughts" is nailed to the mountain, becoming a work of art in himself, but one which is made useless by a tyrannical part of the self, Kratos (Strength or Power):

> KRATOS: You're wrongly named, Prometheus, Wise-before-the-
> event!
> Wisdom is just the thing you want, if you've a mind
> To squirm your way out of this blacksmith's masterpiece!
> (ll. 82–84)

As Prometheus keeps reiterating, he already "knows about" all the various tortures he is doomed to undergo; and despite this he "wills to be wrong". There is a need for a new type of "foresight". Yet the new values – epitomised by the meaning of Prometheus' own name – have yet to be established: what indeed is foreknowledge? Whenever Prometheus utters the phrase "I know" – as he frequently does – he means "I knew but I did not know the meaning." This is a play whose action is entirely verbal, until the final spectacular catastrophe. Indeed we could say Prometheus' ordeal images the shift from "knowing *about*" his fate to fully experiencing or "knowing" it (as in Bion's [1970] distinction). The fixing of Prometheus to the rock figures what Bion calls 'the point of origin of a thought', which is equated with its mythical phase of development, an advance on its somatic or bodily origins. Pain arises when the growing thought becomes "fixed in dream-myth" (Meltzer, 1978, p. 64), and this symbolic fixing of the originating point engenders the thinking process.

Prometheus' initial speechlessness gives the impression not merely of intense agony but also of a preverbal state, helping to establish the sense in which he represents mankind in all its phases, including that of the infant helpless to comprehend its own story through means other than sensory intensity (pain), until modulated via maternal reverie. He is Lear's "poor bare forked animal", naked and prey to hyperstimulation – the frozen sky at night, the heat of the midday sun:

> HEPHAESTOS: Glad you will be to see the night
> Cloaking the day with her dark spangled robe; and glad
> Again when the sun's warmth scatters the frost at dawn.
> Each changing hour will bring successive pain to rack
> Your body; and no man yet born shall set you free. (ll.23–27)

The beautiful lines nonetheless suggest a majestic openness to natural rhythms here, of cold–warm and dark–light, equivalent to the infant's first perceptions of the external world. The "god of mountainous thoughts" is appropriately nailed to the mountain in order to explore his internal contents (protomental thoughts), later imaged in his eagle-ravaged liver – the *splanchna* which, according to Padel (1982, p. 131), referred in ancient Greece to characterological contents not merely bodily entrails. Prometheus with his fire proved himself a "great teacher in every art", but his job is barely started: what is to be done about these poor forked creatures who do not know themselves? Throughout, he reiterates how it is his "duty" to remain on the rock and suffer, renouncing the various temptations to compromise that are offered by his visitors. His job is to demonstrate to men how to convert sensuous hyperstimulation into useful suffering, on the lines of Bion's (1970) distinction between pain and suffering – the latter being pain, or indeed pleasure, that has been symbolically transformed. Like a proto-Christ (as Shelley saw him) his plight suggests a common mythico-religious source in human nature. Like Atlas, the other brother-Titan with whom he specifically identifies, he bridges heaven and earth, taking the strain in his mind rather than on his arms. For the sake of man, he harrows Tartarus. Meaning has to be earned; and this is particularly evident in ancient tragedy where the outcome of the myth is already known in the literal sense, but not in the metaphoric sense of the precise symbolisation of a particular pain.

When Prometheus has been clamped to the rock, so tightly that he can barely see, his other senses are heightened: he feels, smells, and listens:

> PROMETHEUS: Ah! Who is there?
>   What sound, what fragrant air
>   Floats by me – whence, I cannot see? …
>   Ah, I hear it again, close by me!
>   A rustling – is it of birds? …
>   Whatever comes, brings fear. (ll. 114–127)

They are the Oceanids, daughters of Oceanus and therefore his relatives, and they make up the Chorus. They have been brought out of their submarine cave by the sound of ringing steel on rock that shook them out of their "quiet bashfulness" and drew forth their female sympathy. The other side of omnipotence (Zeus) is helplessness; Prometheus is the "miserable sport of every wind", but these winds suggest a soothing sensuous contact that makes it possible

10   THE ART OF PERSONALITY

for him to begin to review and tell his story. The solid, painful perspective of the present moment – chained to the rock – widens both backwards and forwards in time, in an attempt to sketch an evolutionary pattern. "Grief is a wanderer who visits many", and Prometheus who used to be so active is now immobile, forced to listen to his feelings, those wandering "griefs" who are now part of himself. Can these wandering windborne visitors "share the suffering of one whose turn is now" (ll. 274–275)? This passage is later echoed by Milton in "the breath of heaven fresh-blowing, pure and sweet" (*Samson Agonistes*, l. 10) that first awakens Samson – also unable to see – from his mental servitude. As often in Greek tragedy, the Chorus voices humanity's ordinary or normal concern for the sufferer – within the bounds of existing convention. Yet even the fragrant air that bears them is not pure solace; like any new experience, it brings fear.

Prometheus' self-analysis, like Samson's, is conducted by means of his dream-visitors: Oceanus, Io and Hermes. In between each of them, he adjusts and revaluates his own position, chained to the rock of suffering – what it means and what it may lead to in the future. The central and most substantial dream in the play is the chance arrival of Io, the feminine counterpart of Prometheus and fellow victim of tyrannical Zeus. This long and lyrical episode is framed in sharp relief by the two shorter visitations of Oceanus and Hermes, each satirically characterised.

Oceanus is a smooth talker, bluff and blunt, who advises against Prometheus' "proudspeaking". His motto is "know yourself", but by this he means to "take upon yourself new ways to suit the time" – adaptation to circumstance, political savvy. Prometheus easily sees through this and tells Oceanus directly to "save himself" from the wrath of Zeus – he prefers to "drink [his] painful cup to the dregs". As with Hermes later, there is a touch of comedy in Oceanus' bustle and complacent belief in his own powers of guidance, even directing the winged beast who pulls his car through the air "by will, without any bridle". "Your way of speaking plainly sends me home again", says Oceanus, fearful of endangering himself through an alliance with this straight talker. He departs in his airborne carriage, saying that his horse wants to go and "lie down comfortably in his stall at home". Although the Aeschylean vision is always about reconciliation, this does not mean mere political compromise. Oceanus – who represents the false poet or rhetorician – is later satirised by Keats in the same vein in his poem *Hyperion*. No real knowledge or insight can be gained when avoidance of suffering is the main goal.

In reaction to Oceanus, Prometheus formulates clearly the values he is promoting – basically the attempt to provide mankind with mind and reason, to bring contemplation into the sense-based process of living, to give life meaning:

> At first
> Mindless, I gave them mind and reason . . .
> In those days they had eyes, but sight was meaningless;
> Heard sounds, but could not listen; all their length of life
> They passed like shapes in dreams, confused and
>   purposeless … (ll. 443–454)

Prometheus taught the hidden life of sense – the instinctive spiritual colouring of the sights and sounds encountered on the road of life, and by implication language itself as a tool for endowing men with meaning (as Prospero said to Caliban, or Shelley in his own *Prometheus*). This capacity to interpret reality is not so much forethought as thought itself.

> Their every act was without knowledge, till I came …
> Then I distinguished various modes of prophecy,
> And was the first to tell from dreams what Fate ordained
> Should come about; interpreted the hidden sense
> Of voices, sounds, sights met by chance upon the road.
>   (ll. 484–487)

Such knowledge is dangerous: it entails the relaxation of division and hierarchy, a process inherent in mythmaking and creativity; it is associated with Prometheus' feminine identifications (which were ignored by early psychoanalytic readings). All Prometheus' gifts are variants on the use of fire, either literal or metaphorical. What disturbs everyone other than Prometheus himself is the possibility of evolution itself – which, as psychoanalysis is aware, is instinctively resisted by the status quo of the personality. And evolution is not in the hands of the tyrant Zeus but of Necessity: "cunning is feeble beside Necessity" and even Zeus (he reminds the Chorus) "cannot fly from Fate". We begin to understand there is a power, or source of ideas, beyond both Zeus and Prometheus, which could either bring further disaster or guide their potential reconciliation. (In Bion's terminology, cunning is K and Necessity is O.)

After Oceanus comes the maiden Io, midway through her vast migratory wanderings across Europe. She is crowned with cow's horns, testifying to Zeus' sexual tyrannising. Her part is central not so much to the overt plot as to the mental qualities and sympathies

12   THE ART OF PERSONALITY

that are being established. It is often thought a digression: the playwright brings it in rather than paying attention to more standard features of the mythical network, such as the story of Pandora, or Prometheus' own brother Epimetheus (Hindsight). The justification for the long account of Io's wanderings, both past and future, is not to advance the plot but to establish new perspectives. Unlike the other characters she enters on the scene unintentionally, whilst in the midst of her flight from the prophecy that she will be raped by Zeus, and immediately after the Chorus' mention of Prometheus' wife Hesione, as if summoned by memory to be another avatar of the feminine principle. In a sense, maddened, Ophelia-like Io is a dream of Prometheus', a visitation from the inner world. It is often said that Prometheus is an entirely male myth, but this is not so in either Aeschylus' or Shelley's versions, which are both much concerned with marrying the separated male and female principles.

Io's own father Inachus, an obedient follower of Zeus, has cast her out for having adolescent sexual visions about the loss of virginity:

> At night in my own room visions would visit me,
> Repeating in seductive words, "Most blessed maid,
> Why live a virgin for so long? Love waits for you –
> The greatest: Zeus, inflamed with arrows of desire,
> Longs to unite with you in love." (ll. 649–653)

Her annunciation-style dreams advise her to go out to the fields amongst the grazing cattle so that "the eye of Zeus may rest from longing and be satisfied", resulting in her transformation into a cow, under constant surveillance by the hundred eyes of Argus (or his ghost) – Hera's hound and the most persecutory of superegos.

The "hot spasms" of the "gadfly" that goads Io on are another kind of false fire, a type of sexual excitement that appears to madden her so that "words rush out at random" – her cries and words representing ungoverned and shapeless instinct that she needs to outgrow. While she spins erratically around the stage, Prometheus' fixity is accentuated – the still point of her turning world. Io's journey through the world has been seen as a progressive theodicy (Bollack, 2006) – mapping geographically the gradual civilisation of the countries where gods are worshipped. It could equally be seen as a map of Io's growing up, which Prometheus prophesises will eventually take place. Amongst the travels that he indicates is a visit to the man-hating Amazons (like a type of girls' boarding school, a refuge from goading men). His catalogue opens up the horizons of the play, quite literally flooding it with variety

PROMETHEUS AND THE MYTHOLOGICAL CONSCIOUSNESS   13

and potentiality, including even the dangerous areas and tribes that Io is counselled to avoid. Imagining her future story enables him to fore-think further the possible nature of a new kind of Zeus whose ethics are no longer founded on tyranny and violence. This takes the form of reminding Io that once, in the grove of "speaking oaks", Zeus had propositioned her honourably as "destined bride" rather than viewing her as a cow (ll. 832–35). It is as though Io had forgotten this dream of her own: rejected by her father she needs assistance in reinstating this alternative model of manhood. Prometheus then points to her future as a mother and how it is linked to his own eventual freedom: "My child shall set you free from these chains?" wonders Io. This freedom – essentially, for future man to think and be creative – can only occur in the context of a change in the nature of Zeus himself, as pictured in the prophecy:

> PROMETHEUS: And here at last Zeus shall restore your mind, and come
> Upon you, not with terror, with a gentle touch;
> His hand laid on you shall put life into your womb …
> (ll. 847–849)

The "hand" penis rather than the gadfly-goad will result in the "child of a touch, Epaphos" who will eventually become ancestor to the new (ancient) Greeks and be associated with the release of Prometheus. This will be also a release for Zeus, who was otherwise doomed to a self-destructive liaison with a dangerous woman whose offspring would destroy him. The "child of a touch" is the primordial prototype of creativity (as in Jung and Kerenyi).

Only at Io's absolute insistence does Prometheus proceed with hi prophesying. He is afraid the truth will "shatter her heart" but she insists on knowing "the whole truth" for she does not wish to be "comforted with lies" (l. 687). However painful the content of a story, its transformation into narrative gives its own pleasure, and the Chorus too want their share (Freud's two principles enhancing one another rather than merely being in equilibrium). A certain amount of bargaining goes on, punctuating each stage of the story, as when Prometheus offers Io a choice of prophecies: to hear about either the rest of her journey, or about his own deliverer. They are of course the same story, and the Chorus make an active intervention to join the strands together:

> CHORUS: Of these two favours, if you please, grant one to her,
> And one to me, Prometheus; do not grudge the telling.

14   THE ART OF PERSONALITY

> Reveal to Io all her future wandering,
> And tell me who shall set you free. I long to know.
>
> PROMETHEUS : Since you are eager, I will not refuse to tell
> Everything you desire ...
> Write what I tell you in your book of memory. (ll. 784–790)

What is repeatedly emphasised is that the listener must be sufficiently "eager" to hear the story; and also that it must be true. Prometheus says that "simple words" are best, not elaborate rhetoric. He shrinks from causing Io pain, but telling lies is worse than the gadfly – and lies depend on intentionality. Prometheus' intention – like that of the psychoanalyst – is to help Io to bear her suffering as he bears his own, by means of true storytelling, an aid to thinking about emotional experience. By reflection this strengthens his own resolve. This episode therefore makes a contrast with the episodes on either side, which counsel avoidance of suffering and entail the abuse of clear truth-telling language.

The language of Necessity

Prometheus' last visitor is the unpleasant joker Hermes, mouthpiece of Zeus in his existing tyrannical form. His sneering arrogance clashes with Prometheus' "proudspeaking" to bring on the clash or "cataclysm" of the next catastrophic change. It is the dialogue with Hermes that allows it to become clearer that there is a problem about what kind of knowledge is needed for the advancement of knowledge in the sense of creative thought. Repeatedly, from the very beginning, the topic of Prometheus' "secret" has come up – the knowledge that will eventually feature in his release – and always he refuses to name the answer. We wonder, like Hermes, whether he has been guarding his prophetic knowledge in the form of a secret, using the immortal fire in the fennel stalk as ammunition. Yet as has been suggested (Bollack, 2006), this may be an over-literal interpretation of the prophecy: the Chorus make clear that the secret is actually "a holy truth cloaked in mystery" (l. 521) which is different from something he knows himself yet conceals even from his friends. The fact is Prometheus is not yet in possession of the "truth"; he is like a doctor who helps mankind yet cannot cure himself (ll. 475–76). Sometimes he talks as though his release and Zeus' overthrow is inevitable; sometimes that it is impossible – at the same time knowing from the start that in some way or other he and Zeus must eventually make a "pact of friendship" (ll. 191–92). When he

PROMETHEUS AND THE MYTHOLOGICAL CONSCIOUSNESS

says it is "not time" to reveal the secret he is still puzzling over its nature: not over names and events but their meaning – the psychic truth behind the cloak of the myth. As Bollack writes: "This future is still under construction… Prometheus is someone who explores rather than someone who has knowledge" (2006, p. 83). Indeed a fragment of *Prometheus Unbound* indicates that later in the story, a different side of Zeus' nature will appear, for which shooting the tormenting eagle becomes a partial symbol – heralding the unfolding of future meanings. Mankind needs a new pattern of mentality that does not split law and reason from emotion and creativity (as Shelley interpreted the duel between Zeus and Prometheus). In Protagoras' view, Prometheus' gifts were not enough on their own since it was Zeus who held the key to social organisation and living in communities.

But meanwhile, the split between the two generations of gods comes to its cataclysmic head. There is an element of truth in Hermes' diagnosis of Prometheus as a "sour-hearted master-mind". Hermes demands the facts, the official "secret", not "clever riddles" (l. 950). But he, like young Zeus, has a limited notion of truth. He wants to know the name of the one mortal woman (Thetis) whom Zeus must not seduce since this would result in his fall from power, figuring an oedipal revenge-story which would repeat that of Zeus' overthrow of his father Cronos, reiterating the old Titanic values. Hermes has no conception that the "truth" might take some form other than a message of this sort. Zeus and Hermes belong to the new race of young gods ("You and all your crew are young", l. 954); and Prometheus treats Hermes as the child he is: "You banter with me – do you think I am a child?" (l. 985). The message he bears through his own bearing is that Zeus is a little boy playing with his special toys thunder and lightning, a picture of narcissistic omnipotence. Zeus may hurl Prometheus to "black Tartarus" but not, through external fire, quench his inner fire:

> PROMETHEUS: Understand this: I would not change my painful plight,
> On any terms, for your servile humility.
>
> HERMES: Being bondslave to this rock is preferable, no doubt,
> To being the trusted messenger of Father Zeus. (ll. 965–968)

Zeus, he boasts, has never known the word "Alas". But, retorts Prometheus, "Time teaches everything"; Zeus is merely inexperienced. Not knowing the experience of "alas" is nothing to boast about. If men are "creatures of a day", it is all the more necessary

16   THE ART OF PERSONALITY

for their imagination to reach beyond their own day – backwards (into the mythical consciousness) and forwards (into abstract thought). The word "alas" brings the consciousness of time and history and the tolerance of suffering, and ultimately leads to a type of immortality or redemption for the race of man. As Keats said, when incubating his own poem about evolution, *Hyperion*, there really is a "grand march of intellect".

Although Prometheus says he will not plead "like a woman" in the sense of the kind of womanliness approved by the hierarchy (l. 202), his confined condition ("bondslave to a rock") and the female company he prefers figure a strong feminine identification; this was reinforced via Io and led to the reaction and confrontation with the little-boy tyrannical parts represented by Zeus. At the very end of the play, as the cataclysm advances, he reasserts the reliance on his earth-mother whose prophetic advice had originally set him on his idiosyncratic quest for knowledge: "O earth, my holy mother ... You see how I am wronged!" (ll. 1090–1093). The final cataclysm, in which Prometheus is swallowed back into the earth, may be seen as a metaphor for what Bion (1970) has called "catastrophic change" – the way each new phase of knowledge is absorbed by the personality, becoming the basis for the next phase. Zeus too is heading for "a flame hotter than lightning-strokes". Founded in psychic prehistory on the newborn infant's fear of falling, it constitutes the rhythm of thinking – the way preconception becomes thought, myth becomes *muthos* (Burian, 1997) in a continual process of dissolving to recreate. It is the end of one play or phase and preparation for the next; indeed the next play opens with Prometheus reconstituted on his rock. Prometheus' own psychic journey has barely commenced; but meanwhile, in addition to encouraging Io, he has educated the Chorus by example: inspiring not only sympathy but ultimately courage in the women who ultimately acquire the courage to stick with him rather than preserve their own comfort. "If you want to persuade me, use a different tone / And give other advice", they tell Hermes; they are offended by his unpoetic language that does not correspond to what they have now begun to understand about Necessity – a force to which both the old and the new gods are subject.

Necessity will shape evolving mankind, but it will be based on a proper acknowledgement of the Titanic mythological consciousness and its place in a more grownup Olympian theodicy. Creativity is the life-force, a law beyond any temporary formulation; it is mysterious but not secretive. In any situation of conflict it is the "evolving O" (Bion) that shapes evolution according to its own internal logic, and every new thought is experienced as foreign or monstrous, just like the wondrous fire prophesied by Prometheus (l. 121). It is a characteristic of the mythological consciousness, according to Cassirer, to think in phases; and "every phase of a man's life is a new self" (1946, p. 51).

The early psychoanalysts did not consider the mythological consciousness in terms of "presentational forms" (Langer) that could hold meaning later to become verbalised. Yet Abraham viewed the child's dream or fantasy world in parallel with the "infantile psychic life of the race", and in a sense the drama between these two modes (whether cultural or individual) is the theme of the ancient play. Edith Hall (1997a) has argued that the thinking in Greek tragedy is more sophisticated than the society that generated it. A modern psychoanalytic view would say that in fact the child enters the world with an embryonic philosophical predisposition in the form of the object relations in his fantasy world which later find other symbolic forms in language and argument. Aeschylus, we may guess, aimed to find a way of integrating these two mental modes in order to convey an evolutionary thinking process in which Zeus acknowledges he is a descendant of the Titans, just as in the *Oresteia* the Furies are given a home beneath the Areopagus of Athens.

Prometheus' "binding" was ultimately commemorated in the garlands that bound the forehead of victors in all contests, transforming his crown of nails (Sommerstein, 2010, p. 226). In poetry and intellectual pursuits, it becomes the binding power of thought. Using Aeschylus as inspiration, Shelley in his *Defence of Poetry* redefined Foresight as Poetry, that can see the shadow of the future cast before, and making use of myth and metaphor, can symbolise ideas that mankind will only be able to formulate discursively or put into action centuries later. Prometheus may be seen as a type not only of prophet and poet but also of the psychoanalyst who – as Bion says – is always in the process of "becoming a psychoanalyst", just as man himself is always evolving through thinking about himself. What the ancient Greeks saw as the language of Necessity, psychoanalysts following Bion (himself following the Romantic poets) would call the "language of achievement". The sons-of-Aeschylus suggest the fire of salvation does not depend on Prometheus (or any other "seldom-appearing Socrates" as Keats put it) but on the Promethean within each individual; the man is not yet born who can save mankind.

CHAPTER TWO

Electra complexities across three dramatists

Although Freud was probably wrong in naming the Oedipus complex after Sophocles' version of the myth,[1] Jung was probably right in finding it instead in somewhat pathological form in the female wing of the Orestes story, which he denominated the Electra complex. It is interesting to survey its treatment by the three great ancient dramatists Aeschylus, Sophocles and Euripides; interesting also that this segment of the family drama of the house of Atreus is the only theme that they all treated in their extant works; beginning with the brother–sister recognition scene and ending in the murder of the parents. This may be a coincidence of survival, or it may have something to do with the sense that the three Electra plays are organically linked, and certainly (as many scholars have shown) the later ones engage with and comment on the first version, that of Aeschylus in *Choephori (The Libation Bearers)*. It is not known whether that of Sophocles or Euripides was performed first; in the case of each dramatist they were all plays of maturity; and they were all anti-war, even those who fought for democratic Athens at the "moment of tragedy" (Vernant), the brief century of fluidity between myth and rhetorical debate. It therefore

---

1   I have discussed this in "A man of achievement: Sophocles' *Oedipus* plays" (*British Journal of Psychotherapy*, 1994) and in *The Vale of Soulmaking* (Karnac, 2005).

20 THE ART OF PERSONALITY

makes some sense to consider the three versions of the story as part of a wider pursuit.

In approaching the plays from a modern perspective it is worth bearing in mind three points: firstly, as Edith Hall has written, Greek tragedy "does its thinking in a form which is vastly more politically advanced than the society which produced Greek tragedy" (1997a, p. 125) – and we can say the same of its psychological advancement; the dramatists were working out ethics as well as politics. Secondly, as Bion points out, poets of the past can "penetrate states of mind which did not then exist – ours" (1987, p. 232). Thirdly, according to Money-Kyrle, the fantasy of the parental intercourse is at the root of concept-formation, and patients seem to come up with almost every variety *except the right one* (1978, p. 417): in other words, the capacity to think logically is impaired by misconceptions derived from the colouring of this fantasy. And the house of Pelops (father of Atreus and Thyestes), who came to grief after a tricksy chariot race, is the original modern "accidental family" as Dostoevsky would put it.

The name Electra is considered to be synonymous with A-lectra, meaning woman without a marriage bed – in effect a virgin, but not quite the same; it stresses not the untouched purity of marital expectancy (as in the characterisation of Iphigeneia) but the sense of something lacking in her identity or sense of self. She has no possibilities of action without the presence of her brother Orestes, no useful role in life. Electra is not listed as a daughter of Agamemnon in Homer; but from Aeschylus on, her parent-killing alliance with Orestes seems a fundamental part of the psychological investigation. Orestes is held up as a model to both Telemachus and Hamlet, but neither of these youthful "far-thinkers" chooses to follow it; the name Telemachus means "far-fighter" and is associated with both Odysseus' skill as an archer and his thinking powers – an alternative mode of fighting; Hamlet seeks "thoughts beyond the reaches of our souls"; both define their identity in relation to their internal father-image and his thinking-sexuality. Instead of following Orestes' Apollonian example however they each seek for other internal-deity guidance, with varied success. Indeed Apollo with his provocative Delphic oracle gets an increasingly bad name as the ancient plays unravel, though it becomes a formal denunciation only in Euripides; the same applies to wartime *kleos* (glory) and its attendant notion of Achillean heroism, and to the Hermetic mode of guile or cunning used in crossing boundaries between different worlds, such as those of life and death, past and present, male and female, conscious and unconscious, outside and inside, men and gods. The wily Odysseus who specialised in such crossings was saved from psychosis by his wife and son – but not everyone is so lucky, as Agamemnon discovered. Another mode of communication is needed, another form of *nostos* (homecoming) from a situation of war.

Everyone is aware that "blood for blood" is not a good enough law of conduct in either family or state relations. Aeschylus in *The Oresteian Trilogy* makes clear that his vision of an ethical advance is achieved through the establishment of clear paternalism and the rule of law, whilst allowing the other fifty per cent of the votes (those in favour of the female Furies) a voice that may be heard in its chthonian cave beneath the court, even if it is not obeyed. Sophocles, it is said, presents a balanced view of both sides of the argument; though in my view there is a Brechtian horror in the curt military denouement of the parable, such that we almost wish the Furies could somehow enter Orestes' pragmatic mind as they do in both the other dramatists. Euripides' version is characteristically the most undermining of established beliefs and systems, and the murdering duo are put back in contact with their feelings of despair; yet he is in effect building on the poetic implications displayed by Aeschylus (and possibly Sophocles as well). It is not so much an answer to the older dramatist as a continuation of his unconscious poetic thought, minus the overarching divine schema of justice that the trilogy discursively or consciously proclaims.

In all the dramatists the view is given of a manlike, dominant Clytemnestra and a womanish Aegisthus, consort rather than king in his own right. Agamemnon, commander of all the Greeks, has been entangled in a Hermetic net, a caricature of a female container full of dagger-holes. The person who emerges as king after this violent female-led consummation is Aegisthus. Although Aegisthus is sometimes presented as a decadent foreigner, Clytemnestra's two husbands are in fact cousins, sons of the quarrelling brothers Atreus and Thyestes respectively. It is impossible not to read the story through the hindsight of *Hamlet* where the "uncle-father" echoes this conversion of a heroic warrior (with clean heroic values) into a soft sensual "adulterer", resulting in a mixed-up view of the marriage-bed of the king and queen, and confusion of identity in the adolescent children who are not sure what ethical system the house operates under – a domestic or a warlike one. However in none of the plays can we forget the sacrifice of Iphigeneia, recounted by Aeschylus in graphic (almost pornographic) terms of a gang-rape by bored soldiers on the seashore, and excused by Agamemnon in terms of the claim that he was prepared to sacrifice

22   THE ART OF PERSONALITY

his own feelings as an individual for the benefit of the army as a whole. (Everyone would be aware of the contrast with the story of Odysseus who refused to drive his plough over his baby son Telemachus on the beach.) Even if we consider this, in modern terms, as a dream or fantasy, and even if Iphigeneia is really just an aspect of Agamemnon himself, the violence is clearly a pollution of the idea of manhood which Agamemnon needs to erase or split from his family life, as represented by the sacrificial bath and stabbing at his own hearth on his return from Troy.

Aeschylus' Choephori

In *Choephori (Libation Bearers)*, the second play in the *Oresteia* trilogy, the revenge action is heralded by Clytemnestra's dream of the serpent coming to suck at her breast. We do not hear the dream's content until later: just the fact that the "dream-prophet of the house" has caused a shriek of terror from its heart – the female body (1. 33).[2] However it is associated with the idea of the man's return, as if from the underworld, so Electra has been sent to pour libations into the depths of the earth to appease his spirit. Later Clytemnestra realises it is Orestes rather than the ghost of Agamemnon that is the serpent, but as in *Hamlet*, the vengeful ghost is a type of projection of the son's, with his bid for "lordship of the house" and ownership of his "possessions". Electra is stirred up by the Chorus of (Trojan?) slave-women whom she deferentially requests to "instruct her inexperience" and to "prescribe" her conduct, saying she is a "slave" herself (1. 118). The emotional interaction seems to bring to the surface the famous signs of recognition – Orestes' lock of hair and footprint – followed by the emergence of Orestes himself and his companion Pylades. Hands, feet and hair were considered peculiarly individual indications of a whole person; it is as though Electra's male counterpart has materialised from the earth. The fact that there are two of him (in the form of Pylades, in all the plays a constant companion) is slightly sinister, especially as later it is Pylades who, in his only speech, orders Orestes to kill his mother, while Orestes is vacillating. The two figures represent two sides of Orestes; and one of them admits he is merely following the oracle – the old revenge-law – rather than his own feelings: "such were the oracles and ... even if I lack belief, the deed must be done" since that comfort-obsessed "pair of women" (Clytemnestra and Aegisthus)

---

2   Line references are to H. Lloyd-Jones (ed.), *The Libation Bearers by Aeschylus* (Prentice-Hall, 1970).

cannot be allowed to rule a household (1. 304). (In *Hamlet* too there is criticism of "th'imposthume of too much wealth and peace" [IV. iv. 27], a self-indulgent Oblomovian sexuality.)

Following on the recognition scene is the conjuration scene, in which the Chorus (who play an unusually active role) – in their *kommos* with dancing and head-beating stir a state of sanctimonious excitement in Orestes: "the thud of this double scourge strikes home – our cause has champions already below the earth – it is for you, children, to act!" (1. 379). They want to be granted the "piercing cry of triumph" after the murders of the king and queen. Orestes hesitates "which way to turn"; Electra herself is in "two minds" and again asks the Chorus how to "find the target", claiming she was shut in her chamber "like a savage dog" when Agamemnon returned home: "hear this and write it in your mind, father!" she cries (1. 450) – like Hamlet and the Ghost ("meet it is I set it down / That one may smile and smile and be a villain" [I. v. 97]). The primitive conjuration-dance is intended to bring up Agamemnon's ghost from the grave – "come to the light and hear us!" The children (eagle "nestlings") are compared to corks holding up a net, "reaching up from the deep" – from the earth, the sea, the unconscious – in a metaphor recalling Clytemnestra's net, so with similar implications of orgiastic sexual activity – "to act".

Their "Arian dirge" is the emotional core of the play (1. 423), translating fantasy into action in a way equivalent to Euripides' Bacchae. After this Electra leaves the scene and for the rest of the play Clytemnestra is the prime protagonist opposite Orestes. It is not only because of the limited number of speaking actors (Aeschylus had only two), but because Electra's soul has in a sense migrated into Orestes, imbuing him with Agamemnon-like revenge not really part of his nature, and she herself has been set up to a significant degree by the Chorus, the multiple voice of slaves whose motivation in troublemaking is never questioned but definitely seems to belong to a fight-flight basic assumption organisation. Why should they be loyal to Agamemnon who brought them from Troy as captives, thereby casting them outside family structures, deprived of their own men? It is no wonder they are critical of "shameless passions" that overrule the female parts of "beasts and men".

When Clytemnestra takes the stage she appears in two aspects, representative of femininity – the shamelessly passionate queen and the lowborn, earthy nurse who fed Orestes as a baby. It is sometimes said that the vitality of the characterisation of the nurse, Cilissa, acts as a foil to the queen, showing up her hypocrisy by contrast with Orestes' "real" mother. (Part of the justification for

24   THE ART OF PERSONALITY

killing Clytemnestra is that she isn't the real mother – as Electra claims in Sophocles' version also.) However it also has the effect of opening our eyes to another aspect of womanhood within Clytemnestra, that she projects into the figure of Cilissa, who in effect represents Clytemnestra-as-nurse – a feature that her regality does not allow her to display in her own person (as indeed remained the case in upper-class families everywhere for the next 2000 years). "To guess at these needs I had to be a prophet, and often I know my prophecy proved false", says Cilissa: that is, as "washerwoman and nurse combined" (l. 760), she had to interpret the baby's distress, whether as feeding- or toilet-breast (in Meltzer's [1970] term). Yet Clytemnestra also reminds Orestes of the times he was fed at her own breast, that is, when she was Cilissa (l. 897). This linkage across the societal split between the upper and lower-class women is borne out by Clytemnestra's dream of the serpent-baby that draws blood as well as milk, and her attempt to "cut away distress" by pouring libations into the earth and lower world, sating the chthonic lust for blood, milk and honey – passions which have to be appeased in order to remain contained.

The dream is a kind of prophecy, reminding Clytemnestra of her son's infancy. Orestes however takes it in literal, concrete terms as another command of Fate or Necessity: "so must she die by violence, and it is I that turn into a snake and slay her as this dream announces". The Chorus of course second his interpretation – "I choose your reading" – they want to see some action (l. 551). But it is only an interpretation. Loxias (Apollo) is brought in again, which as always, reminds us of his doublespeak. His prophecies like those received by Cilissa on the baby's behalf can only be "guessed at". Moreover as Hugh Lloyd-Jones points out (1970, p. 54), their prayers "appeal to the deity's self-interest" – that is to a self-indulgent or tyrannical internal object. We become increasingly dubious about the cleansing nature of Orestes' attack on his mother. It is not like Odysseus' *nostos* – a self-revelation – but rather a reversal of it, the enactment of a confusion.

Clytemnestra herself appears sincere in her cry of woe when told of Orestes' death: she had hoped he was "well bestowed out of the way" of the family "mire of ruin" (l. 697), that is, mentally secure. But Orestes has orphaned himself, and is compared to an "orphaned colt harnessed in the chariot of calamity" (a metaphor taken up by the other dramatists), his own wits driving him off-course (l. 1022). The Chorus still egg him on by insisting he is only his father's child not his mother's: "utter your father's name, your father's, and accomplish an act of horror none can blame". Inside the house (intrusive penetration of mother's body) he is to "work bloody ruin". His lingering indecision comes to a head after the attack on Aegisthus, when he asks Pylades (his rigid counterpart) what to do and is told to get on with it. Aegisthus describes himself as having "a mind whose eyes are open" – and in all three dramatists he gives the impression of a comfort-loving, easygoing, liberal type, openminded but not in the sense of any great psychological acuity, which is his downfall (he never appears with guards, but always alone, for which a variety of excuses are given). Clytemnestra calls him "dearest one" which immediately inflames Orestes, who declares he will kill her "by his side, for in life you preferred him to my father" (l. 905) – that is, to the imaginary father he never had, Agamemnon, warrior king, top dog of the Greeks. To prove the justice of his case he brings out the old "hunting net" cloak that was said to have trapped Agamemnon in feminine wiles before the weapon was plunged in, filling it with holes. It is his vision of a destroyed mother, via a destroyed father. It is hardly surprising that we are not convinced when the Chorus sing that now the curse on the house is lifted; at the same time, calling on the "web that slew my father", which has become his concept-guiding metaphor, Orestes remembers that he is in a chariot going off-course, "losing the battle" against insanity as the invisible Furies materialise around him forming a reciprocal net of revenge.

Sophocles' Electra

In Sophocles the Platonic chariot metaphor of rising madness is continued, but its results are more visually evident in Electra who appears on stage unkempt and undignified, whereas Orestes is cool and businesslike, his madness well under control, that is, split off – even to the extent of conjuring up (via the mouth of the Pedagogue) a magnificent piece of lying rhetoric describing his own death in a chariot race. He is above superstition; he doesn't care about the implications of this "crafty tale", since as he pragmatically points out, "what harm does it do me to say I'm dead?" (ll. 58-59).[3] It is a "trick" he has often seen used by "clever philosophers". Now, come of age at last, he enjoys the opportunity given him by Apollo to proceed to shed blood "by lone deceit and stealthy craft"; and the idea of his own "charred remains" being carried around in an urn

---

3   Line references are to D. Raeburn (ed.), *Sophocles: Electra and Other Plays* (Penguin, 2008).

26   THE ART OF PERSONALITY

in his own hands satisfies a quirky sense of humour – a toy chariot race of his own devising.

The play begins with Orestes, Pylades and their teacher-slave (known as Old Slave or Pedagogue), surveying the plain of Argos from the viewpoint of the palace of Mycenae. It is a "crossroads" not just scenically but in terms of Orestes' life – he has come to claim his own, "rich in gold, rich in blood" as the Pedagogue's motto nicely encapsulates it. The Pedagogue may be a good poet in terms of the manipulation of words, but the substance of what he has taught Orestes is not poetic: "Get your talking done", he instructs Orestes and Pylades, "This is the final crossroads. The time for flinching [thinking?] is past. To action now!" With this trio, masculine common sense rules, and will be contrasted with frantic feminine interference in the form of Electra who nonetheless has to be given her say as she is essential to the plot. Her eery wailing cry *"Io moi moi!"* issues from within the palace and penetrates their businesslike machinations. They cannot listen to her lament at that time, being occupied with Apollo's instructions to pour libations; the audience however have to.

Without Orestes, Electra is convinced that in herself she has no family, though the Chorus try to convince her that "others are in your house" – she has sisters, and she is not the first to experience bereavement. Her "strength is ebbing" and almost, her sense of identity, "wasting to nothing without any children, without husband" (ll. 186–187). Orestes is the only family who counts, the husband-substitute. Yet for him she is just a stepping-stone towards his takeover; he comes not to please her but to please himself. Electra lives in the past, in her own lamentations, vividly kept alive by self-scourging like her cut hair. The Chorus empathise with her fantasy of a "night of horror", a "monstrous union" caused by lust in which, in identification with her father, she imagines the "two hands looming near" (l. 207). Mixing up all the family metaphors of birth, rape, and sacrifice, her mother's hands are felt to have captured her in a deadly net, and her cries of "blood for blood" (l. 247) are stifled, ineffective. Her mother, she complains, has made the day of "trapping" Agamemnon and marrying Aegisthus, that "polluting criminal" (as in Hamlet's view of a marriage-funeral) a celebration. This murder-marriage is an "obscene feast" held in her father's name. The father that exists is a no-father – the real father is absent, just as Orestes her own husband-baby is absent. The equivalence of Agamemnon–Aegisthus is suggested in her description of one superimposed on the other: Aegisthus "sitting on my father's throne, wearing the same royal robes", and her supposed "witness" to the parental intercourse – the "crowning outrage" of "my father's murderer sharing my father's bed with that brazen mother of mine" (l. 271).

The Chorus, while empathic, try to point out in a "motherly" way that her "sullen soul keeps breeding wars which cannot be won"; but Electra feeds on her own sense of grievance. She is a model of sulky teenage rebellion of the oratorical type, ranging from lyrical whining to logical litigation, as given full play in the interviews with Clytemnestra and Chrysothemis. She taunts her sister with being her mother's not her father's daughter (in Aeschylus, the Chorus incite Orestes in similar vein), though the Chorus insist "she's Agamemnon's daughter as much as your mother's" (l. 325); and she is also sensitive to status. Chrysothemis contrasts with her acceptance of realities; she accepts the abstract "right" of Electra's case but her definition of "freedom" is to obey human necessity: "if I want to be free, our lords and masters must be obeyed" (l. 340); and later points out that "You can be right and do a lot of harm" (l. 1042). For Chrysothemis self-respect (freedom) is measured in terms of "having a care for the life that you have"; for Electra her life is "not much but enough for me" provided she can "annoy *them*" (the rulers), as in this way she proves her respect for the dead (a strangely negative argument, suggesting "the dead" are a fantasy of her own, and indeed she adds "if the dead can enjoy respect"). Her sense of identity is founded primarily on aggravating the parents; "The only sustenance I need is a clear conscience" (l. 362). This brings forth a message from Chrysothemis purporting to come from the parents: that their plan is to immure Electra in a cave, buried alive to "chant her miseries there". It is a returned projection, like a dream, of Electra's own self-burial; later she admits she wants to immure herself, ready to "forgo the joy of sunlight" if only she could convict the two "Furies" (Clytemnestra and Aegisthus) and "be true to her noble father".

In this the dialogue between the sisters echoes that between the romantic but fanatical Antigone and the empathic Ismene in Sophocles' *Antigone*; but Electra exhibits from the beginning a fixed masochistic identification with the claustral world of the dead and non-existent. She doesn't have Antigone's justification of an unburied brother, despite her attempt to maintain that Agamemnon had not been buried – we know he had. Chrysothemis, hoping to cheer Electra, then tells her their mother's frightening dream. Instead of Aeschylus' serpent, Sophocles' Clytemnestra dreams of a sort of phallic resurrection of Agamemnon – the kind of husband she hated – in the form of his staff (currently wielded by Aegisthus) being planted on the palace hearth and growing to overshadow

28   THE ART OF PERSONALITY

the whole of Mycenae. That is, she dreams of the pliable Aegisthus turning back into Agamemnon, as will happen in the return of Orestes who is in a sense his father's long lost ghost. Electra promises that if Chrysothemis switches around the grave offerings, not carrying out Clytemnestra's instructions, then Agamemnon will "come himself from the world below" and be their champion; indeed, she believes, "*he* was minded to send her this ugly dream" (ll. 459–460). It is in effect his ugly mind in the shape of Orestes that she is conjuring into consciousness. And the Chorus in their next song bring back the metaphor of Pelops' fateful chariot race, recalling the conjuration scene in *Choephori* in which the powers of Nemesis are awoken by the "soul's deep eye" and set in unstoppable motion like the chariot of Pelops that was cursed by his charioteer, initiating the house's troubles.

Clytemnestra then enters, like the traditional stepmother, brusque and efficient, and immediately challenges Electra's moping and railing with "Out and about again and off the leash!' (l. 516): adding, "If I curse you it's due to the taunts you're always hurling at me." The style of the *agon* (debate) is very different in tone from that with Chrysothemis, but we begin to see where Electra gets it from – she is her mother's daughter. All right, says Clytemnestra, I did kill your father but he deserved it for his barbaric crime – "he sacrificed your sister to the gods". She speaks for Iphigeneia who "would say the same if she could speak for herself". Electra, as if observing proprieties, asks permission to "straighten the record" in defence of both her father and sister, and Clytemnestra answers in the same mode: "I wish you always began in a tone like that – you'd be a pleasure to listen to." It is a rhetorical mode of sizing up the opponent and soon they are head to head like unfeminine combatants in the Assembly, "speaking their minds". Electra however wins the skirmish by using the time-honoured accusation that she gets all her bad deportment, argumentativeness and combative language from her mother: "Shameful ways are learned by shameful example ... If such behaviour reflects my nature,/ The world can say, 'she takes after her mother'!" (l. 609).

Clytemnestra, enraged and unsettled, demands to conclude her case in the form of a prayer to Apollo; interestingly Electra is allowed to listen to it, and keeps her promise not to interrupt: "Sacrifice away! I shan't interrupt – my lips are locked." It shows a different side to Clytemnestra – uncertain of her "doubtful dreams" and her own status as mother, rocked by children's hostility. This prayer is usually considered blasphemous, as Clytemnestra is in effect asking to keep her role as "governor of Atreus' sons and all this realm" along with the comfortable life acquired by disposing of Agamemnon and fulfilling her own masculine nature. Is it so unreasonable to ask to live "in prosperous joy with friends I love and those children who bear no malice"? But we know whose side Apollo is on.

Her prayer immediately conjures her new enemies into her presence (Apollo's answer, as has been said). The Old Slave / Pedagogue enters with his news of Orestes' death, and in his highly polished and dramatic messenger speech details the chariot race that caused his apparent demise. Apollo as god of poetry had a hand in it, as it is clearly not constructed by any Old Slave. It far outdoes anything the uneducated Electra is capable of producing; her eloquence is confined as Clytemnestra says to "spiteful chatterings", however effectively they may hit the familiar mark of her mother. "I've never known a man with such an amazing run of success" says the covert orator of his protégé Orestes. The story of the race undertaken by "Orestes of Argos, son of Agamemnon, supreme commander of Greece" makes the race immortal in a way that only poetry can do, leaving the impression that, though supposedly tipped over the wheel-axle into death, Orestes is still running, his story is not yet finished. It is his own heroic Trojan war; the mangled body at the end reflects that of Agamemnon, linking father and son; yet somehow the heroic glamour does not correspond to the cool pragmatic Orestes whom we have already met. But then it doesn't correspond to an Agamemnon who has turned into Aegisthus, either. Heroic glamour and real life are different psychic worlds.

Clytemnestra, in her softened mood after both praying and listening (as distinct from when she was battling with Electra), "looks distressed", according to the Pedagogue. And surely there is sincerity – not mere hypocrisy – in her reaction, as we saw also in Aeschylus' version when she tries to reconcile her mixed emotions of sadness and gladness – is this "happy news or sad"?

> CLYTEMNESTRA: Motherhood is a strange thing. No wrong
> Can make you hate the child you've borne. (ll. 770-771)

Unlike her Aeschylean counterpart, she did not send Orestes away for his own safety; rather he "tore himself form my nurturing breast for exile/ In a foreign land". She is aware that her own life has lain in the balance; not unnaturally, she wants to save it: "Now I am free from fear". This however is not the same as "gloating" as Electra accuses in her reaction; but as soon as Electra's voice re-enters, Clytemnestra reverts to her coarse, hardened persona,

30   THE ART OF PERSONALITY

and insists Electra be left outside "to moan away for herself and her poor lost brother". "There's maternal grief for you!" says Electra sarcastically, unaware of her own influence on her mother's reaction. Again she is "quite alone" (despite the continuous presence of the Chorus who are unequivocally her supporters), a "slave" again, never to set foot in "that hateful house" but determined to "sink to the ground and wither away my days unloved" (ll. 819-120).

Electra's reaction to the Pedagogue's news is: "Orestes dead – this is the death of *me!*" In a kind of tomboy substitute existence she puts all her life into her absent male counterpart. (Doubleness seems a structural necessity in murdering the parental figures.) Yet no blame is attached to the trick the three strangers now callously play on her when they hand her the urn supposedly containing her brother's ashes, which is closely identified with the lost father or his lost heroic image:

> ELECTRA: It's true, it must be him –
> This tiny urn in front of my eyes! (ll. 1115–1116).

By contrast with Aeschylus (and with the recognition drama in Sophocles' *Oedipus Tyrannus*), a recognition scene is not necessary for the plot since Orestes and co are well aware of Electra's identity; they are indeed in front of her eyes. (There is a lot in the play about the evidence of one's eyes, and its subjectivity.) In fact the long lamenting road to Electra's recognition of Orestes has the dramatic function of analysing her emotional disturbance, her inner world of objects. She tries first to convert Chrysothemis into the necessary fellow-murderer, saying they could gain male *kleos* or glory. Already she has poured scorn on her sister's way of seeing: Chrysothemis, returning from the grave where she came across the traditional lock of hair, has had "visible proof" of Orestes' presence, and in her eyes he is not an urn of ashes but a face, springing to life in her mind: "As soon as my eyes fell on it, a familiar face flashed in front of my mind" (ll. 902–903). Her reaction serves to contrast the different varieties of identification in the two sisters; Chrysothemis imagines however mistakenly that his arrival might improve the atmosphere of the house. More realistic than Electra, she observes that dying isn't so terrible, but staying alive under torture makes for a far more desolate house.

When Electra is handed the urn, everyone watches detachedly as she turns the shrunken male remnants into a false baby, a doll, with more repetition of "tiny" ("your tiny weight has come home in a tiny urn"), pretending that she has always been Orestes' real

ELECTRA COMPLEXITIES IN THREE DRAMATISTS   31

mother and Clytemnestra is a "fraud". At the same time she imagines almost ghoulishly penetrating the container in order to unite with its contents: "Let me come into this little house of yours, nothingness into nothing", like the fantasy of parental incarceration relayed by Chrysothemis (a returned projection of the fantasy of intercourse), or the "tomb" or "wall" that her mother calls her. Only when she releases the urn from her hands does she see Orestes alive before her; though for us he is already a mock-heroic figure.

Orestes, watching this display, seems to need to be sure of Electra's capacity for self-immolation before the murder can be effected; she is his passageway into the house (his perverse version of marrying his mother, through being taken as her baby). All the same he is worried that she is overdoing it and this will interfere with the business: "Enough of words, Electra" (l. 1289). The Pedagogue reinforces this with "You crazy fools … stop this endless talking … Be shot of your task" (1335–1338). Together, Orestes and the Pedagogue represent the old Agamemnon-father risen from the grave, as if conjured into her fantasy via the urn. To Orestes she says, "If father came back to life, I'd believe *my eyes*; and with Sophoclean irony, "no *nostos* [homecoming] was ever like this"; and to the Pedagogue, "Welcome father … father is how I see you" (l. 1361). "Enough", he pronounces, arresting her outpourings. In effect, the spirit of Agamemnon is conjured up as in Aeschylus, only to cause a lot of trouble to those amongst whom it is distributed.

After the old Pedagogue has said there has been "enough" of talk, Orestes gets his alter-ego Pylades, partner in action, ready to "move inside at once" after a brief salutation to the ancestral gods of the porch. As in *Macbeth*, action means murder ("Be it thought and done" [IV. i. 149]) – extreme bodily intrusion – and is a male prerogative in this play; Electra is left outside the house door while "the men are at work". But she demonstrates her form of action in the words she shouts through the door when she urges them to "strike a second blow" at Clytemnestra, who laments "My house is empty of friends" such that even the Chorus, Electra's friends, sense a chill in the air (l. 1409). In the context of this unglamorous confusion only the cynical Orestes can imagine that "All is well indoors – if Apollo prophesied well". When Aegisthus turns up after his afternoon stroll and encounters his murderers, he is attended by none of the pomp or armed guard that we might expect to accompany a king, such as that attending Agamemnon in the *Oresteia*; and when he declaims that Orestes deserves a whipping we are not entirely unsympathetic. As soon as he pragmatically reckons up the odds against him, he accepts his fate without making a fuss.

32   THE ART OF PERSONALITY

The definitiveness of the opposition finds symbolic display in the weighty form of Clytemnestra's shrouded body which is wheeled from the inside to the outside, taking centre stage, proving how the violent intrusion has "found its way to her heart". The inner world becomes manifest in the outer.

The fact that there is no mention of the Furies (those carriers of conscience), as in the other two dramatists, contributes to the play's ominous tone at the end: the pace is brutal, coarse, matter of fact, as in all efficient dictatorships. Aegisthus is not allowed to speak even "one word – just one" as he pleads; instead he is ordered by Orestes (egged on by Electra) to "stop bandying words – you're wasting time – now move!" He is marched to the very spot where in the past he was Agamemnon. But now Orestes is the new Agamemnon: he has emerged from the urn that symbolises his decrepit father and come to "life": a new man whose old teacher has apparently taught him to value deeds above words and indeed the thoughts and feelings which they may convey. Kitto (1939) pointed out that the Chorus had no entry-song in this play but are summoned one by one to the tune of Electra's anapaests, a primitive drumbeat rather than a lyrical invocation. Now, shocked out of song, they are given just three brief and ambiguous lines to round off the play, inform-ing us that the seed of Atreus have "come to the ending" – of what? Where are the signs of mental breakdown we expect, and get in the other dramatists' versions, and which offer us some relief from this particularly dark and deadpan irony?

Euripides' Electra

Euripides is writing a different type of tragedy, deliberately undermining the dignified-heroic and bringing into play a strange mixture of tragic-comic and thwarted Shakespearean romance. It is not known whether he wrote his play before or after Sophocles', though it is hard to imagine how Sophocles could have presented his after seeing this even more emphatic indictment of the revenge motif. Not only does he parody Aeschylus' poetic metaphors (in the signs of recognition – the hair, the footprint etc.) but he seems to take Sophocles' implications one stage further. (Euripides also later wrote an *Orestes*, the equivalent of Aeschylus' *Eumenides*, telling the final stage of the story; and two about Iphigeneia, going back to the beginning.) Euripides (according to Kitto) saw Apollo of Delphi as "an immoral and reactionary institution" – something which is in fact latent in the other dramatists, becoming increasingly evident over time. There are gods, but they are not to be found "sitting on the tripod" as Euripides' Electra naively puts it. Euripides stresses the absurdity of the fanatical murdering trio with their jihadist attitudes (Electra, Orestes, Pylades); and the ordinariness of the parental couple Clytemnestra and Aegisthus.

Euripides' Electra is a country girl believing she should have been a princess; she is obsessed with mourning that which she feels she has lost, or (Euripides emphasises) that of which she has deliberately deprived herself – hair, father, ornaments, riches and status; though in her commonsense aspect she is aware that she has been married for her own wellbeing to a man who, though poor, is virtuous, hardworking and of respectable birth, as in many subsequent Shakespearean avatars. She rejects his potential advances and therefore he doesn't make any; he observes her princess-like qualities and treats her "with respect". He is not downtrodden however, and his retort to Electra when she calls him a fool for inviting quality guests into his house is that if they're really noble they will be equally at home in a cottage orgrand surrounding; and anyway, a full belly is the same for rich or poor (l. 430).[4] Euripides is a notable leveller, though some say the Farmer's virtue depends on his obscured noble birth; one could equally say his birth is just a metaphor and that his innate consideration is what makes him noble. As such he contrasts with all the other characters, even though they are much preoccupied with the difference between "is and seems" (as Hamlet puts it), with illusion, and with the nature of true nobility or gentleness.

Electra carries a water-pitcher on her head, instead of a libation jar or an urn of ashes, to emblematise her condition as a "tuneful swan" caught in a river net's snares just as her father was caught in the tricky net of her mother (ll. 151–154). There is a certain self-dramatisation, distinct from the genuine phobia of Sophocles' Electra when she sees the urn; her cropped hair and rags are flaunted to emphasise that they are the higher ascetic equivalent of the bright clothes and golden necklaces which the other women will wear at the celebration for unmarried women. As a virgin she feels she has no place with either the girls or the matrons. She rejects the Chorus' offer to lend her fine garments and their advice to offer prayers rather than groans to the gods. Groans are more musical, swan-like. Yet her poetic-ascetic image is instantly undermined by her irrational cowardice when Orestes and Pylades appear from

---

4   Line references are to J. Davie (trans.), *Euripides: Electra and Other Plays* (Penguin, 1998).

34   THE ART OF PERSONALITY

behind a rock and she fears (or pretends to fear) they intend to murder her (as if she really wore valuable ornaments or possessed a valuable virginity): "Let's get away from these villains – you run along the track, I'll dash into the cottage!" (l. 218). It is as if she is play-acting with herself as audience, mindful of great dramas of the past. The scene outside the humble hut is a caricature of how in the other two dramatists the dangerous duo approach the palace with murder in mind. She seems to have watched their plays and to make her own home the scene of an oedipal murder – and it is her home, as we are minded by domestic references to weaving cloth, fetching water, preparing food etc., which she performs despite the Farmer reminding her she's a princess and needn't do it. Somebody needs to be murdered in the house and if it is not she then it is her mother. Her fantasy of intercourse is that Agamemnon's blood has got inside Aegisthus who then mounts her father's chariot (mother's body) "grasping in his bloody hand the very sceptre" (the phallic weapon) carried by Agamemnon when he led Hellas to war.

Reassured by the strangers, she continues in the same vein, explaining that she has a "marriage like death" (l. 247), meaning that her husband is not rich enough for her. Nonetheless, on behalf of her farmer husband, she does get into Orestes' head a distinction between fear of consequences and integrity. Orestes tries hard to grasp the concept of an uncowardly man. We are aware of an ironic subtext in the long recognition scene, namely that Electra suspects who Orestes is but is unconsciously testing his resolve, making clear how she expects him to act and behave. He is walking into her net as Agamemnon walked into Clytemnestra's: he must stop lurking in shadows, hovering about the countryside where he can make a quick getaway, etc, and instead behave like a hero as in Aeschylus and Sophocles, going straight to the point. Her "brave Orestes", she says, would not arrive in secret from fear of Aegisthus.

Meanwhile Orestes talks about himself as if he were not there, merely his "messenger": complaining that a man in exile "cannot rely on his own resources" (l. 237), a sentiment echoed by Electra but with a menacing tinge of accusation. Orestes is "somewhere else", she says to his face (l. 245), meaning that her heroic warlike expectation of a brother has not yet proved itself. Gradually, through her taunts and insistence, Orestes is being brought to the point and there is no escape. In the midst of this the Chorus sing a song about the glories of the Trojan war as epitomised in Achilles' shield. The effect of this is to make us aware of the huge gap in worlds and values; Achilles is just a folk hero of no relevance to the real everyday world of tilling the fields and herding the goats.

The Old Man (the Pedagogue) is brought in from the country to bolster the contents of the larder and to distance the protagonists yet further from heroic legend: "Who is this old relic of manhood?" asks his former pupil (l. 553), and is taken aback when he realises he owes his safe escape to the old man. The comedy builds as the old man walks around Orestes "recognising" him, as if staking out the net ("perhaps he thinks I am like someone"), and as proof he has been caught, he points out a childhood scar on his forehead that Orestes acquired while chasing a fawn with Electra (not hunting a wild boar like Odysseus) – emphasising his childishness. Orestes' identity is secured; now he is a pawn in Electra's hands – she who once led his (delinquent?) games and is later herself compared to a fawn dancing. The three pray for vengeance in mock heroic style; Electra declares her readiness to plunge a sword into her heart if Orestes does not "prove himself a man" and murder Aegisthus (l. 690).

The Chorus at this point deliver a song about the family history, all murder and glamour, concluding that frightening tales are useful because they promote reverence for the gods; if only Clytemnestra had remembered such stories perhaps she wouldn't have killed her husband (l. 745). Electra hears noises and – just as in her reaction to the first appearance of Orestes and Pylades – indulges her tragic persona, rushing to the conclusion that now she must kill herself: "Quick! Let me do the deed!" (l. 758). Orestes has not failed – but the story of his success, in slaughtering Aegisthus like an ox when his guest at a festival – is no more savoury. Yet in a sense it is all playacting. Plato would say the trouble with this pair of siblings is that they take the old frightening tales too seriously, and imitate them, rather than ignoring them. Drama unlike philosophy can only set a bad example – too much theatre-going and fawn-chasing. Electra welcomes him as the son of the conqueror of Troy and brings out her stock of triumphal wreaths and garlands from the dressing-up box. Orestes in return brings forth the head of Aegisthus from his sack and offers it to her, saying "Before you called him master, but now he is your slave." (l. 898).

Despite this, the dispatching of Aegisthus has an unreal quality; he is not the main enemy here any more than in Sophocles – the real venom is reserved for Clytemnestra; it is a matricidal tale. It is as if Electra has to get rid of her mother before she can choose a "proper" husband for herself – not a girl-faced fop who only serves the dance but "a man who looks the part" and whose children serve the war-god (l. 943). (The girl-face is Aegisthus, but is also Orestes if he does not do as commanded.) As the elder sister, Electra directs

36   THE ART OF PERSONALITY

the children's games. She invents the plot to entrap Clytemnestra, using the bait of her supposed childbirth and admitting her mother is sufficiently fond of her to visit. (The plot has an ungodly quality, making light of serious matters – similar to Orestes in Sophocles saying he doesn't care if he fakes his own death.) Electra is prepared to use the sacred rituals of birth and motherhood in perverted form: "Now you shall offer to the gods the sacrifice that is due."

Clytemnestra arrives in her chariot, echoing Agamemnon and Cassandra and the chariot-body that Electra fantasised in inter-course. She is stepping straight into our net, says Electra, in her fine clothes and carriage. Orestes tries to get out of it, not know-ing who to obey: "Your word was that I must kill my mother ... I shall be sent into exile" (ll. 973–975). He is unsure who will punish him most, whose is the stronger arm. Electra, just as she chose to be convinced by the scar on his forehead (but not before), now chooses to be convinced by the idea that whoever retains his seat on Apollo's tripod proves he is the god's agent, owing to this mark of unquestionable authority:

> ORESTES: Did some evil spirit make that pronouncement,
>   taking the god's shape?
> ELECTRA: And take his seat on the sacred tripod? I doubt it.
> ORESTES: I cannot believe this command from the oracle was well
>   made.
> ELECTRA: Do not turn coward or lose your manhood! Go on
>   to set the same trap for her as she used with Aegisthus to
>   kill her husband! (ll. 979-983)

Clytemnestra speaks in homely language, in stark contrast to Electra's melodramatic jargon:

> ELECTRA: Well then mother (as a slave myself, banished from my
>   ancestral home and living in a wretched hovel), let me take hold
>   of your royal hand. (ll. 1004-1005).

Clytemnestra gives her side of the story, reminding us of Iphigeneia the lost child – a real tragedy rather than Electra's fake one of demo-tion. "When Tyndareus gave me in marriage to your father, it was not a condition that I or any child of mine should be put to death" (ll. 1018–1019). She advises a logical approach and ascertaining the facts before judging. Nor did she wish to be one of "two wives", alongside Cassandra. She says she followed Agamemnon's exam-ple in getting another lover (as Sophocles' Electra blamed her harsh tongue on imitation of her mother's). Electra however continues to

ELECTRA COMPLEXITIES IN THREE DRAMATISTS 37

harp on the old heroic values and how her mother missed a favour-
able chance to "win great renown" by contrasting her virtue with
her sister Helen's bad behaviour. Clytemnestra isn't interested in
making her name, and though aware of being judged by others,
states clearly why she disapproves of it. She accepts Electra's natural oedipal preference for her father: "My child, it has always been
your nature to love your father. This is a fact of life" (l. 1102). That is,
she loved one kind of father (the glamorous sort) but not the other
one – Aegisthus whose nature is similar to her own: "That is the
way he is; and you too have shown stubbornness." Our picture of
Electra as a difficult child expands via her mother's eyes. Moreover
Clytemnestra says she regrets her anger and revenge. Older and
wiser, she has come to terms with both the lost and the divorced,
and tries to make the best of her life with its present comforts, yet
without the self-revenge of heartlessness, as Euripides emphasises.

The murder of Clytemnestra therefore takes on the quality of a
self-deluding, omnipotent game that has gone wrong, under the
aegis of a false father-god composed of bits attributed to Apollo
and Agamemnon. It is conducted like a bodged execution, with
Electra dropping her sword and hanging onto her brother's arm in
order to take part, whilst he also nearly drops his sword.

> ORESTES: O Earth, O Zeus who sees all that men do, look
> upon these foul and bloody deeds, two bodies stretched
> upon the ground, struck down by my hand in recompense
> for my woes.
> ELECTRA: A sight indeed to make one weep, my brother, but I
> am responsible. Oh what have I done, venting my fury on our
> mother here, the woman who was the mother of her little girl!
> (ll. 1178–1183)

Finally the "wind of truth" clears the air of Electra's self-obfusca-
tions and manic delusions, the "curse" she has inherited from her
ancestors. Euripides' answer to the Sophoclean Orestes' muddled
claim that "all is well indoors – if Apollo prophesied well" is
unequivocal. Apollo, or rather the pseudo-god that men have
invented for themselves, has wrought havoc. The murder has taken
place not exactly onstage, but far nearer to us than that of Aegisthus
out in the fields; we feel we know the inside of the hut, Electra's
shabby home or mind, where she belongs or is at least tolerated by
her farmer-father. Realism and emotional complications take over
from the mock-heroic, stylish execution of Aegisthus which was
efficiently accomplished by regarding him as a mere ox to be split

THE ART OF PERSONALITY

and slitted. Or did that only appear efficient because it happened so far backstage – can we trust the account related back to us over such a distance? A typically Euripidean question: the overt meaning of words is not necessarily any more transparent than the countenance of human beings.

When the Dioscori appear on the godwalk they state unequivocally that Apollo was wise but "wisdom was absent from the command he gave you" (l. 1247). Euripides disperses all the divine equivocations not because he is a psychologist rather than a religious poet (for he is both), but because psychology changed religion as it had been commonly understood – the dramatists leading the way.

Further considerations

None of these three tragedies is of the same type as *Oedipus Tyrannus*, the great prototype for the movement in which death is a metaphor for "catastrophic change" – that is psychic development – in the way described by Aristotle and centuries later taken up by Bion in psychoanalytic theory. They portray the other type of catastrophe – the disaster of internal revenge where nothing is learned except that it has all been wrong, which is a message ultimately for the audience not the protagonists.

Looking at the trio of plays we seem to be able to trace a logical progression in which the great dramatists explore the psychosis behind Electra's oedipal complex-gone-wrong. Sophocles picks up the psychotic traces behind Aeschylus' attempt at the balance and reconciliation of male and female deities. His play ends with a certain horrifying blankness, like an echo from the Marabar caves, full of sound and fury but signifying nothing. It takes Euripides (building on this) to state explicitly that the whole business is psychotic. No kind of internal lawcourt – no religious rationalisation or psychoanalytic interpretation – can smooth over the psychic disease that misinterprets the nature of the combined internal object as in matricide. Apollo's rulings via the Pythian drug-induced smog just do not carry emotional weight. "Faded, far-flung Apollo" as Keats said centuries later, likewise discarding him as a god for poetry, and turning instead to the mysterious mother-like muse.

Is this just some inappropriate modern reaction? Or is it one of those states of mind that Bion said had "not happened yet" – because it is "ours"? Certainly Shakespeare thought so when he re-examined the return of the father's ghost in *Hamlet*. He, as we, preferred the Claudius-Aegisthus model of fatherhood, despite its evident failings, to the heroic butcher or the fag-and-prefect model of Orestes and his silent shadow Pylades. We would rather have feminine, "foolish" Yorick than the sinister Old Pedagogue playing with our children and teaching them how to "act" rather than spend time thinking – which has further implications for the wider models of society.

The state of mind (the ethical orientation) did not then "exist" because in the cultural sense, Aeschylus saw the future hope for humanity as lying in the establishment of a secure patriarchal democracy, epitomised by the Areopagitica, governing the female furious passions in their cave below the hill and appeasing them with regular rites and offerings. He hoped his plays would help to establish this patriarchal democracy and its ethics. But even though this vision was politically young and would take centuries of oscillation in the attempt to gain a hold, it was already out of date in poetic and psychological terms. When the emotional elements settle after the dazed state induced by these astounding plays, what remains to govern our Electra identification like sunlight entering the underground cave, is the searing poetry of the *Agamemnon* – the gang rape of Iphigeneia at her father's command to appease the internal "soldiers" (the basic assumptions), the purple carpet of her blood leading the murderer to the mother's revenge, and the humble watchman who finally awakes on the palace roof and notices what is going on in this wartorn mind – imagining the sequence of flaring beacons that have linked up the conscious with the unconscious, hitherto so distant. At last there is an observer. The moment when, on its original performance, dawn rose over the hills of the open-air theatre, is surely the most powerful in theatre history. And perhaps the state of mind has not happened to us yet either. When we dead awaken ...

CHAPTER THREE

Women, gods and witches: Euripides and the roots of perversity

It can be hard to gauge the tone and psychological viewpoint of the plays of Euripides. Their complexity and even their poetry has an experimental quality, as if he upturns conventional views to see what they look like from the other side. In this chapter I would like to discuss two of his most brilliant and puzzling plays, *Medea* and *The Bacchae*, which have left a most powerful impact on readers over the centuries, and are well known for their psychological depths.

Euripides by the twentieth century had acquired a dual reputation for both misogyny and feminism. In his lifetime he was never as popular as Aeschylus (the old master) or Sophocles; although subsequently over the centuries he became the best known and most emulated of the ancient authors, and served in translation as an indirect source of many Shakespearean themes and plots. Euripides was interested in philosophy and philosophical argument; his plays are more overtly intellectual than those of the other dramatists, and the *agon* or rhetorical debate constitutes an important structural part; moreover in these debates, his women characters are generally given a powerful voice that is equal with or superior to that of the men. At the same time his Chorus members are frequently ordinary (as distinct from intellectual) women; and their dramatic function is to add emotional atmosphere to the logic of the debates, through poetry, singing and dancing.

42   THE ART OF PERSONALITY

Euripides and Sophocles were contemporaries (Sophocles being only slightly older) and both were in a theatrical sense sons of Aeschylus, but they developed the tradition in different ways, not least in terms of their mindview or worldview. Euripides was familiar with the Pythagorean table of opposites, set down later by Aristotle, in which the male principle – associated with limit, unity, straightness, light etc – exists in tension with the female principle of plurality, unlimitedness, twisting, darkness, evil. To these we can add the associations of city versus country, overground versus underground, manmade order versus wild nature, conscious versus unconscious, ego versus id. These divisions are a visible part of the core framework of his plays and (from our point of view, with hindsight) give them a classical Freudian quality. The repressed is revealed in the process of the play's evolution, giving the opposites a voice. How can the opposites be harmonised and what are the types of false link that destroy, disharmonise? Indeed if Sophocles with his poetic empathy for the mind's roots in infancy may be considered a Kleinian, and Aeschylus with his archetypal characters a Jungian, then Euripides' revelations about the twists of pathology in relation to punitive superegos is perhaps the most Freudian of the great dramatists.

The general pessimism of Euripides might seem remarkable so soon after Aeschylus had worked through his vision of a new world of inner and external harmony in the *Oresteia*, which Euripides saw performed when he was age 26. In the *Oresteia* the primitive Furies are transformed into the Eumenides who have a rightful place in the structure of both mind and state, so no longer need to be repressed or outcast. The period of Athens' glory lasted only a century, and the *Oresteia* in a way marked what has been called "the moment of tragedy" (Vernant and Vidal-Naquet, 1988) – marking also the height of imperial power. At that very moment the seeds of its own destruction were sown with the beginning of the long wars that would end in Athens' defeat at the hands of former allies who had revolted against her imperialism. Euripides' plays indicate that he was highly sensitive to these reverberations and tried to make hidden uncomfortable things visible and audible. Aristophanes in one of his satires made Euripides claim that he was a true "democrat" because he gave all types of character a significant voice in his plays – women, slaves, children and old people, in other words the less powerful or low in status make a contribution to his mindpicture equal to that of heroes and gods. He amplifies the orchestration of tragedy's voice, whilst at the same time curtailing its power to resolve uncomfortable issues into a major key.

Nietzsche famously accused Euripides of causing the "death of tragedy" by bringing gods and myth back down to earth. Indeed Euripides' gods are not internal objects, they are more like instinctual impulses, manifestations of the id rather than the superego, demanding recognition. The Furies may take the form not only of hissing harpies but of beautiful intelligent women or smiling vine-wreathed gods. All audiences are disturbed by Dionysus' cruelty, just as they are disturbed by Medea's infanticide. Neither of these acts of violence have the cathartic significance of Oedipus' putting out his eyes, which in Sophocles (see Williams, 2005b) represents a triumphant resolution of aesthetic conflict, a step forward in self-knowledge. But in a different way they have the same artistic aim of doing what Louise Bourgeois called "seeing what is, not what I would like"; Bourgeois (who in fact cites *Medea* at one point, identifying with her) also points out that the representation of murderous feelings in her art was the precise opposite of enacting murder in real life (cited in Williams, 2014, p. 21). Euripides' method is to research the darkest recesses of the psyche in order to calculate the most fitting revenge on the personality. This method has an aesthetic reciprocity of its own, which is particularly evident in tightly constructed plays such as *Medea* and *The Bacchae*. Euripides probes the forces that pervert or deflect the aesthetic conflict. For all these artists, the route to civilisation and sanity lies in making the unconscious conscious, the obscure transparent. What is difficult about Euripides is his intellectualism: the extent to which one is left wondering, is this emotional conflict real, or has he invented it, pursued it to a *reductio ad absurdum*? Unlike Sophocles, or Shakespeare, we are never entirely clear where his heart lies. But perhaps this is why he is a "democrat".

Medea: from woman to witch

Euripides wrote *Medea* about halfway through his career. The play portrays what is in certain respects a commonplace scenario of a poisoned bourgeois marriage, with the murder of the children being a vivid or heightened metaphor for the way in which children are liable to become the primary victims in their parents' divorce. The extravagance of the play's action and its denouement, when Medea flies above the stage in the Sun's chariot transporting the dead bodies of her children, may appear to place it beyond the reach of everyday normality. But when viewed as a symbolisation of feelings, her transformation into a witch flying on a broomstick

44   THE ART OF PERSONALITY

seems fitting and familiar. While Jason, the hero of the Argonaut, is revealed as an impotent figure who is not even granted the heroism of dying. Medea's final curse prophesies how he will "die a humiliating death, struck on the head by a fragment of the Argo ... the bitter conclusion to your marriage with me" (l. 1389).[1] Euripides has made sure that we feel he deserved his fate, and that he is not enough of a man to be worth killing; his voyages have all been those of self-promotion, comfort and security, not of passion and adventure; and it is fitting that the phallic prow of his own ship should put an end to his potency.

The scene is set by the dialogue between the Nurse and Tutor, outside Medea's house; their colloquial conversation is punctuated by the piercing cry of Medea from within, having learned of her desertion by Jason and his new marriage to Glauce the daughter of Creon, king of Corinth. Her repeated loud cry from the depths of the house vividly brings to the fore the depths of Fury-like despair and rage at the core of her personality, in the context of the impotence of the internal parents who are in the position of mere servants ("Poor fool!" says the Tutor "if one may speak of one's mistress like that" [l. 62)]). Their attempts to protect the children are semi–comical – telling them to enter their mother's house, but to stay away from their mother in her dangerous mood – a self-contradictory instruction.

At the very beginning of the play the Nurse recounts the sexual history of Jason and Medea – a retrospective view of the famous voyage which brought them together in Colchis and then landed them as foreigners in Corinth:

> NURSE: How I wish that the Argo had not flown through the dark
> Clashing Rocks on its sea-journey to the Colchians' land – that
> the pine had never fallen, hewn amid the glens of Mount Pelion,
> and furnished oars for the hands of those heroic men who went
> to win the golden fleece for Pelias. (ll. 1–5)

This is the background to their marriage, and it is referred to several times in the play, along with Medea's betrayal of her father and murder of her brother. The clashing rocks suggest the dangerous passage in and out of Medea's body. The Argo with its vigorous rowing hands, split from a single pine (a representation of Jason's body) robbed Medea's own fatherland of its golden fleece, in a story of serial episodes of violence in which Medea herself was

---

1   Line references are to J. Morwood (trans.), *Euripides: Medea and Other Plays* (1997).

WOMEN, GODS, AND WITCHES IN EURIPIDES 45

not merely complicit but instrumental, "her heart unhinged in her love for Jason". It is her daunting sexual appetite, as much as her foreignness, that makes her position that of an alien or "barbarian" in civilised Greek society; yet it is also her cleverness that marks her out from the norm or average, in relation to both men and women. Her Asiatic origin is a metaphor for her association with wild unknown forces – something that applies to the idea of the female in ancient Greek culture. The hidden wildness of femininity complements the everyday domesticity of women.

And at the beginning of the play Medea's talents are ambiguous with potential for good or evil; after the turning-point at the middle of the play Medea commits herself to evil, driven by a desire for revenge which is stronger than any other emotion. Already in the opening scene the Nurse is alarmed for the children, who represent the possibility of a civilised future. She knows more than Medea herself consciously knows – that they will be the first victims of an intercourse more violent than passionate:

> NURSE: But she hates her children ... I know her, and I fear that
> she may go silently into the house where her bed is laid and
> drive a sharpened sword into their heart ... For she is fearsome.
> (ll. 36–43)

The house is the place where "her bed is laid" and from which Jason has moved out, and the Nurse's phrasing suggests there is a certain inevitability in the result of this being the death of the children. The marriage bed and the children are an entity. This is the Nurse's insight; it contrasts with the respectable forms of revenge that everyone more or less expects Medea will take – killing Jason, or the royal family, or Medea herself. For at this point Medea does not yet know what the Nurse has already glimpsed, just as she sees the wild animal in Medea's eyes – "that fierce look she throws at any servant who approaches her with a message, it reminds me of a lioness with cubs!" (l. 187). Ironically, this lioness will turn on her own cubs. But it is not yet certain, and indeed was not a feature of the original myth. The drama of the play consists in the gradual clarification of Medea's intention to kill the children, the perverse fulfilment of her marriage. The logicality of the perversion has an aesthetic precision.

The Nurse complains that the bards make "unnecessary song" at banquets when men are already sensuously comfortable, rather than soothing their spirits at times of distress. Euripides seems to imply that comfort is no answer to distress as wild or sharp as Medea's:

46   THE ART OF PERSONALITY

what is needed is penetrating investigation of its non-rational source. He is himself an alternative type of bard, whose ambition is to disturb rather than to soothe the minds of his audience.

When Medea emerges from the house, we see what a skilled speaker and politician she is. The house – her body or mind – is contrasted with the normality of life outside: we have children running races, old men playing draughts, and a Chorus of ordinary women who for the first half of the play sympathise with Medea in her abandonment, and who even hope that as a woman of special abilities she will use the opportunity to speak up for the cause of women in general. The contrast is often noted between the inside-Medea who shrieks incoherently, and the outside-Medea with her dignified bearing and devastatingly logical arguments. Yet the inside-Medea and the outside-Medea are the same person, and this is what interests Euripides.

When she comes outside, she carefully adjusts her position relative to the Chorus. Her emotional turbulence is left behind in the house, and her famous first speech is a masterpiece of self-control and of her capacity to scrutinise her effect upon others. She points out that she is different from the other women, but in such a way as to elicit their sympathy and perhaps admiration:

> The same reasoning does not apply to you and to me. You have this city, your father's house, a fulfilled life and the company of your friends, while I, a desolate woman without a city, shamefully injured by my husband who carried me as plunder from a foreign land, have no haven from this disaster, no mother, no brother, no relative at all. ... When [a woman] is wronged in her marriage bed, no creature has a mind more murderous. (ll. 252–267)

The voyage of the Argo set her on a sea of troubles, friendless, a metaphor governing the first half of the play, forming the pattern for the original sexual act while Medea is still turbulent in her own mind and has not made the decision (which she considers irrevocable) to murder the children.

Her speech begins tentatively but builds up as she gradually gathers the Chorus within her power. She presents herself as spokeswoman for all the others (indeed, parts of her speech were adopted by the Suffragettes):

> Of everything that is alive and has a mind, we women are the most wretched creatures. First of all, we have to buy a husband with a vast outlay of money – we have to take a master for our body.

WOMEN, GODS, AND WITCHES IN EURIPIDES   47

> The latter is still more painful than the former. And here lies the most critical issue – whether we take a good husband or a bad. For divorce brings shame on a woman's reputation and we cannot refuse a husband his rights. ... We need prophetic powers to tell us specifically what sort of husband we shall have to deal with.
> (ll. 230–240)

She says her "confidence has been wrecked" by Jason's desertion, yet her speech in its supremely measured rhetoric belies this. We are so impressed (seduced) that, like the Chorus, we pass over the sophistication of its primary intent to conquer the audience. Even her claim that it is better to face the enemy three times in battle than to bear one child, is not very convincing, though it is an effective piece of rhetoric (it is not the sentiment of a mother whose son has gone to war). The constraints she lists in her speech may indeed apply to women in general, in a patriarchal society – but they don't apply in her own case. Medea was not given by her father in marriage, nor was she seized as a slave (as "plunder"). On the contrary, she was the one who mastered Jason and led him through every step of his sea-voyage, removing the obstacles and murdering inconvenient persons on the way. We might even begin to suspect that Jason is tired of being raped by Medea – "playing the tyrant" with his body and also his brain, via the "wearisome storm of her words" as he complains (l. 523). Jason was captured by Medea and did not know whether he was getting a good woman or a bad; he was not intelligent enough to see the difference, and in any case he had no choice at the time. Medea was in a better position to judge a man's character; but back in Colchis when she arranged the rape of the golden fleece she was more interested in sensuality than in character. Indeed Jason attributes his escape in the Argo to Aphrodite rather than to Medea herself.

Eventually Medea's argument for the rights of woman takes her to the crucial point at which she demands the other women's silence as an indication of their oyalty and fellow-feeling: "And so there is one small kindness I ask of you, if I devise some ways and means of making my husband pay for this suffering of mine: your silence" (l. 260). We now understand that this has been the point of the entire speech: a masterpiece of insincere political rhetoric. She has not yet decided on the form her revenge will take; and the Chorus agree that it is "just" she should take revenge on her husband – this is something they can understand, after she has invoked their solidarity as women and her allegiance to womanhood. In Greek tragedy, the Chorus are always ineffective; their role is not to affect the

48   THE ART OF PERSONALITY

action, but to provide perspective and emotional atmosphere. The scene in which the children scream from inside the house before they are killed echoes that in the *Oresteia* when Orestes kills his mother. In each case the Chorus, as if paralysed, wonder out loud whether to go in and help. Medea however creates a kind of false solidarity, sealed by a pact. It demonstrates that what she seeks is their silence as allies, not their friendship as women. In doing so she stifles her own womanliness, and when the Chorus later explicitly forbid her to kill her children, their command falls on deaf ears because she has already alienated her femininity.

Euripides focuses on the tension that makes Medea an outsider from both the world of women and the world of men. The perverse model is refined and brought to prominence in the context of the series of men who represent the patriarchal values of the status quo, the respectable city-state. Interviews or debates (*agon*) take place in turn with Creon, Jason and Aegeus. Each one embodies or reinforces some feature of masculine blindness, weakness or stupidity – Creon is fearful, Jason is bombastically complacent, and Aegeus avows his impotence and his low intelligence. Honing her identity against the limitations of these men, Medea moves relentlessly closer to metamorphosing into a witch.

Central to this process is the fact that all the representatives of masculinity want children, because children seal the respectability of their lives and the security of the state. They all feel it is unfortunate that this entails getting mixed up with women. Medea's first male antagonist, Creon, appears on the scene as soon as she has secured her first victory over her fellow-women. She achieves mastery over Creon despite his suspicions by "fawning" on him, she says, in a way that overlays his natural timidity and fear of her powers. She begins with the same tone of self-pity that engaged the sympathy of the Chorus: "Oh, I am ruined, utterly ruined! Oh, misery! My enemies are running up full sail and there is no place for me to escape from ruin" (l. 280).

Like a ship under sail herself, she tries different tacks. Her first tactic – appealing to Creon's pity – fails (though it worked with the women), because he is dominated by his fear of her:

> CREON: You are a clever woman, skilled in many evil wiles. You are distressed at the breakdown of your marriage and the loss of your groom. I hear that you are threatening to take some action against the husband and his bride and me, who gave my daughter to him. And so I shall take precautions against these things before we fall victim to them. (ll. 285–290)

WOMEN, GODS, AND WITCHES IN EURIPIDES 49

Medea explains how her "special knowledge", her cleverness, itself makes her a victim in the eyes of others: she is "clever beyond the norm": "Because I have special knowledge, some view me with resentment, others again with distaste". Her cleverness is unjustly envied, she says, but is not irrational, and it would not be clever to harm Creon, only Jason, the one who has wronged her. At no point does Creon manage to come up with a counter-argument; he just voices his instinctive fear that she is dangerous: "Your words are soothing to the ear but I have a terrible misgiving that in your heart you are hatching some evil plan."

By the end of the debate, however, she has contrived to make a link with him via the idea of children, which puts him in her power. He lets her know how precisely she can hurt him most – through his family and children. At this point she seizes his hand in supplication (a powerful gesture), and demands pity for her own children:

> MEDEA: You too are a father, you have children. You are likely to be sympathetic to mine ... I weep for them, the victims of ill fortune.
> (ll. 343–348)

Thus she wins this round in the debate. Creon, despite his doubts, does not wish to be thought – or think himself – a tyrant: "I am no tyrant in my heart but a king." She has found his vulnerable point, his self-image.

In this way the idea of the children as the crucial instrument of victory gains ascendancy. Each stage brings on their fate – pawns in the deadly game between humans, rather than between gods as is more usual in Greek tragedy. Yet Medea herself has still not decided on her plan of action; she has "some scheme in mind", she says, yet at this point is still thinking of killing "three enemies" – father, daughter and husband. With the Chorus sworn to silence, she can consider openly the merits of fire, the sword and poison – which she calls the "most direct" way and one in which she is "particularly expert".

During this phase she draws attention to the fact that her co-worker and guide is Hecate, queen of witches, whose image she keeps "in a recess of my hearth" – intimately in a corner of her mind, like a parody of an internal object (as when Milton's Satan says: "Evil, be thou my good"). The recess is associated with finding "a secure place of refuge". She is in search of "an act of ruthless daring" that will fittingly express her mastery over the men who have tried to drive her out. What is hardening in Medea all this time is her determination not to be "laughed at", and this becomes key

50   THE ART OF PERSONALITY

to the play's denouement. If she is caught, she fears, her enemies will have a chance to laugh at her:

> MEDEA: You must not bring laughter on yourself through Jason's marriage into the house of that traitor Sisyphus, you the daughter of a good father and grandchild of the Sun. You have the skill – and what is more we are women, supremely helpless when there's good to be done, supreme in clever craftsmanship of all bad deeds. (l. 405)

Again she rallies her fellow-women. Her satirical tone exposes the standard patriarchal view of how effective women are in working evil. But the Chorus interpret her message as intimating a new age for women, who will be celebrated by poets instead of condemned for faithlessness: "Honour is coming to the female sex" they sing. Medea with her talent, intellect and dark arts becomes a type of perverted poetess.

It is something that Jason too suggests in his confused way – adding that one of the benefits he brought Medea was that of bringing her to a civilised country where she could "win a reputation". He, like the Chorus, recognise that for Medea as for the poets, reputation and not being "laughed at" are of more significance than comfort and stability. Killing the children – which no-one else would dare – will ensure eternal fame. Through his heroine (or anti-heroine), Euripides takes a wry look at his own activity as playwright.

It is in this context that Medea says: "Truth to tell, I often view matters differently from many people" (l. 579). In the confrontation with Jason, Medea, like Lady Macbeth, accuses her husband of being "a man who is no man", and uses this diagnosis as a basis for her disquisition on the difference between appearance and reality: why do men carry no "stamp" of authenticity on their body to identify whether their coinage is true or "counterfeit"? She proceeds to "stamp" Jason herself by exposing his specious arguments about how his marriage into the royal family would benefit all those around him including even his cast-off wife; concluding that women are a nuisance and it would be better if children could be produced without them; then there would be no need for a female sex to exist and "Then mankind would be free from every evil". The surrounding presence of the female Chorus on the stage enhances the absurdity of the declaration, though we are also conscious that it is merely a sharpened formulation of the underlying assumptions of the rational, prevailing patriarchy. Children,

WOMEN, GODS, AND WITCHES IN EURIPIDES   51

like wealth and other possessions, are considered to be an attribute of the patriarchy, cementing order and security. Paradoxically, this is what puts Medea's children in danger.

"Get on with your marriage" is how she dismisses Jason at the end of their first interview. She says he must be "overwhelmed" by desire for his new wife. Again her words are sarcastic; Jason's attitude indicates that his motivation is not sexual desire but political expediency and the wish for a quiet life, away from the "wearisome storm" of Medea's words. The general lack of sexual and emotional vitality in the world of men is borne out by the visitation of Aegeus that follows next. Again Medea's cleverness is emphasised by contrast with this representative of the male world. Aegeus, king of Athens, has been to Apollo's oracle at Delphi to ask him why he does not have any children, and is now on his way back home with a message that he does not understand:

MEDEA: What did Phoebus say to you about children?
AEGEUS: His words were too clever for a mere man to interpret.
  (ll. 674–675)

The oracle told him not to "unloose the wineskin's hanging foot" before returning to his own country – that is not to spill his (limited) sexual energies outside his home; these needed to be conserved and directed, to become effective. The answer is clear to the audience and to Medea, though she does not make an immediate interpretation, but rather, promises to "cure his childlessness" when she herself gets to Athens (the implication is that she brings both cleverness and sexuality with her). The "mere man" is infertile both in the physical sense of begetting children on his own, and in the intuitive or artful sense of interpreting the words of a god. He is unaware of his reliance on the female principle in both ways.

When Medea complains that Jason has deserted her, Aegeus asks ingenuously: "Was he in love or couldn't he bear his relationship with you?" (It is as if he suspects she would be an unbearable partner.) Jason, she explains sarcastically, has remarried "for love" – but then adds, "He conceived a passion to marry into the royal house". It was not love of a woman but of status and security that made him reorganise his life. Meanwhile, with this promise of "cure" in the background, Medea extracts a promise of protection from Aegeus, in preparation for her flight from Thebes after taking revenge on Jason. She demands he swear by the Earth and Sun, the "father of her father" – silencing his future objections in the same way as with the Chorus.

52   THE ART OF PERSONALITY

The Aegeus episode, at the centre of the play, though sometimes seen as a digression with an incongruously comic quality, is central to the emotional progression of the plot. Medea has secured her refuge by exporting the secret of engendering children: the very thing which seems to engender her own perfect form of revenge on Jason. For her own plot seems to hatch between the lines during this interview. No longer tempest-tossed, she concludes that at last "I am on the way" and she has "fastened her stern cable" to Aegeus of Athens. It is the ruler of the world's most civilised city who will ensure the success of her uncivilised revenge and be forced to harbour infanticide, the price of Aegeus' infertility – an aspect of the play's perverse aesthetic reciprocity. In a similar way she gets her vitality and power from the Sun, the source of life but also of death (transferred to the golden headband which kills Glauce). She genuinely feels it is inevitable that she must kill her children, to perfect the pattern of revenge:

> I cry out when I think what kind of deed I must do afterwards. For I shall kill the children, my own ones. Nobody is going to take them away from me …
>
> Let no one think of me as weak and submissive, a cipher – but as a woman of a very different kind, dangerous to my enemies and good to my friends. Such people's lives win the greatest renown.
> (ll. 790–811)

It is the poet's goal of fame, the seal on her artistic murder. Worse than sexual rejection for her is to be disparaged: "Laughter from my enemies is not to be endured, my friends" (l. 797) The children (her work) will contribute to this only if she is the person who destroys them. It is the exact antithesis of the Judgement of Solomon.

This is the point at which Medea says she is ready to exchange words for deeds: "Until the deed is done, all words are wasted" (like Macbeth's "Be it thought and done" [IV. i. 141]). Edith Hall (1997b) has pointed out that after this, the imagery of sea turbulence is superseded by that of "hands". The women have been sworn to silence, and the Nurse is a slave – though ironically Medea instructs her to behave as "a true woman" and keep silence also.

Medea's perverse vision is that the children should themselves carry the poisoned robes to Glauce, the empty-headed girl who is easily seduced by appearances: "When she saw the adornments, she could not resist" (p. 31). Emphasis is laid on how the children are linked to her by their hands, and this is what seals their doom:

WOMEN, GODS, AND WITCHES IN EURIPIDES 53

> CHORUS: No longer have I any hope now for the children's lives,
> No longer. Already they are going to their death.
> The bride will accept the golden headband ... (ll. 976–978)

The golden headband and the robe with its "loveliness and divine brightness" are dangerous gifts from the Sun, "concealing death": "Take these bridal gifts into your hands, children." There is a certain quality of a drama of part-objects in the tableau which contributes to the perversity. The phallic shape of the girl is wrapped in a tight-fitting skin that becomes poisonous so that her body crumples and collapses on the throne. The Sun's rays through the golden headband spout poison not semen. Medea has made the children part of this poisoned tableau, a parody of creative sexuality, and this is why she has to complete the process with the sword. Her gloating over the details of the princess's death reinforces her perverse artistry and sexuality: she tells the Messenger she will get "double the pleasure" to hear that Glauce and Creon died "the foulest of deaths".

The pathos is increased by Medea's moment of indecision, when she momentarily says "I will not do it" and struggles briefly with her *thumos* (emotional base); but again it is the prospect of being "laughed at" that clinches her resolve: "Do I want to make myself ridiculous by letting my enemies go unpunished?"

> MEDEA: There's no alternative – they must die. And since they must,
> I who gave them birth shall kill them. In any case, the thing is
> done and the princess will not escape. Even now the garland is
> on her head; in the robe the royal bride is dying. (ll. 1061–1065)

When Jason confronts her at the end he describes her as an "artist in obscenity" (as indeed is Euripides in the off-scene events of his own art-form). At first Jason is still egotistically obsessed, believing that as a final outrage Medea might even be intending to kill him: "Can she be wanting to kill me too?" When he realises his own death is irrelevant to Medea's spectacular vision, he begins to change, showing signs of curiosity:

> JASON: Where did she kill them? In or out of the house?
> CHORUS: If you open the doors, you will see your children's
> corpses. (ll. 1312–1313)

Medea's ultimate artistic *coup de theatre* turns the inside (feminine, emotional) out – but not in the conventional manner, although

54   THE ART OF PERSONALITY

Jason seems to have some inkling of it when he imagines her either hiding beneath the earth or "flying with winged body into the deep heaven". Instead of the house doors opening to reveal the corpses, she appears with them above the house in the Sun's chariot – a witch riding on a broomstick. Yet at the same time it is a manifestation of her divine origins and thus of the link with hidden emotionality which she represents – that resides both below and above normal everyday existence. It is the final transformation of her cry from within the house.

Jason is the person who learns most about his own feelings by the end of the play. Medea through her art has taught him how to be hurt: "These children are no more. This will hurt you." He laments that even their traditional role of laying out his corpse will be denied him. Up to now his arrogance in relation to women has stifled his capacity for feeling: when Medea originally suggested he should plead with his new wife that the children should not be sent into exile, he replied "If she is like the rest of her sex, I think I shall persuade her" (l. 946). Unable to analyse his preconceptions about the female sex, he has never been in touch with his feelings. He did not love either Glauce or Medea, only himself. Now Medea has shown him his love for his children, and that they are not mere adornments or status symbols.

> MEDEA: You are still a novice in grief. Wait till you grow old.
> JASON: O my dearest children.
> MEDEA: Dearest to their mother, not to you.
> JASON: So why did you kill them?
> MEDEA: To cause you pain. (ll. 1396–1398)

Is Medea a fanatic or a prophet, a bad or a good witch? This final passage of *stichomythia* has a quality of genuine, direct emotional communication, which is different from Medea's previous plotting and manipulation (a language of secret hidden meanings). It is different too from her "wearisome storm" of abuse; it is the language of the "sword", emotionally piercing. Perhaps there is hope for Jason in the future now that his complacency has been shattered, and he becomes aware of the necessary link between children and mother. Only the children's death *in this manner* had the power to do this. Medea's witchcraft has hit its mark: pain has become meaningful to him, and thereby, to every man. He could yet be the hero of the Argonaut, and the death from its falling prow that Medea prophesies for him could be as ambiguous as a Delphic oracle. It could turn out to mean, for example, the death of his narcissism, and the consequent birth of a new type of man, beyond the confines of the patriarchy. We shall never know, but the crucial point is that owing to these final unexpected moments of genuine emotionality, Euripides has ensured that the potentiality is hinted at. The action of the play could be considered a type of premonitory bad dream, warning against the consequences of enacting certain fantasies, from which the dreamer can gain insight and – as Louise Bourgeois said – ensure that real murder does not take place.

The mountain of dreams: The Bacchae

The Bacchae was Euripides' last play, performed posthumously and written when he was away from Athens in Macedonia, possibly in political exile of some kind. It is the only play in which a god is a protagonist; and we remember that for Euripides the gods are not forces of wisdom but forces of power, from the irrational unconscious; and man's best hope is to acknowledge this power and investigate its complexity and forms of manifestation (or disguise). This has to be done in a way that acknowledges the beauty as well as the ugliness of the internal Furies – their association with intelligence and creativity, as well as with blood and revenge. It also has to be done in a way that is sincere, authentic, not merely a superstitious lip-service such as that paid here by the old men Teiresias and Cadmus.

Dionysus, the "god of theatre" (Easterling, 1997), is the perfect vehicle for Euripides' ultimate demonstration of this philosophy. The *Bacchae* pictures the delicate balance inherent in poetic *furor* itself between joy/creativity and frenzy/destruction. (Democritus, E. R. Dodds tells us [1951], was the first to speak of poetic *furor*.) If Medea is a cruel analytic mother to Jason, Dionysus is a cruel analytic mother-father figure. For Pentheus the "man of sorrows", he is the type of god pictured in Christ's "Father, why hast thou forsaken me?" There are many strange premonitions of the Christian story here, and indeed according to Sophie Mills (2006) Agave's lament for Pentheus served as a model for a twelfth century author's *Christus Patiens*.

Some critics interpret the play as a failed initiation rite, and this seems a helpful way of approaching it. We could also call it a failed psychoanalysis. Pentheus, like Hamlet, is on the verge of adolescence, and his turbulent feelings (the females of the city) have been banished to the mountain Cithaeron, where wild things happen – they have gone "mad" and, he suspects, are obsessed

56   THE ART OF PERSONALITY

with sexual desires and practices outside the city's social institutions and mores. There is an interesting split between the "good" Bacchae of the Chorus, Dionysus' confirmed followers, with their emphasis on natural joy and desire, and the unstable Bacchae who are on the mountain and who can switch in a moment from peace to rapacity. (We never see these Bacchae; they are only imagined or dreamed, their activities recounted by messengers.) It has also been suggested that this pattern might be based on a difference between the Dionysus of Athens and of Thebes: there are two types of Dionysus, or he has two faces, ecstatic and violent. The mad Bacchae on the mountain, flesh-tearers rather than joyous fawn-like dancers and singers, are those who have denied the god: "You did not believe that he was a god" as Cadmus tells his daughter Agave at the end (he likewise was not a believer and is likewise punished).

Dionysus himself opens the play, announcing that he is the son of Zeus and of Semele, Cadmus' daughter, who was consumed by Zeus' lightning-flame; and the evidence is on stage in the form of her still-smoking tomb, covered in vines, a symbol of Dionysiac energies. Dionysus himself was twice-born, first from his mother's womb then from Zeus' thigh where his gestation was completed. His birth suits his own ambiguous sex, a male god with feminine characteristics. He presents himself as a new god who has come to Greece from the East, the land of the barbarians (like Medea – the source of alien emotionality). Yet at the same time, he has come home – to the Theban palace where he was partly born, and where Cadmus still resides though he has handed over his rule to his grandson Pentheus. Thus Dionysus is both an alien and a member of the family, Pentheus' cousin. This is the paradox which confronts Pentheus though he does not know it. How can an ambiguous, ambivalent, attractive yet repulsive figure such as Dionysus find a place in his own mind? What can he make of such a kinship? Not only is Dionysus a new god: he is a new kind of god, who merges boundaries – and shows the inside outside, face to face with the unconscious, the gods within.

For the object of Dionysus' quest is to open men's eyes and ears so that they can learn to see what is in front of them – that is, what is inside them. He says he has come in defence of his mother Semele to prove that her lightning-blasted death is a testimony to divine insemination, not divine punishment for sexual transgression.

He is a god who disturbs the status quo – the established order, the rule of reason, logic, daylight, patriarchy, the city, etc. – and opens channels of communication with the female, irrational, emotional,

WOMEN, GODS, AND WITCHES IN EURIPIDES 57

wild nature. At the same time, bringing polarities together has the effect of making visible a split in the mind's unity. Thus at the beginning of the play Dionysus describes how he has made the women of Thebes mad, driving them out of their established social roles and divisions. In a departure from the social norm, slaves and aristocrats have congregated together on the mountain:

> DIONYSUS: Mixing with the daughters of Cadmus they sit together beneath the green firs on the roofless rocks. For this city must learn to the full – even if it does not wish to – that it is still uninitiated in my bacchanals and I must speak on my mother Semele's behalf by appearing to mortals as a god whom Zeus begot. (ll. 36–42)[2]

He then calls in the Chorus of his eastern-bred Bacchante, his follow-ers, who will represent the Dionysiac spirit onstage even when the god himself is not there: or rather, they represent the joyous creative aspects of the Dionysiac, through dance, song and poetic imagery, whilst the destructive Bacchic action takes place later off stage. The good Bacchantes sing of the joy in flinging off the constraints of society and the city, and the upsurgence of creative spirit:

> Euoi!
> The soil flows with milk, it flows with wine, it flows
> With the nectar of bees.
> The Bacchic god, holding on high
> The blazing flame of the pine torch
> Like the smoke of Syrian frankincense,
> Lets it stream from his wand
> As he spurs on the stragglers
> While they run and dance,
> And rouses them with his joyous cries,
> Flinging his delicate locks into the air …
> Happily then, like a foal beside its grazing mother,
> The bacchant skips with quick feet as she runs. (ll. 142–169)

Their words poetically evoke life on the "mountain", where city rules do not apply. By contrast, immediately afterwards is the semi-comic episode when Teiresias and Cadmus appear dressed as maenads. They represent entrenched city values trying to keep up with the latest religion, which they can embrace only in theory

---

2   Line references are to J. Morwood (transl.), *Euripides: Bacchae and Other Plays* (1999).

58   THE ART OF PERSONALITY

but not in spirit. Their concern, like bad actors, is with looking the part – not with identifying with the inner nature of the character.

> TEIRESIAS: I see that you feel in the same state as I do. For I am young too and shall join the dance.
> CADMUS: Shall we go to the mountain in a carriage?
> TEIRESIAS: If we do, the god will not have the same honour. (ll. 190–193)

The Bacchic rules state that nobody, however old, can go to the mountain in a carriage. Even Teiresias' assurance that in this new religion there is no distinction between young and old – "all should dance" – sounds like the result of academic study (he is a "professional ecclesiastic" as Kitto [1939] put it). Teiresias is careful to speak impeccably correctly. But Cadmus, who is less confident, advises Pentheus to "tell a lie for credit's sake" and pretend that Dionysus is Semele's son: "Even if this Dionysus is not a god, he should still be called one by you" (l. 333).

The irony is that despite his hostility, Pentheus is closer to the spirit of his divine cousin: his emotional reaction of disgust or hate thinly veiling a prurient curiosity which is only a slightly offkey version of love. He is potentially a genuine initiate, unlike his uncle. As a new and inexperienced king, he believes it is his role to control the madness of the women, for the safety of the city. He is immature both as a man and as a king, but his interest is in what drives the Bacchae on and makes them dance – an energy which he takes to be flagrant sexuality. (And despite the fact that the women are reported as "chaste", the communal dance does have this aura of sexual manic celebration, verging on the sinister when it tips into devouring and dismembering – the aspect of the ritual indicating possessive greed, an extreme form of introjection.) His vision of cutting off Dionysus' head (in the form of the stranger) reflects the Dionysiac nature as it later redounds on himself, when his head is speared on his mother's *thyrsus* – the "violent fennel wand". He understands what Dionysus would do in so far as he is like Dionysus; and the god responds to the perceptions of his subject.

Pentheus will be hunted like a wild animal by the Bacchae. But it is a hunt that he initiates himself, in the form of the seeking out the stranger who is Dionysus and who is at same time (in a certain sense) a facet of himself. The servant reports:

> SERVANT: Pentheus, we have come here after hunting down the quarry which you sent us for ... But we found this wild beast tame. (ll. 434–436)

The wild beast-god is caught without resistance, by the curiosity of Pentheus embodied in his "servant". Dionysus in the form of the "stranger" kindles his curiosity, which indicates a hidden desire to search for a mirror that will reflect the Dionysus within himself. Euripides here probes the very structure of identification.

The two protagonists become increasingly entangled through step-by-step stichomythia (dialogue in alternating lines). Much of the dramatic tension in these confrontations comes from this questioning of identity (enhanced by the actors wearing masks) and the strange sense that the answer to the "hunt" is there in the mirror all the time. Pentheus has caught Dionysus in his "net", unaware that he himself is the one who is trapped:

> SERVANT: It is up to you to decide what comes next.
> PENTHEUS: Let go of his hands. Now that he is in the net, he is not
> so nimble that he will escape me. Well, physically you are not
> unhandsome, stranger, to a woman's taste at any rate ... you
> have long flowing locks, whch prove you no wrestler. They fall
> right by your cheek, laden with desire. (ll. 450–456).

There is already a homosexual erotic attraction in the nature of Pentheus' feminine identification – "not unattractive to a woman's taste". There is emphasis on Dionysus' hair – the flowing locks which express abandon and dissolution of boundaries; Pentheus threatens to "cut off your love-locks". The narcissism that goes along with the delusion that he is in control, the king, the one who "decides what comes next", is what will be shattered in the ensuing course of events (symbolised by the dismemberment of his body).

There is a contrast between the old men's shallow pretence and Pentheus' emotional engagement, however ambivalent. This is led on and stimulated by Dionysus' answers which Pentheus calls "sophistical". Thus he asks about the rituals and is told that the uninitiated "must not know", to which Pentheus reacts: "You faked that answer skilfully to make me want to hear". How, asks Pentheus, did this stranger become initiated by Dionysus himself, and did it happen "in a dream or face to face"? The stranger mediates between Pentheus and the god, as if representing an aspect of both of them. There is a passage at the end of the play, where Agave is gradually released by her father from her delusion, which is sometimes known as the "psychotherapy scene". Before that, however, the debate between Pentheus and his alter-ego the god resembles psychotherapy in its suspicious, emotionally loaded skirting around problems of knowledge, recognition and

60 THE ART OF PERSONALITY

identification. Pentheus (says Dionysus-as-therapist) must "pay for [his] ignorance and impiety". The payment is his therapy and also his dismemberment. The role of the therapist is not merely to be a comforter; it also entails a type of cruelty owing to its rearrangement of parts of the self (catastrophic change); and the recognition process – which is self-recognition – begins early on.

Their discussion hinges on the nature of words and their meaningfulness, and the problems of appearance and reality:

> PENTHEUS:The god, just what was he like? Tell me, for you say
> you saw him clearly.
> DIONYSUS: He appeared in the form he chose. I did not arrange
> this.
> PENTHEUS: Here again you have sidetracked me with fine but
> empty words. (ll. 477–480)

The scene is reminiscent of the Pauline concept of "seeing through a glass darkly" as distinct from "face to face". Pentheus is clearly curious about the "face to face" experience; and this is what leads to his downfall – or conversion? The wordplay suggests how in being unable to recognise the god who is facing him, he is also unable to see himself and his own nature:

> DIONYSUS: You do not know what your life is, or what you are
> doing, or who you are.
> PENTHEUS: I am Pentheus, the son of Agave and of my father
> Echion.
> DIONYSUS:You have a name fit to sorrow for. (ll. 507–509)

The spiritual definition of identity is contrasted with the legal or familial label that identifies a man within his society. As Shakespeare puts the problem: "Is it possible he should know what he is, and be that he is?" (*All's Well*, IV. i. 35). Divorced from spiritual knowledge, Pentheus becomes a man of sorrows, entering into the implications of his name (now explicit), when he shuts Dionysus in the stables of his palace to "do his dancing ... in the black darkness" (with anal connotations): the claustrophobic alternative to the freedom of the mountain of dreams. The Chorus say he is "revealing his earth-born ancestry, the old dragon's brood" (referring to the myth of the founding of Thebes). These Theban foundations refer also to faecal mass, shortly to be expelled by Dionysus-Bromius who is "lord of thunder" – in the sense that thunder may also be equated with rectal activity (as in the Victorian term "thunderbox" for toilet). At the same time as his identity as man of sorrows is

WOMEN, GODS, AND WITCHES IN EURIPIDES   61

becoming clarified, Pentheus becomes a type of Everyman as in the medieval mystery plays. His body in the form of his house is shaken and struck by lightning like a caricature of his aunt Semele, by Dionysus-Bromius whose thundering shows him to be a true avatar of Zeus the thunderer:

CHORUS: Ah, ah,
  Can you not see the fire, do you not perceive
  Around this holy tomb of Semele
  The flame which Zeus' thunder-flung bolt
  Left here long ago?
  Throw throw your trembling bodies
  To the ground, maenads. (ll. 596–601)

Dionysus' name echoes in sound the recurring word "deinos" – meaning strange or terrible, ambiguous in its connotations, yet becoming increasingly synonymous with disaster or revenge, symbolised by rectal mass returned to the ground, rather than dancing figures in the air-space. The palace fire is a kind of dream: semi-fictional since it appears to take place in the imagination of the Bacchae, and Dionysus himself is in two places at once; thus he recounts his adventures in Pentheus' stables-bottom with his raging, panting and dripping sweat, adding that he was all the time "nearby / sitting quietly watching". Meanwhile the language of the Chorus' ecstatic adoration prefigures Christian worship in a way unusual in classical plays:

CHORUS: O light of our day, our leader in the ecstatic rituals,
  How joyful I am to see you, all alone in my isolation.
DIONYSUS: Did you fall into despair when I was being taken
    inside –
  Thinking that I was about to fall into the snares of Pentheus'
  dark dungeon? (ll. 608–611)

Pentheus the "man of sin" has attempted to manage the women of his house – his emotions – by tyrannical means, but is out of his depth. It is when he appears to realise this (they always escape) that he "converts" to following Dionysus, although it is a false conversion, founded on the dominance of his intrusive or voyeuristic curiosity about his internal mother (Agave). The intrusive curiosity comes to the fore in response to the Messenger's account of the crazy or "bad" Bacchae who are on the mountain: young mothers have deserted their own infants to give milk to wild animals. They tear cattle asunder with bare hands and their *thyrsi* turn to weapons:

"Women did these things to men. A god certainly helped them" (p. 65). Pentheus listens with fascinated disgust to the upturning of established order – it is "beyond endurance" to suffer "at the hands of women". Yet all the time he is drawn closer to Dionysus:

> PENTHEUS: I am locked together with this stranger and can find no escape from the hold. He will be silent neither when he offers nor when he acts. (l. 800)
> DIONYSUS: Sir, it is still possible to set this matter right.
> PENTHEUS: By doing what? By being a slave to my own women?
> DIONYSUS: I will bring those women here without the use of weapons. (ll. 800–804)

It is a type of psychoanalytic wrestling match – perhaps the stranger is a wrestler after all. Pentheus is convinced Dionysus will come up with some new "trick", verbal or psychological. Dionysus asks: "How can it be a trick if I am willing to save you by my skills?". But Pentheus does not want to be saved, he wants to get inside; he calls again for weapons, and tells Dionysus to "stop talking". This irritates Dionysus to the extent that he is in a sense seduced by Pentheus' own psychosis:

> PENTHEUS: Bring me out weapons here, and you, stop talking!
> DIONYSUS: Ah! So you want to see them sitting together on the mountain? (ll. 809–810)

This "Ah!" has been identified as the turning point of the play (Hall, 1999). If Pentheus will not allow the women to be brought to him, he will be brought to the women, in a woman's dress – the mountain will go to Mahomed. The child-Pentheus' intrusive curiosity leads to the type of projective identification that makes Agave a bad or at least a punitive mother, rounding vengefully on the lordly child who is obsessed with his perverse vision of his combined-object "sitting together" in a sexual orgy. Dionysus, like an impatient psychoanalyst, prepares to "save" Pentheus ruthlessly, by the sacrifice of his egotistical self, demonstrating his vanity and fragile exoskeleton. In some respects similar to the destruction of Glauce in *Medea* by means of poisoned clothes, Dionysus tells Pentheus he will personally dress him inside his palace. But the externalities represent false emotions, like the superficial homage paid by Cadmus and Teiresias. Now Pentheus is going to become a bad actor. He takes on long hair like Dionysus, and women's robes which will mark him out not as one of the Bacchae but as one to be "slaughtered at his mother's hands" – a projective or voyeuristic type of identification, "eager to see what you should not" (l. 912). "How do I look then?" asks Pentheus, becoming like a young girl who feels she is walking with a bull, groomed by the god who tells him how to wear his clothes and hair, etc: "This lock of your hair has slipped from its place. It isn't as I tucked it beneath your headband" says Dionysus, in fake reprimand. We are reminded of primitive marriage rites such as those in which the bride's virginity is proved to the expectant crowd, waiting outside, by waving the bloodstained white wedding sheet. A complicit mother may indeed have felt she was sacrificing her daughter to a bull (one of Zeus' own manifestations).

The mad *sparagmos*-dance or dream involves Pentheus in a phallic delusion, perched in the crown of a pine-tree, where Dionysus "with smiling face" throws his "deadly noose" around him, a cruel way of showing him his identity, mirroring his own tyrannical (masturbatory) imprisonings with the use of the white "iron hands" of the female gang, a form of self-rape in fantasy. The Bacchae on stage imagine what is happening, and then the Messenger reports the denouement:

> MESSENGER: Agave spoke: "Come, stand round in a circle and take hold of the trunk, maenads, so that we can capture this climbing beast and stop him reporting the secret dances of the god … Perched on high, he fell … Pentheus the sorrowful." (ll. 1106–1113)

The implications of Pentheus' name are fulfilled. Finally, Agave enters, returning slowly to everyday consciousness from the mountain of dreams or madness – exiting her claustrophobic position of imprisonment in an intrusive identification. In Donald Meltzer's (1992) account of the claustrum it is not possible to engage in the true transference–countertransference until the patient has managed to exit from a state of mind in which internal objects are locked in mutual intrusive identification; it is possible only to describe the features of the internal world in which the patient lives.[3] Although the classical play is far more stylised than the Shakespearean, the interchange of masks and roles has a modern ring of internal identifications being enacted. The actor who played Pentheus returns wearing the mask of his mother, with his head (mask) on the spike of her *thyrsus*:

> CADMUS: Look at it closely and you will reach a clearer understanding.
> AGAVE: I see a sight that brings me infinite pain and misery.
> (ll. 1281–1282)

---

3 This was pointed out by Marina Vanali during a seminar at Biella.

64   THE ART OF PERSONALITY

Is any true reintegration is possible after this catastrophe? It appears there is only exile for Cadmus and Agave, and a reassembling of dead parts for Pentheus: "Is every limb laid decently by limb?" asks Agave in the pathos of this mere shadow of reparation.

At the same time however, the catastrophe points to the myth of Dionysus' own dismemberment and regeneration – the only god who (like Christ) takes on flesh and dies in order to save mankind by his skills. Is there a sense in which he has "saved" Pentheus as he promised, through this identification? Perhaps it was the only way Pentheus could be brought to recognise Dionysus as the son of Zeus, a force which is ambiguously and by turns "a most terrifying and a most gentle god to mortals". Or as it says in the Bible after the Resurrection, "Surely this was the son of God." There is a sense in which the entire drama is also about the reactions of the theatre audience (or the reading process). Since Dionysus is the theatre-god, perhaps Euripides' ultimate message to his viewers is that in order to ensure his powers are therapeutic, rather than inflammatory, we need to focus on the nature of our own emotional involvement, analysing our attitude to the artform to ensure that it is fuelled by introspective rather than intrusive curiosity. We too are Bacchae, but of what kind – good or bad? On the frontiers of new psychic horizons, is "catastrophic change" possible for us in its developmental sense, or merely its destructive sense? The answer is not the sole responsibility of the playwright, but lies in our own individual identifications.

CHAPTER FOUR

Reversing perversion: a musical resolution to *Wuthering Heights*[1]

The "aesthetic conflict" (Meltzer & Williams, 1988), namely the passionate turbulence of love and hate in the face of beauty and truth of the object, may be engaged in or retreated from; it is the perennial human predicament in all situations that demand development or "catastrophic change" (Bion), and is the underlying theme of most enduring literature.

In *Wuthering Heights*, Emily Bronte set herself the task of filtering the genuine or passionate elements of love and hate from their destructive imitations that tend towards entropy, emotional paralysis and revenge – the claustrum that stifles personality development. Key to this process of filtration was her ambiguous Byronic hero Heathcliff, who functions as an organising principle in the novel and as a magnet for both positive and negative emotions; he has the potential both to promote and to retard growth. And her method of filtration was essentially musical, as I wish to demonstrate: the revolution that blew through the exposed levels of the moor-mind when "Byron" entered the Heights ultimately found a musical resolution.

---

1   This chapter on musical structure is based on the analysis of poetic structure in my book *A Strange Way of Killing: The Poetic Structure of Wuthering Heights* (1987). A version was previously published as "The hieroglyphics of Catherine: Emily Bronte and the musical matrix" in S. Hagan & J. Wells (eds.), *The Brontes in the World of the Arts* (Ashgate, 2008).

66   THE ART OF PERSONALITY

The Byronic hero and psychoanalysis

The Byronic hero was a cultural construct that originated in Shakespeare's Hamlet and in Milton's Satan, with the addition of some local colouring from contemporary popular tales of ghosts and vampires in the Gothic novel. The denomination attached itself to Lord Byron owing to his flamboyant public persona – "mad, bad and dangerous to know" as he was described by one of his lovers (Lady Caroline Lamb); also because of the apparent similarity between himself and the heroes of his poems. The Byronic hero had, typically, a passionate but melancholic nature; mysterious origins – that is, unknown or disguised parentage; a childhood in some respects happy, even idealised, yet darkened by hints of incest or some other crime. He was a restless character, stigmatised by society for "murkiness of mind" (*The Giaour*), though "not all degraded" and showing "brighter traits with evil mixed". In other words, he was an adolescent. The Romantics invented not just psychoanalysis but also the Teenager – a type that the rational Enlightenment seemed to have forgotten, at least since Shakespeare. Byron was the celebrity of the age like a modern pop-star, and all the young Brontes hero-worshipped him. He died in 1824 when the Brontes were teenagers, and they knew about his more complex side from Thomas Moore's publication of his letters (1933), in which – like Hamlet – he championed the melancholic, haunted, obsessive type of thinking that accompanied the sense of being an outcast from society and seen as a menace or a "devil", whilst always driven by a "quest of hidden knowledge" (*Manfred*). For these antisocial propensities were inextricable from the metaphysical concerns that characterised the Romantic movement – that is, what kind of substance is *a mind*? Byron wrote:

> Man is born passionate of body, but with an innate though secret tendency to the love of Good in his Mainspring of Mind. But God help us all! It is at present a sad jar of atoms. (Byron, 1973, p. 278)

Emily Bronte's moor landscape is a metaphor for just such an adolescent mind, full of conflicting characters that make it a "sad jar of atoms". This appears first in the famous dream in which a storm of snowflakes merges with the letters of Catherine Earnshaw's name, whirling around in Lockwood's brain. The child's hand bleeding as it thrusts through the broken glass of his bedroom window, indicates the sadomasochistic background to the idea of the deprived or excluded child. "Terror made me cruel", says Lockwood – the apparently civilised city-dweller who has come to the moors filled with romantic notions about country life and quietness, but ignorant of the violent emotions that lie buried beneath a latency mentality. It is a Byronic dream associated with the loss of a female sister-lover or mother-figure, resulting in an eternal haunted restlessness which the dreamer is perpetually trying to fight off or sublimate through other mismatched and vaguely incestuous relationships. After the dream Lockwood finds the moorland covered in snow, obliterating all his familiar landmarks; he takes to his bed for some weeks in order to digest the involved romantic history of the protagonists that the housekeeper Nelly relates to him in stages.

Wuthering Heights thus begins with a swirl of unintelligible hieroglyphics, a sad jar of atoms, a state of mental disorientation. As the story becomes gradually revealed to Lockwood, this chaos is traced back to the turbulence caused by the arrival of the mysterious Heathcliff a generation ago – a "gift of God" who is nonetheless "as dark as the devil". Heathcliff is a variant on the Byronic hero, the outcast who is nonetheless essential to the moor-mind's vitality and continued existence, and who is adhesively identified with the first Catherine, as in the famous romantic declaration "I *am* Heathcliff". When this adhesiveness is split, as is required by psychic development, there is a danger of the mind taking revenge on itself: "catastrophic change" is on the horizon. The challenge is how to integrate the vitality without the destructiveness: how to reform the idea of egocentric romantic love, how to defeat death by detoxifying the perversity of the Byronic hero.

Love, hate, and perversity are closely entwined in the first generation, and an element of perversity has been bequeathed to the next generation; they have to find their own way of dealing with this inheritance – a way of selecting the ghost's vital aspects and discarding the tyrannical vengeful ones. Money-Kyrle stresses how the process of revitalising is one of clarifying and withdrawing the perverse projections, rather than of inventing something new. The death impulse is entropy; the life impulse is synthesis (Money-Kyrle, 2014, p. 38). This is a progressive clarification, in stages. For it is a significant feature of the book's structure that a single generation is not considered enough to cope with the turmoil aroused by the impact of the "new idea" on the moor-mind. The idea is introduced in the form of the ambiguous gifts imported by old Earnshaw in his greatcoat after his journey to Liverpool – a whip for Cathy, a fiddle for Hindley, and the young Heathcliff who thrashes about and in the process

68 THE ART OF PERSONALITY

crushes the fiddle, prefiguring his crushing of Hindley and his fragile but musical soul. It takes three generations to constructively absorb the impact of the new idea and to make a fruitful catastrophic change in the mind's structure. We can view these three generations not just in the literal sense, but also as a metaphor for the multiple levels of working-through that are necessary to achieve integration or synthesis of the useful parts, and to accept without denial the uselessness of the perverse ones (the Linton Heathcliffs) and the waste of vitality that they incur. This understanding is founded on a progressive process of filtration, across linear time and also in a transverse dimension, crossing backwards and forwards between the two houses at either end of the moor, weaving the web of a new mentality.

The new generation differs from its predecessors in developing a capacity for "suffering" in the sense that Bion distinguishes as developmental rather than sadomasochistic. They are associated with the elasticity of steel rather than the brittleness of iron. Where their parents collapsed into selfish tantrums, the new generation learn to nurse and digest their wounded feelings and survive their humiliations, by means of internalising their inner gods rather than demanding to possess them. Instead of attempting to bend their objects to their will, they respond to an underlying principle of development, sensed through internal movements. This process is facilitated by the "housekeeper" Nelly Dean, a containing housekeeper-mother-analyst-storyteller. Yet her helplessness reminds us that modern psychoanalysis may often stress the need for containment, at the expense of neglecting the religious concept of suffering. Nelly empathises, reflects and observes, and on a level of practical necessity she participates and promotes life. But, alone, she cannot achieve catastrophic change in the moor-mind. The religious dimension is represented for Emily Bronte by the walking, purgatorial ghosts, ever-present on rainy nights. It was not the religion of her father's church – at the end of the novel the church slates are on the point of falling off into the turf. But perhaps it was her perception of his internal religion, after his own crossing of the Irish sea and romantic marriage to Maria.

Byron himself never stayed long enough in one place to truly suffer. A brilliant poet, he always sought action: "*Onward! - Now is the time to act!*" as he wrote in a letter. His most popular, and beautiful, lyric is the one beginning "So we'll go no more a-roving". Pursued through Europe by Poetry, Dreams and Woman, he ended up like Hamlet with "a soldier's grave" in the Greek war of independence. Containment alone ends in the coffin. It cannot deal with perversity. Emily Bronte split Byron's story between Lockwood and Heathcliff – forcing him to lie on the couch and listen to his internal conflicts – and in a sense rewrote the inner life of her own adolescent hero.

When Lockwood (Emily Bronte's pun) is introduced – and introduces us – to the moor-mind it is at its nadir, and the principle of revenge appears to have triumphed; but his capacity for dreaming "unlocks" the psychic impasse. Heathcliff, the victorious tyrant, is the most persecuted and self-imprisoned, haunted not by an inspiring spirit but by a persecutory "collection of memoranda" of a lost love whose meaning is ever absent, a spectral teasing. Yet ultimately, Heathcliff "thwarts himself"; his revenge is abandoned not through deliberate willpower but through passive inspiration, in fact against his will. This represents the de-perverting of the Byronic hero in his satanic glamour.

It has been said by Hans Loewald that the way out of tragic impasse and the standard revenge cycle is to "convert ghosts into ancestors" (Mitchell, 1998). The problem confronting Emily Bronte at the culmination of the era of the Byronic hero was: will the mind lapse into self-destruction, persisting in its revenge on its internal forebears, or will it find a way of using stormy adolescent energies constructively to "remake itself" (as Yeats put it) – perhaps by reviewing its own ancestry and effecting a transformation from persecutor to muse or facilitator? This is the area in which the Byronic hero merges with the metaphysical preoccupations about the nature of existence and of mind itself that Emily Bronte imbibed from the Romantic poets – or in internal objects and in what sense they become the mind's ancestors.

The musical matrix

How did Emily Bronte achieve this constructive reversal of perversion, this metaphysical revolution? The remarkable quality of her novel lies not in its content, characters and situations which are in many ways standard Gothic; not even, solely, in the embedding of these features in her moorland landscape. Rather it lies in their orchestration: in a polyphonic combination of voices and vertices that seem to emerge from their matrix in the moor of soul-making and swarm like Catherine's snowstorm of "hieroglyphics" around the reader's head. As Forster (1927) said, the characters' emotions, instead of inhabiting them, surround them like thunderclouds. The realistic landscape becomes a mental one.

70   THE ART OF PERSONALITY

Charlotte Bronte defined the originality of Emily's poetry in terms of its "peculiar music – wild, melancholy and elevating" (C. Bronte, 1972, p. 4). What are the elements of this "music"? As always in artistic creativity, the greatest originality of expression coincides with the deepest absorption of artistic teaching, the point at which the artist is most in contact with the essential inspiration of his or her predecessors – learning by assimilation rather than by precept. And Emily, like most poets, makes her contact by musical means. She hears the music above everything else, puts her trust in it and follows where it leads, casting her "anchor of Desire/ Deep in unknown Eternity" (Bronte, 1941, p. 232). Unknown eternity is the infinite Platonic source of musical ideas (equivalent to Bion's "O"), and its messages are brought like soundwaves by the "glorious wind" she so frequently invokes. The "spirit's sky" is a source of "strange minstrelsy" where "a thousand thousand silvery lyres/ Resound far and near" (Bronte, 1941, p. 199), or where, as with Caliban, "a thousand twangling instruments" may "hum about [the] ears". Shakespeare, Milton, Byron and Coleridge are primary influences on the music of her own language; their phrases are stored as sound in her Aeolian bag, awaiting the release of inspiration. Milton's early poetry, with its explicitly musical themes, frequently finds an echo in her own voice. Like him she sees a transforming power in music, "Dead things with inbreathed sense able to pierce" (Milton, 1966, p. 107). The inspiring wind is not a purely natural phenomenon but a container for the voices of all those who form part of her emotional legacy and who help to shape its theme-tunes. The mindset which has traditionally been termed "mysticism" is in Emily Bronte an inherent musicality. It accounts for the sense of autonomous powers at work which – as many readers have remarked – characterises the novel's progression. The music of the wind, in accordance with its Romantic embrace of the terror that lies in beauty, ranges from "flashes of storm" to "mute music", from "tempest's roaring" to "tempest's fall"; it combines both the beautiful (with its pleasing qualities) and the sublime with its awesome qualities:

> My spirit drank a mingled tone
> Of seraph's song, and demon's moan – (Bronte, 1941, p. 196)

It mingles sounds and contrary perspectives, dissolving in order to recreate, just as Catherine insists on the validity of both angelic-Linton and devilish-Heathcliff elements in her soul.

In one of Emily's poems, memory has "dyes" like the sounds from a harp.[2] As aestheticians have observed, sounds and colours are fundamental sensuous units of expressiveness – "feelings", the starting-point for a more complex evolution of symbolic structure. Their development may be spatial or tonal or both. Catherine speaks of the difficulty of expressing "a feeling of how I feel", and says her dreams flow "like wine through water", changing the colour of her mind (1972, p. 72). Creativity begins when "the hearts real feeling/ Has entire unbiased sway" (Bronte, 1941, p. 69) – a state of initial confusion or darkness. Catherine needs to find a symbolic mode that can artistically contain her state of mind and enable her to understand herself. Emily Bronte knew Moore's *Life of Byron*, published in 1833, and like Byron when he described his mind as a "sad jar of atoms", Catherine's emotional hieroglyphics are not combined aesthetically. How can the snowstorm of adolescent turbulence organise its contradictory emotions into a "love for life"? (p. 58). The question of whom she should marry brings to the fore the problem of how she might expand her constricted, egocentric identity through a creative otherness. Such an expansion, or exploration, begins when feelings start to combine into *motifs*, as in a lyric poem. This enables them to engage in a subject-and-answer arrangement as in music, seeking their partner or antithesis. This is what Susanne Langer termed "the morphology of feeling" in her *Philosophy in a New Key*, which used music as a starting-point for a theory of aesthetics. Music, she writes, "reveals the rationale of feelings, the rhythm and pattern of their rise and decline and intertwining", and in this way "becomes a force in our mental life, our awareness and understanding, and not only our affective experience (1942, pp. 238–39). In other words, musical form converts emotions into thoughts, or at least into patterns of understanding which are thinkable and interpretable. Emily Bronte pursues this process by means of her protagonists, in particular her heroine. At the beginning of the story the bewildered Lockwood – like the reader – is assailed by the whirling of Catherine's indecipherable hieroglyphics. By the end, this enigmatic notation has arranged itself into a new symbolism in which Catherine as wind-goddess gently animates the wild grasses, presiding over subsequent lovers and future emotional storms. When she achieves legibility she becomes a force in Lockwood's, Emily's, and our own mental life.

Wuthering Heights is unusual among novels in that it responds

---

2   One modern edition has "mournful dyes" but others read the manuscript as "memory's dyes".

72   THE ART OF PERSONALITY

to being considered in musical terms. Its literary descent may be traced back to the song–and–dance media at the very roots of culture: the odal and choric structure of Greek tragedy, the fatal inevitability of the ballad, the epic manner of interweaving narratives into singable episodes as in the oral tradition. The greater part of the novel is written in dialogue, tying it to drama, and insisting on the supremacy of the speaking voice. Music requires us only to describe, not to explain, its emotive effect on us. It is a liberating critical analogy, and has been invoked by readers who seek a means of describing the novel's poetic formal qualities. David Cecil's seminal essay saw the drama of the story in terms of the interaction of storm and calm. J. F. Goodridge wrote of its "cosmic polyphony" and saw it in terms of overture and opera (15, 78). The variety and driving force of its verbs, the subtle momentum of its syntax, and the organising function of key lyrical and dramatic passages, have been noted and admired by many critics. Stevie Davies compares the novel to a symphony, with its structure of exposition, development and recapitulation, and analyses its diction and its dynamics, which vary from storm to stagnation, tantrum to lullaby, soliloquy/recitative to duet or polyphony, single-strand lyricism to the cacophony of conflicting views (Davies, 1998, 96–107). She writes of the "volatile rhythm" of its dialogue structure, which "resembles less a voyage to the 'empty' heart of darkness than a musical exploration of themes extending their logic to its limit" (Davies, 2002, 96–97). The novel is structurally a mesh of repetitions and variations, and these have the "organic unity" characteristic of poetry and music rather than the usual "heterogeneity" described by J. Hillis Miller in his classic study *Fiction and Repetition* (1982). In *The Disappearance of God* (1963), Miller locates the "transcendent" quality of the novel in the way the second generation story is necessarily engendered by the first, "liberating energies" which "radiate back" to create the new religion: "The storm is greatest near the center. At the center is peace" (p. 209). This overall rhythmic patterning is a standard structural feature of longer musical works. The first movement is not an alternative to the last, but rather, its necessary harmonic ground.

Wuthering Heights has its motifs; its tendencies; its repeated themes and cadences; its contrapuntal interplay of voices; is dissonances and its harmony; its tonal distances and direction; and its significant timing. Firstly, however, it is a musical work on the fundamental level of sound-sensuousness. Even such a simple description as "the infant ruffian continued sucking" has its internal rhyme and rhythm (p. 120), that perfectly captures without sentimentality the child's childishness, as does the sound-cluster of "stammer a word ... totter a step ... despot's sceptre in his heart" (p. 152). It is no wonder Lockwood finds listening to Nelly"s story, from the enforced swaddling of his bedclothes, a "tiresomely active" process; it takes somatic possession of his body, leaving him "feeble as a kitten" (p. 35). Its music has got into him – from the "teasing sound" of his dream onwards, with its accompaniment of the "feeble scratching" of fir-fingers, "rappings and counter–rappings", and the "swarming" of snow-letters (like bees – not "storming"), modulating in the morning into the string of curses as Hareton performs his "orisons *sotto voce*" (p. 33). Hareton has learned his curses from his "devil-daddy" – an integral part of his earliest stammerings – and they are just as much a part of his musical education as is the dialect of Joseph, though both are in a conventional sense extra-curricular. Indeed Joseph's structural importance in the novel derives from the sound of his guttural uncouth drawl as much as from his ensconced Calvinistic illwill. He has no power to influence any of the characters, yet his existence is somehow indispensable, a parallel to Heathcliff"s "eternal rocks beneath" (p. 74); his deep timbre helps to maintain the overall orchestration, grounded in the northern moorland's authenticity. The fugal explorations of the protagonists depend in some way on his immovable antagonism, like a held note or chord, as the others in oblique motion weave their way round about his primitive tenacity.

The complex narrative structure of the novel entails a series of key motifs being presented for comparison like harmonic intervals: motifs such as the petted versus the neglected child; life versus its false semblance (as in the question of Catherine's "eyes"); angelic and devilish sides of the soul; fire or light in darkness; earthly versus ghostly existence; boundaries which may imprison or be broken through; the baby or creative spirit that emerges from "death"; the points of passionate transition or conflict – often marked by blood or violence – as in the "teething" motif, the menarche, or the "window" motif which was explored by Dorothy Van Ghent (1961). The underlying pulse of the novel derives from the way in which motifs and sequences are echoed and contrasted, accruing significance. A major source of disagreement between critics is the success of the second-generation story, the novel's denouement: is it merely a watered-down version of the first – an authorial imposition intended to correct a more exciting romantic fantasy – or can we find in its perfection of form a new and evolutionary morality? Thomas Vogler, for example, examines the pulsing dialectic of its "images of change" but concludes that there is no ultimate

74   THE ART OF PERSONALITY

resolution. It is, as is often acknowledged, a strangely "abstract" work – prompting Charlotte to call her sister a "theorist", or Heger to reflect on the power of Emily's "logic" (Gérin, p. 229; Gaskell, p. 151). If it were abstract in the sense of a mathematical formula, it probably would not capture our imagination – we would regard it as *merely* theoretical. But being abstract in the musical sense, it relies on its sensuous context – the evocation of the realities of nature and human nature – to engage our identification. Mark Schorer said Emily Bronte was "educated" by means of her own analogical matrix, as her narrative progressed (Schorer, 1972, p. 376). Strictly, it is the way the metaphors are linked – the *musical matrix* – that is the educational force, allowing the author to transcend her own romantic fantasy, but through expanding rather than negating its origins.

According to the *Oxford Dictionary of Music* the purpose of a musical form is to hold the musical Idea such that it is neither too repetitive nor too full of novelties to be able to *hold attention*. As the feeling of inevitable progression becomes established, our impression is reinforced that the novel is being driven forward like the Ancient Mariner's ship by "spirits beneath" – the current or windsong of its own ghosts; the author is listening to these pattern-shifting forces rather than imposing a preconceived framework. Langer explains the nature of the "commanding Idea" in a musical piece:

> In music the *fundamental movement* has this power of shaping the whole piece by a sort of implicit logic that all conscious artistry serves to make explicit... the great moment of creation is the recognition of the matrix, for in this lie all the *motives* of the specific work; not all the themes... but the tendencies of the piece, the need for dissonance and consonance, novelty and reiteration, length of phrase and timing of cadences ... Under the influence of the total "Idea", the musician *composes* every part of his piece. (Langer, 1953, p. 122)

The interleaved narratives of *Wuthering Heights* unfold according to this type of organic necessity, with the sense that they have not been imposed by the author but rather derive from a musical logicality. The author, like a composer, is listening to and following the musical Idea as it works itself out. At the deepest level of appreciation, it is the musical Idea that we – with Lockwood – listen to as we read the novel. Yet it is the musical, sensuous immediacy that holds our attention such that the Idea can operate; the mystical concept of eternity (a fount of potential energy) has to be manifest in the form of actual energies – which happen to take the shape of people, animals, land and weather formations on the moor.

The moor-landscape and its weather are for Emily Bronte the grounds of spiritual being, together with the birds and vegetation which like musical sounds testify to its life. For her the moors (as Charlotte said) were not a "spectacle" but "what she lived in and by" (C. Bronte, 1972, p. 10). She was reared herself in the "breeze-rocked cradle" of the second Catherine, and the myriad voices of the leaves rustling are "instinct with spirit" (1941, p. 146). One of her earliest known poems, "High waving heather", runs like a piece of organ–music between the registers of air and earth in what Milton in a description of organ-music called "perfect diapason": bending/blending/descending/sending/jubilee rending ... Bursting the fetters and breaking the bars" (p. 31). Indeed Patrick Bronte, her father, introduced an organ to the church at Haworth. Emily finds "jubilee" in this wind-induced intermingling – a key word in the novel, where it refers to both Catherine's reception of the returned Heathcliff, and the second Catherine's idea of heaven. Like Shelley's West Wind scattering words and dead leaves over the landscape, her visitor that "comes with western winds" insists on the death without which there can be no rebirth:

> When the ear begins to hear, and the eye begins to see;
> When the pulse begins to throb, the brain to think again,
> The soul to feel the flesh, and the flesh to feel the chain.
> (1941, p. 239)

This is real hearing and real seeing – when the pulse begins to throb. The rhythm is emphatic and brooks of no denial or turning-back. There can be no knowledge of abstract, mellifluous "eternity" without the concrete, metaphysical yoke of "the anchor of desire". If this is mysticism, it is not so in the escapist sense; the sensuous and the ineffable are inextricable from one another. The rhyme is "chain" not the expected "pain" – a musical surprise. It is only real because it jars, like the wrist of Lockwood's ghost rubbing against the broken glass. Because of the chain the pulse of the music can be felt. Music operates partly by going against its framework – its expected harmony or metre – yet in accordance with its *matrix*.

Emily Bronte navigates this musical matrix like the "great navigator" M. Heger saw in her (Gaskell, 1971, p. 151). Lockwood and Heathcliff "divide the desolation" of the moor–mind between them, as in musical division (p.13). This "suitable pair" create the tension of opposites within which the story is held, establishing its pattern of Subject and Answer. This tension sets the search for

76   THE ART OF PERSONALITY

Catherine's spirit in motion . The "sympathetic chord" between them which Lockwood is convinced he hears goes beyond irony to a higher truth (p. 15); in their apparent dissonance lies a latent potential for co–operation (p. 240). Between them they open a tonal window, a new dimension on the "stalled" condition of the present protagonists who have in various ways lost the meaning in their lives. Lockwood, from his wooden, windowed bed of dreams, hears that Cathy's ghost needs to be "let in", and Heathcliff cannot achieve this internal listening mode by himself; he feels in fact that he has been shut out from his symbolic capacities and these have been replaced by teasing hallucinations – instead of being a "ministering angel" (as in Lockwood's term) Catherine has become "a devil" to him since her death, blocking him from all soul-knowledge. Lockwood's curiosity however begins to open cracks in the rockface. History is brought into the present, through Nelly's masterly performance and Lockwood's listening-time. The "busy world" fades into insignificance as the inner story finds its voice (p. 205). Catherine's search to know herself is overlayered by the need for others to know Catherine (Lockwood, Heathcliff, the second Cathy); and the internalisation of her spirit in their minds is synchronous with Emily Bronte's progress towards symbol-formation in the novel. By this means the decadent, nostalgic music of the moor-mind is rejuvenated, its dead monuments inspired with new life.

The history of the Earnshaw music or creative spirit begins when old Earnshaw imports his ambiguous gifts (from "God or the Devil") in the shape of Cathy's whip and Hindley's fiddle, enclosed within his greatcoat and subject to the young Heathcliff's thrashing about. After his death, the old music of the Christmas celebrations is superseded by Cathy's search for a different music – the sort that sounds "sweetest at the top of the steps", striving towards the soul–knowledge associated with Heathcliff in his attic prison (p. 57). She is the leader in the orchestra, in her quest to absorb the reverberations of this primary theme; and Nelly can be considered the conductor: her "double-dealing" a necessary feature of musical listening (p. 188), hearing both separately and together, recognising the moment at which the next instrument must be allowed its entry, and making her own personal morality subordinate to the overall orchestration. She winds the contrary voices together just as she later twists together in Catherine's locket the contrasting locks of hair belonging to Edgar and Heathcliff (p. 140). When the musical Idea demands that Heathcliff has a final interview with Catherine, Nelly throws open the doors and windows. When it is necessary for the second Catherine to be made a prisoner at the Heights, all Nelly's efforts to release her are to no avail – comically so. Yet when the lawyer tries to override Edgar's instructions about being buried next to his wife, Nelly's "loud protestations" uphold the law. This is psychological necessity, not authorial omnipotence: Catherine's necessity – and the need for others to know Catherine – demands it, therefore the author must find some means of making it plausible. Emily Bronte is herself listening to the musical Idea of Catherine, composing it in her mind and running it through Nelly. The apparent irony of Lockwood's deciding to leave the area at the precise moment of Nelly's suggesting he should marry Catherine, is undermined by the greater irony of his function as catalyst to the latent romance between her and Hareton, on his farewell visit to Heathcliff at the Heights. Nelly's conducting succeeds beyond her hopes. Ultimately the windsong will end in the symbolic music of the "moths fluttering" and the "soft wind breathing" over the grave-mounds, spiritual emanations of the moor-mind's new gods.

The narrative progresses through consonance and dissonance, stress and release, and in the final cadences of each movement are sown the seeds of the next melody. None of the "accidents" in the story are accidental. It is no accident that Hindley chooses for a wife a flute-like "rush of a lass" (p. 60) whose music-loving "gay spirit" will imminently succumb to her already established tuberculosis, just as his fiddle was crushed by Heathcliff under the dubious protection of his father's greatcoat. This led to his giving up his horse – his stake in life – to the Heathcliff within, whom he interprets pessimistically as an impulse to destruction as lethal as tuberculosis itself. He then surrenders his home and child – Hareton being the final exposition of this particular theme-tune, last of the Earnshaw stock. Through Hareton, the musical spirit is transposed from Hindley's register to Heathcliff's and the tones mingle. It becomes the foundation for Heathcliff's ultimately "thwarting himself", his revenge paralysed by unin-tended but reciprocated feelings of love, the result of another striking modulation. This "thwarting" became inevitable from the moment when Heathcliff unwittingly caught Hareton at the precise moment of his father's dropping him from the banisters, bassing his trespass in a moment of climactic and far-sounding diapason, and testifying to his own obdurate link with the "rocks beneath". We may be impressed by the near-almanacal accuracy of Emily Bronte's chronology, but the essential feature is not the dating (the metre) but the *pulse* – the illusion of significant timing.

78   THE ART OF PERSONALITY

The "essence of rhythm", according to Langer, is "the preparation of a new event by the ending of a previous one ... everything
that begets expectation prepares the future"; musical rhythm is a
function of "tonal motion" not of "time division" (Langer, 1953, pp.
126–29).

All this unfolds in parallel motion to the antiphonal polyphony of the contrasting "fire" and "moonbeam" voices within
Catherine's soul, like "seraph's song and demon's moan". She
seeks an expansion or musical development from the monotony of
her egocentric identity ("I *am* Heathcliff"), which has become stale
and tiresome – "stalled" to use the word that the second generation adopt to express the absence of dynamic motion (pp. 235, 237).
It is no accident that when the first Catherine tries to explain to
Nelly her idea of an "existence beyond myself", the baby Hareton
is sleeping beside her, dreaming of a "mother beneath the mould";
and Heathcliff – whom she has called "dumb or a baby"– is lying
in a type of sound-shadow, cradled in the gap behind the settle
(pp. 72–4). He hears what is necessary to separate him from her,
and nothing more. Meanwhile Nelly recoils from being used as
Catherine's sounding-board, but as always, Catherine's push
towards symbolic expression is more powerful. Between them they
establish an interplay of voices which cannot find verbal expression yet which all contribute to the meaning of dreams told and
untold, a "feeling of how I feel". We, too, know there is *something
beyond* the state of mind which Catherine embodies at the time she
delivers her famous rhapsodic speech to Nelly's unwilling ears.
She sounds the leading note and our curiosity is aroused – what
does she mean? All we gather, from the total orchestration of this
tableau, is that her "prophesy" has to do with her future, unknown
existence. One day she too will be a mother beneath the mould,
and what then will be the condition of the Earnshaw "baby" – its
creative spirit? Heathcliff says her "will" is responsible for his
banishment, but in reality they are driven apart by something
deeper than self-controlled willpower. Their adhesiveness has been
stifling the voice of creative fulfilment, and the underlying musical
Idea demands progression. In a symphonic crescendo, the clatter
of soot and rattle of thunder sound the emotional thunderbolt that
has fallen in the midst of the hearth, at the mind's core. After this
storm Catherine's mind is split: her brainfever leaves her changed,
fragile, for she cannot achieve symbolic integration of her mind's
fire and moon colours by herself, in her own earthly existence. It
will require another movement, another generation, to reorganise
her straining emotional contraries.

It is the same with the other significant rites of passage. The deaths of Catherine, Isabella and Edgar occur when the younger generation are emotionally ready to supersede them as protagonists, neither sooner nor later; just as previously, the elder generation of Earnshaw and Linton parents fell away, in cadence, when their creative potential had been stretched to its limit. Pubertal ventures are laid down in sequence, then layered in memory so they augment in significance, resonating. Thus at the age of thirteen the second Catherine feels impelled to jump the bounds of her home in order to investigate the life on the other side of the moor, resonating with her mother's exploration of the opposite household at the same age where she became seduced by her new status as a princess. The red blood-spots of the menarche that mark these adventures are sound-colours indicating the urge to seek new harmonies beyond the known horizons. The static, simplistic princess-existence of the second Cathy requires enrichment: to know her mother she also has to know Heathcliff. Thus when she clambers down from her red-hipped, rose-covered wall (an autumnal echo of her breeze-rocked cradle) to find herself trapped on the other side, Heathcliff emerges on cue, at the roadside. She is then described as "dancing" to the tune of his horse's hoofbeats, in a type of pas-de-deux, with Nelly's concealed voice countering yet at the same time supporting its rhythms, in a form of syncopation (p. 188).

There is a sense in which the second Catherine has to become Heathcliff's child, not instead of but in addition to being Edgar's. This is not in the literal sense, any more than we need take Heathcliff to be literally an illegitimate child of Earnshaw's. Hareton matches this, in his own way, with his own adoption of Heathcliff as father – a love whose mystery has to be accepted by Cathy even though never understood. They both learn to absorb the volcanic implications of the Heathcliffian fire-and-rock stratum of the mind, that rumbles and jars in its unconscious depths. Cathy is a product of Heathcliff's transposition into a new key, beginning on the evening of the harvest moon when he returns to the district and emerges from the shadows of the Grange; he is recognisable by his "deep voice" (p. 82). The pulse of the story demands his reappearance, to disturb the tranquil but sterile harmony of Catherine and Edgar's marriage. "Nelly, is that you?" is a sound both familiar and unfamiliar, an instrumental entry announcing the next movement – which will culminate in death, and birth. He is the herald of Catherine's pregnancy and her existence beyond herself. He brings dissonance like a clashing chord, both "calamity" and "jubilee", enriching and stirring the latent creativity. His departure, and his return,

80   THE ART OF PERSONALITY

are opposite directions, yet both are necessary to the symphonic development.

The death-and-birth theme that began inside Earnshaw's pregnant greatcoat finds its most operatic expression in Catherine's delirium, near the centre of the novel. Here her wailing ghost takes shape, and links up with motifs that reach backwards and forwards in time. The ghost-elements are notes that we recognise from Lockwood's dream, and we now learn that they have been generated and flung to the winds to undergo a process of "moral teething" as Heathcliff calls it (p. 128). They spread through identification into her "pet" Isabella whom she calls her "child" and whose fascination with Heathcliff makes her (in Catherine's eyes) as vulnerable as a "canary in the park on a winter's day" (p. 89). She prophetically anticipates the recapitulation of this theme in the second part of the novel. However she is unable to anticipate her actual daughter's resilience – something beyond her own knowledge and capacity, and which represents not just the recapitulation of a theme but its further development. In the second movement the Catherine Earnshaw-Linton-Heathcliff hieroglyphics are shaken up like Byron's jar of atoms and the personality characteristics are redistributed, spreading their colours like wine through water, or blood through snow. The teeth of the new personality are later symbolised in the image of the triple headstones pushing through the earth's crust.

The "teething" motif thus aptly describes the chaotic swirl of notes during this central symphonic development, characterised by prolonged dissonance and *stretto*, like the process of birth itself. The feather–snowflake imagery, a multitude of white dots seeking formal arrangement, reappears in various forms, from the "score of glittering moons" reflected in the lattice at the time of Heathcliff's return (and originating in the glass chandelier of the Lintons' sitting-room), through the "spatters of milk" scattered over the stairs from Isabella's shattered jug, to Heathcliff's white "cannibal teeth" and snow-spattered shoulders at the Heights window. The chaotic spatterings of raw emotion (colour-sounds) are gathered together harmoniously for the "great occasion" of Catherine's last meeting with Heathcliff, which is characterised by the splashes of white seen in her book and dress and the stirrings of air that suggest her bird-soul fluttering, about to depart through the open window. Meanwhile Isabella and the image of her twitching little dog carry away the masochistic elements of Catherine's soul, leaving Catherine free to become the muse of the moor. The moment of change is underscored by the music of the moor, which always comes into being when we sense spiritual communication between the Grange and the Heights: the sound of the brook blends with the chapel bells through the onomatopeia of "bell–valley–mellow–flow–soothingly", modulating into the fulfilling cadence of "sweet substitute for the yet absent murmur of the summer foliage, which drowned that music about the Grange when the trees were in leaf" (p. 131). It is the music of communication between contraries, the beginning of the new symbol-formation.

By the time the second-generation recapitulation commences, the dissonance of the teething period has already achieved a measure of organisation. The ugly or destructive aspects of Heathcliff have either played themselves out, as in the death of Hindley, or been channelled into a distinct theme of their own which counterpoints with the developmental one, to be compared and contrasted. Isabella's residence at the Heights precipitates Hindley's death and releases him from his torment. It is, says Heathliff, a "labour of Hercules" to disentangle her "delusion" of him as a (Byronic) "hero of romance" (p. 127); but his labour bears fruit, as does Catherine's during her simultaneous experience of pregnancy. The white and red-marked feathers of her teeth-torn pillow are echoed by the sharp "i" sounds that recur in her ultimate reception of Heathcliff ("wild vindictiveness/ white/ lip/ scintillating eye", p. 133). These are reflected in the blue crescents impressed on her arm, and are repeated in Isabella's knife-cut and bruises, which she learns how to transpose into the more abstract mode of verbal form: "sticking in darts" and "pulling out the nerves with red-hot pincers", her "eyes sparkling irefully" (pp. 143, 148). Isabella, and later the second Catherine, have a capacity to taunt with psychic accuracy in a way that can penetrate Heathcliff's rockiness: "*Nobody* loves you – *nobody* will cry for you when you die!" sings Cathy (p. 228). Their vitality contrasts with the doomed blundering of Hindley, whose dead eyes express his loss of inner music: the vestigial remnants of Catherine, without colour, spark or expression. In him her hieroglyphics are purely notational, lacking that musical miracle of "breathing sense into dead things". Heathcliff however is emotionally pierced, and the ultimate dissolution of his body – after it is found rainsoaked by Catherine's window – starts here in "suffocating sighs" among the ashes (p. 149). Emily Bronte's "iron man" begins to melt internally, his fire quenched, following not the Byronic but the Miltonic model of the devil who can resist all power but music – as when Orpheus "Drew iron tears down Pluto's cheek/ And made hell grant what love did seek" (Milton, 1966, p. 94).

82   THE ART OF PERSONALITY

For the second generation derive their *energies* from the first, but their *strength* from battling with their inheritance. Like Cathy, who is "elastic as steel", Hareton is "tough as tempered steel" (p. 264). In them the Heathcliffian iron undergoes a chemical transformation. The first Catherine, finding herself incomprehensibly in an adult's body, wonders why she can no longer "laugh at injuries" as she could when a girl, "half savage, and hardy, and free", and not pregnant (p. 107). She is brittle, and breaks like the chimney-stack in the storm; her inner fire is self-destructive. The second Catherine however does not laugh away her injuries, in cavalier escapism, nor does she succumb to them – she *suffers* them, in the sense of passionate vibration, tuning her "temper" against them with mental elasticity. So she learns to conquer her humiliation and to differentiate real sorrows from wounded vanity. She "wuthers" the storm in the sense of Bion's "suffering". It is the counterpart to Heathcliff's "strange way" of being killed, where the vision of Catherine holds his body in an intolerable tautness of nerves. Emotional thunder and lightning do not break her; they are absorbed into her spiritual fabric, musically resolved.

The keynote of Cathy's spirituality is the "breeze–rocked cradle", which represents her idea of where her mother has placed her; it has a varied music of "rocking/ rustling/ dusky dells/ great swells/ undulating" to the breeze (pp. 198–9). It is a gentler variant on wuthering, ever-moving without being tempestuous. From this basis she confronts the strangeness of Hareton's rough music – his "vulgar accent", as she refers to it – and his periodic "thundercloud" brows that (like Heathcliff himself) ruffle her equanimity. When she is startled by his emerging from the roadside shadows, echoing Nelly's reaction to Heathcliff's reappearance at the Grange eighteen years earlier, we sense more than repetition – we sense *simultaneity* (p. 202). The novel creates its resonance through this essentially musical quality. It is an illusion in literature but not in music, since music is an art of time not of space. When Emily Bronte says it is "the same room, the same moon, the same landscape" as on another occasion years earlier (p. 227), this is precisely what she means. In one sense, the time is always the present – it is the time of performance, Lockwood's dream-time. The way he listens to the music makes us understand that the first Catherine is alive inside the second, her fluid hieroglyphics sounding notes that we recognise because they are in fact the same notes. Since *now* is when we are hearing it, now is when it is happening. Kierkegaard calls this the "musical erotic", something which is not amenable to "reflection", and says that it is for this reason we use musical

terminology to indicate "the obscure, the unaccountable, the immediate" (Kierkegaard, 1992, pp. 80–81).

The achievement of the musical Idea requires "absolute mutual
penetration" of matter and form, writes Kierkegaard; indeed
"inward mutualities … exist in every classic work" (pp. 66–67). A
concatenation of sounds is not music, any more than Byron's "sad
jar of atoms" or Heathcliff's "collection of memoranda" of the dead
Catherine, or the dead internal babies represented by Catherine's
dream of the nest of birds. These pieces of resemblance are not
alpha-elements (in Bion's terms) but beta-elements – they are
merely physical and not accompanied by soul or spirit. The beta-
elements have no vitality and are no use for thinking or dreaming,
unless some major mental reorientation can take place. Until there
is a synthesising movement, such as that represented by the eyes of
Cathy and Hareton moving together, these elements add up only
to a tantalising, persecutory, superficial reminder with no soul.
Symbol-formation occurs, Bion says, when two objects are "brought
together in a way which leaves each object with its intrinsic qualities intact … yet by their conjunction, are able to produce a new
mental object" (Bion, 1967, p. 50). The new object is the relationship
born of the link between expressive eyes. We come to understand
that Heathcliff has needed the next generation "about him" (p. 227)
not merely in order to torment them (as he supposed), but in order
to decipher the mystery of their vitality.

In his final period, Heathcliff's achievement of his "one
universal idea" – an internalised image of a live Catherine – is
differentiated from the deadness of mere signs, and forms the
countersubject to Lockwood's quest to decipher Catherine's
"faded hieroglyphics". When Heathcliff took revenge on
Catherine's eyes (her soul-windows) he found that she became
"a devil" to him, and therefore "lost", unresponsive to his call. It
is eighteen years before he can rediscover the music of her spirit,
unintentionally, by means of the younger generation and with
the unwitting help of Lockwood. Again it is achieved through a
musical immediacy in which the eyes move in unison, binding
the tonal interval; the separate notes (eyes) mean nothing except
in relationship, when the hieroglyphics fall into order. Now, as
in the poem, "The ear begins to hear and the eye begins to see".
Where Edgar's pulse stopped "almost imperceptibly", Heathcliff
approaches the harmonising crescendo of his death with a full
vibrato – "as a tight–stretched cord vibrates – a strong thrilling
rather than trembling", with "catgut nerves" (pp. 230, 256). His
"sighs succeeding each other so thick" mingle with the music

THE ART OF PERSONALITY

of the beck's murmur and "ripples gurgling" heard through the open window (pp. 259, 262). They are approaching the condition of wine in water – the symbolic transformation when his soul will find its "heaven" or "harbour", its meaningful containment.

Simultaneously with Heathcliff, though travelling a different road, Lockwood completes his own symbol-making journey, after his few months' respite in the "busy world". His fugue with Heathcliff approaches resolution in terms of the knowledge of Catherine, the moor-goddess. His earlier fear of a close encounter with her "second edition" in the form of her daughter modulates to a mingled feeling of discomfort and revelation. At last he comes to recognise his own "malignant" and devilish aspects; now he is no longer the innocent representative of civilisation, but a "skulker", like the dog of that name (p. 243). Emotionally he skulks on the threshold of adolescence, like any scowling teenager, his latency mind unlocked at last. First he becomes acutely aware of his "mingled sense of curiosity and envy" as he listens to the second Cathy teaching Hareton the pronunciation of "contrary!" with the help of a slap and a "voice sweet as a silver bell". She has, he formulates, a "smiting beauty" that had never struck him until it resonated from Hareton's visage, just as Heathcliff could not see Catherine in the eyes of Hareton or Cathy until they met his gaze together. At last the aesthetic conflict of love, hate (envy) and knowledge strikes him both sensuously and spiritually, and he responds to the passionate contrary tensions. Lockwood hears the music, and feels – for the first time – what it is *not* to be in love. But he also sees it is possible to be "not afraid" (p. 265); his education has begun. His final walk on the moor retraces his first one, between the two houses; but instead of a few "dirty dots" in a blankness of snow, he finds he can "see every pebble on the path, and every blade of grass by that splendid moon" – the word "splendid" evoking immediately the "splendid head" of the first Catherine. He has listened to the musical Idea; and now the hieroglyphics of Catherine contain meaning for him. He, too, has learned to read what is before his eyes.

In the course of her self-analytic journey in writing *Wuthering Heights*, Emily Bronte relied on her innate musicality to shape her conceptions, by means of her characters and their relationships. At the same time however there are also indications of her interest in contemporary philosophy, reflecting her informed view of the problems which she was investigating by these musical means. Stevie Davies compares Catherine's famous speech about the possibilities of annihilation of the self to Berkeleyan idealism, and cites an article on the dualistic thinking of Schlegel that was published in *Blackwoods* in 1843. This stated: "Everything would be good were it not for an ABER – for a HOWEVER – for a BUT ... Great indeed, is the virtue of a Schlegelian ABER" (Davies, 1998, p. 52). Emily Bronte would also almost certainly have read Coleridge's *Biographia Literaria* which contains his preoccupation with the German philosophy, and where he insists that "an IDEA cannot be conveyed except by a *symbol*" (Coleridge, 1997, p. 91). There is no "either–or" in a symbol; it is a new mental object. For the "yes but" philosophy is a kind of ideological prison which only the music that "comes with western winds" is capable of piercing. In the same year as the *Blackwoods* article on Schlegel, the young Soren Kierkegaard published his satirical yet deeply serious *Either/Or*, which (though not translated into English for another hundred years) gave a Heathcliffian volcanic blow to the complacency of Hegelian dialectics. It is unlikely but not impossible that Emily Bronte may have come to hear of it; certainly she was struggling, like Coleridge, with the philosophical context which generated it. They were all, from a bedrock of essential Platonism, seeking for a way out – a way that could give proper value to the transcendental powers of artistic expression, as distinct from the limited powers of rational argument.

The portrayal of Heathcliff's "strange change", as he comes to relax his own tyranny, has much in common with Coleridge's distinction between the worldly and powerful man of "commanding genius," and the artistic man of "absolute genius" who actually has a greater inner strength and is able to withstand "times of tumult" (Coleridge, 1997, p. 20). And Bronte has certain natural affinities with the Kierkegaardian cast of mind which make her road to knowledge in some ways parallel to his. They both knew that the acme of common everyday humanity (not just mysticism) consisted in something more than irony or resignation. Her irony is not the pessimistic type of continuous undermining, but the optimistic one of people speaking more than they know, as in ancient Greek drama. Ultimately Kierkegaard formulated his "leap of faith" in a way not unlike Bronte's "Faith ... arming me from Fear" (Bronte, 1941, p. 243); they were both idiosyncratic religious thinkers working out on the pulses their personal alternative to established religion. But it is interesting that in his first work, *Either/Or*, Kierkegaard's analysis of creativity focused not on faith but on music. What is Heathcliff's death-for-love if not a musically induced manifestation of the Kierkegaardian absurd? Music allows for the self to be led rather than to lead, and can therefore approach

86   THE ART OF PERSONALITY

an existence beyond the self. For *listening* is "the primary musical activity" (Langer, 1953, p. 148). Emily listened to the song of the "mother beneath the mould" and discovered how in psychological terms, development is possible: the child can survive spiritual death and become an adult in mind not only in body. She evolved a symbol for a "love for life" that is based on mutual respect not on narcissistic possessiveness or sadomasochistic control: preserving the mystery of the other's incomprehensible loyalties. The hieroglyphics of Catherine, once so swarmy and stormy, find their final composure in a reverie of fluttering moths and harebells, inspired by a "quiet breathing" that by no means precludes future storms, but offers instead the spiritual means of weathering them.

CHAPTER FIVE

The wound and its transformations: some stories by Kafka[1]

Kafka may be placed squarely in the tradition of Hamlet, Kierkegaard, and Dostoevsky, in terms of the struggle with existential *angst* and loneliness in the search for identity; all of whom we have discussed in the course of these seminars. Kierkegaard indeed he regarded as a "friend" whose situation mirrored his own, in that his self-analysis of his lack of faith was honed via an abortive love-affair. To these acknowledged influences (amongst others) Kafka added his reading of Freud: though he disagreed with Freud's hope that analysis could provide a "cure" for what was, in his view, essentially the problem of being alive. And the sense of loneliness or solitude was important to his view of an ongoing inner or spiritual life, to his personal religion in fact, as distinct from his societal religion where he was a committed but nonconformist Jew in the same way that Kierkegaard both denied and depended on his Christianity.

Kafka famously said that all his stories were about his father, or rather, about his conflict with his father, which he recognised to be a "primeval theme" (Janouch, 1969, p. 68). The father or authority who upholds the received values of family or society is often

---

1 Part of this chapter was first published as "The oedipal wound in two stories by Kafka", *Psychodynamic Practice* 23 (2017), pp. 120–132.

88   THE ART OF PERSONALITY

represented metaphorically by "the law" (including a certain type of Jewishness). The aim of this chapter is to consider Kafka's use of this background oedipal conflict as a springboard for the type of "wound" that results in creative writing – Kierkegaard's "wound of the negative" (Kierkegaard, 2009, p. 72, and was also associated with other painful stimuli such as the tuberculosis that overshadowed half his career, and his troubled love affairs with Felice Bauer and Milena Jesenská. It was a double-edged symbol of both life and death: for whose impact on both psyche and soma there was no psychoanalytic "cure" (Kafka, 1953, p. 217).

Kafka invites and exploits this "wound" as an impetus to write more and in his own way; it provides a necessary tension and battleground between training and introspection. His reproach regarding his own education (a standard adolescent one) was that it "tried to make another person out of me than the one I became" as he wrote in his diary (1988, vol. 1, p. 18). For "Man does not grow from below upwards but from within outwards ... It is the condition of man's freedom" (Janouch, p. 36). Based on this conflict between an identity that is shaped from above by social forces, and one that grows outward from within, he sought his "freedom" by means of his writing. Almost provocatively, he once left a piece of writing on his grandparents' table to be picked up, only to receive the comment from an uncle, after a superficial glance, that "It's just the usual stuff" – precisely the negative male response that he expected and perhaps desired: "I had literally been pushed out of their society with a single thrust" (cited in Gray, 1973, p. 31). The break or wound is the equivalent of Bion's idea of "psyche-lodgement" (Bion, 1991, pp. 265, 274) which occurs when any new idea penetrates the existing smooth crust of the psyche. Spiritual development, like the operation of talent in writing, occurs when there is "a gap through which the irrelevant might force its way" (Kafka, 1988, vol. 1, p. 192). This makes possible an "endoskeletonal" rather than "exoskeletonal" development (Bion, 1970, p. 23). Constructive use of the wound ("suffering" it) requires learning to tolerate angst or dread, in the existential or Kierkegaardian sense, something more complex than simply feeling pain.

As always with creative artists, the actual process of writing is his means of self-revelation. Kafka wrote of the "inescapable duty to observe oneself", and of "the wild tempo of the inner process" that results from "introspection, which will suffer no idea to sink tranquilly to rest but must pursue each one into consciousness, only itself to become an idea, in turn to be pursued by renewed introspection" (1988, vol. 2, p. 202). As in Bion's picture of how the mind builds itself in stages through catastrophic change, the completed thought becomes in each case a preconception for the next thought; the self-development of the personality is a continuous process involving a series of deaths and resurrections. One story leads to another, and each time there is "the dread of ascending to a higher life". Each story, struggling into the world after the wound of its birth, embodies a part of the author's psyche: "The beginning of every story is ridiculous at first. There seems no hope that this newborn thing, still incomplete and tender in every joint, will be able to keep alive in the completed organisation of the world" (1988, vol. 2, p. 104). A book's "independent life", he believed, postdates its author, and there is a sense in which even the author "does not develop in his own way until after death, when he is alone" (cited in Danta, 2001, p. 71); he is shaped by his works. Kafka developed after death through his stories.

For Kafka, writing *was* living; and he often, in diaries and letters, makes a contrast between the inner life of the writer and the "normal" life of the working family man in society. "My talent for portraying my dreamlike inner life has thrust all other matters into the background; my life has dwindled dreadfully" he wrote in 1914, the year of writing *The Trial* (1988, vol. 2, p. 77). Trained as a lawyer, with a day job in an insurance office, Kafka wrote at night, when he could enter his other world undisturbed from the outside. The irrational unconscious lies barely beneath the bureaucratic conscious, and is perpetually making unheeded signals of its existence. By contrast with Freud's contemporary theory of dreams as wish-fulfilment, but in line with the view of all artists, Kafka thought that "The dream reveals the reality, which conception lags behind. That is the horror of life – the terror of art" (Janouch, p. 32). Art does not disguise life, it reveals it: hence its terror for the writer.

Kafka's stories often read like inner dialogues between two kinds of person or existence. One of his earliest stories was *The Struggle*, in which one part of himself (the sensual) is possessed of a knife that the other part (the intellectual) is convinced is intended to kill him, although in the event, the sensual part merely drives a knife into his own upper arm. Kafka said wryly of his attendant alter-ego or double that he was "a useless person" who echoed him in a deeper voice like a "bass fiddler"; and that "occasionally I consult with him … as to how I might get rid of him" (1988, vol. 2, p. 171). Sometimes it reads like a dialogue between analyst and analysand; sometimes too there is an implicit distinction between his (internalised) paternal and maternal inheritance – the Kafka

90   THE ART OF PERSONALITY

business head and the "secretive, diffident" Löwy tendency within him – as in the contrast between the uncle who dismissed his story, and the much loved doctor uncle who lies behind *A Country Doctor*.

In Kafka's writings the external imagery of daily movements, including the humdrum and apparently insignificant, is placed in counterpoint with nightmarish fantasy in order to authentically evoke the continuous drama of an internal life. The irrational unconscious lies barely beneath the bureaucratic conscious, and is perpetually making unheeded signals of its existence. He mused on the contrast between his knowledge of his room and his knowledge of himself: "How scanty my self-knowledge is compared with my knowledge of my room … The inner world can only be experienced, not described" (cited in Murray 2004, p. 264). Yet this is what he does describe: the room of his mind, with its many passages – whether it be a castle, a burrow, a torture machine, a locked bedroom, a lecture theatre, or an office in a bank which opens to a "lumber room" of sadistic fantasy. There is not much difference between a room-space and a town or village, like that in *The Castle*: Kafka's Prague is the equivalent of Dostoevsky's Petersburg or Skotoprigonyevsk; each place is traversed by the rat-runs of unconscious brain-activity, like Keats' "wreathed trellis of a working brain". And "The unhealthy old Jewish town within us is far more real than the new hygienic town around us" (Janouch, p. 80).

Kafka identified closely with animal life and described himself as an "animal of the forest" – the forest of the unconscious. It is also the landscape of the senses and their sign-language. He makes "the human (or animal) body the very site and proving ground of literary meaning" (Danta, 2001, p. 71). He often translates the problem of being–becoming into animal imagery, especially of teeth and claws; and many of his stories are implicit metamorphoses of man into animal or vice versa – the dividing line constituting in itself a creative wound that opens up a new perspective on our received picture of humanity.

The Metamorphosis

The dream-situations of Kafka's stories have the quality of being authentically discovered inside himself rather than invented: for as he said, "discovery is harder than invention" (Janouch, p. 111). The famous opening words of *The Metamorphosis* (1912) are: "As Gregor Samsa awoke one morning from uneasy dreams he found himself transformed in his bed into a gigantic insect" (Kafka, 1961,

THE WOUND AND ITS TRANSFORMATIONS: KAFKA   91

p. 9). In the stage adaptation of this story by David Farr and Gisli Örn Gardarsson (2006), the two levels of consciousness are represented by two levels on the stage: an upstairs bedroom in which the insect athletically manoeuvres over all the cube's surfaces, and a downstairs family sitting room where ordinary everyday life is conducted, resulting in a breakdown of decorum whenever the latter is penetrated by the former.

The comic effect, as often in Kafka, is perhaps strongest at the beginning when the hero is in a state between waking and dreaming, trying to orient himself to the picture that has appeared in his mind: "only an image" it may be – yet also, a case of psyche-lodgement; sleep has opened his mind to the unexpected. "What about sleeping a little longer and forgetting all this nonsense, he thought" – but the somatic demands of his new bodily situation keep demanding his attention. There are similarities with Gulliver awakening on Lilliput to find all his limbs bound and a sensation of arrows piercing his skin: or with the sensitivities of a newborn baby adjusting to a harsh gaseous environment. He cannot roll over, he tries to identify an itching spot on his belly and recoils from the contact of his own leg which "sends a cold shiver down him". He feels a "dull ache he had never felt before".

These somatic signals are interspersed with ruminations about the discomforts of his everyday job: in fact they bring to the surface the intolerable tedium of his life, whence his sense of imprisonment really derives. Immediately after the contact between his leg and his belly, he thinks: "This getting up early can make an idiot out of anyone. A man needs his sleep"; and then his secret desire to be free of both his job and his family ties, where he is in effect a kind of prisoner, becomes available for conscious reflection:

> If I didn't have to hold my hand because of my parents I'd have given notice long ago, I'd have gone to the chief and told him exactly what I think of him. That would knock him endways from his desk! It's a queer way of acting, too, this sitting on high at a desk and talking down to employees, especially when they have to come quite near because the chief is hard of hearing. (Kafka, 1961, p. 10)

Gregor is having trouble balancing on his bed, and this brings to mind a reciprocal image of his boss sitting precariously high on his desk. He proposes "cutting his ties" completely with that link: but then the "near future" turns out to be another "five or six years", the same length of time as he has already been in employment. Having never been ill during that time, he decides he could not possibly report sick, since he would merely be accused of laziness. He then formulates the contrary logic: was his position not that of one who, having never missed an hour's work before, was "so tormented by conscience as to be driven out of his mind and actually incapable of leaving his bed?"

He considers the possibilities of "unlocking" himself from this somatic imprisonment: glad at first that his room is locked, he comes to realise it will be necessary to reveal his condition to others: "He felt himself drawn once more into the human circle and hoped for great and remarkable results from both the doctor and the locksmith, without really distinguishing precisely between them." As it turns out, he has to act as his own doctor and locksmith and turn the key with his mouth, "for it seemed that unfortunately, he didn't really have any teeth." This results in his first wound. The newborn creature of this story is "ridiculous" and born from the "filth" of the depths of being; as he describes the creative process in his diary: "[You] came dripping into the world with this burden and will depart unrecognizable again because of it. This filth is the nethermost depth you will find" (Kafka, 1988, vol. 2, p. 114). Indeed, as if prophesying his lung disease, the "repulsive appearance of the insect (which assures his victimization) is in fact an inside: an eventrated respiratory tract replete with cilia and mucus carpet", writes Ian Bamforth (2000). Even before this however, the inside-turned-outside enacts a birth scene.

Meanwhile the voices, and actions, of his family begin to penetrate the morning "fog" that he can perceive outside the window and that applies also to his mental state. His mother's "gentle voice", nagging him anxiously from outside the door ("Didn't you have a train to catch?") is answered by the "horrible twittering squeak" of his own voice which has now become unintelligible to anybody else in the standard human world – just like his writings. "That was the voice of an animal", says the chief clerk suspiciously; and the effect of this alien sound is to deprive him of human speech himself, so that he runs from the building with an animal screech of "Aiee!" It is Kafka's comic depiction of the clerk's failure to comprehend his own terror of looking inwards; the clerk's habitual speech shows him to be a slave of the bureaucracy, but at last he has spoken a true word. The bad poet, says Kafka, can only "shriek", not condense words into language (Janouch, p. 93).

Gregor has taken on the burden of his father's "debts" so that his family can, each in their own way, live a comfortable, carefree existence reading the newspapers, supervising the home, playing the violin, etc., and his attempt to service their requirements (or

THE WOUND AND ITS TRANSFORMATIONS: KAFKA   93

to fit his personality into a "normal" life) has turned him into a monster, much as he would like to believe it is merely a "temporary incapacitation". He cannot squeeze his identity into it, any more than the beetle can squeeze through the half-open double doors of his room without damaging his body:

> Pitilessly Gregor's father drove him back, hissing and crying "Shoo!" like a savage ... He was tilted at an angle in the doorway, his flank was quite bruised, horrid blotches stained the white door ... when from behind his father gave him a strong push which was literally a deliverance and he flew far into the room, bleeding freely. The door was slammed behind him with the stick, and then at last there was silence. (pp. 25–26)

The father, by applying the law with a stick, has at the same time delivered his son from it: his beetle-mind has been born and can no longer be concealed. For Kafka, his father seems to have been a rigid, colourless superego figure who was contemptuous of his writing and focused on social ambition for his children – although he also interpreted this rigidity to Janouch as being a form of "love": "He is anxious about me. Love often wears the face of violence" (Janouch, 24).

Gregor's transformation seemed to happen suddenly, being the dream of one night, and yet he reflects that even the day before he "had a slight presentiment", and he wondered that no-one noticed any "sign" (in the preceding hours, weeks, years, perhaps?). Despite his best intentions, the "inconvenience" of being a beetle rather than a human makes co-existence tricky. As he adapts to his new state, he discovers its true delights, namely "crawling crisscross over the walls and ceiling" of his room, leaving a strange sticky trail of stringy words and arguments that to anybody else looks like a brown mess disfiguring the nice flowered wallpaper that forms the background to bourgeois life. The image also suggests a babe in arms:

> He especially enjoyed hanging suspended from the ceiling; it was much bettter than lying on the floor; one could breathe more freely; one's body swung and rocked lightly; and in the almost blissful absorption induced by this suspension it could happen, to his own surprise, that he let go and fell plump onto the floor. (p. 36)

The tracery of the beetle's long delicate legs constitute what he calls "a seizmographic pencil for the heart"; since for the writer, "the pen is not an instrument but an organ" (Janouch, pp. 47, 95). It is a picture echoed later in *The Burrow*, in which a mole-like animal

94   THE ART OF PERSONALITY

constructs an underground maze which he hopes to make impregnable and which has at its core a Castle Keep, a jealously guarded maternal space:

> I had always pictured this free space, and not without reason, as the loveliest imaginable haunt. What a joy to be pressed against the rounded outer wall, pull oneself up, let oneself slide down again, miss one's footing and fine oneself on firm earth, and play all these games literally upon the Castle Keep and not inside it ... to hold it safe between one's claws. (p. 152)

He once signed himself to Felice, "your cellar dweller" (cited in Robert, 1982, p. 50). In a similar picture, Dostoevsky's mouse-like anti-hero in *The Underground Man* is situated beneath the floorboards, a man of "heightened consciousness" who peers out at life through a crack yet is unable to participate in it. Kafka described writing as a "pleasure-seeking practice" rooted in the cellar of the dark or devilish unconscious, a "solar system of vanity" in which the endless pursuit of grammatical structures enwraps the protagonist in his neuroses, making him "perpetually sorry for himself" (cited in Thorlby, 1972, p. 18).

Now that the animal awakening has brought Gregor's writing out into the open, the other family members revive from their torpor and begin to take responsibility for themselves. Gregor's demise is gradual, as everyday things become "dimmer to his sight". By contrast, the father, whose business had collapsed and who subsequently did nothing but doze over the newspapers, puts on his military uniform and takes a job as a guard; the women take up sewing and Grete begins to blossom and display her "musical" self to the world. Gregor is at first astonished to observe his father's resurrection as a potent figure, albeit of a military disciplinary type, standing "straight as a stick, dressed in a smart blue uniform with gold buttons, such as bank attendants wear". When he advances "with grim visage" towards Gregor who "scuttles" breathlessly away, Gregor is mortally wounded by the apple which seems to "nail him to the floor", and the mother, entering, rushes to the father in a caricatural sexual act:

> He saw his mother rushing toward his father, leaving one after another behind her on the floor her loosened petticoats, stumbling over her petticoats straight to his father and embracing him, in complete union with him – but here Gregor's sight began to fail – with her hands clasped around his father's neck as she begged for her son's life. (p. 44)

THE WOUND AND ITS TRANSFORMATIONS: KAFKA   95

It is as if he receives or almost demands this wound from his father in response to this oedipal fantasy, which he views with "failing sight", and which is reminiscent of popular theatricals – perhaps like the Yiddish acting troupe Kafka saw in his twenties, of which his father disapproved, but which for Franz marked an authentic Jewishness. Kafka wrote in his diary of the "stale tired sheets" of his parents' bed (1988, vol. 2, p. 167); and had suspicions of sex as a "punishment", a "sinister black magic" (Kafka, 1953, p. 136).

At first Gregor's mother has illusions of him somehow returning to them, and for this reason wishes to keep his room "exactly as it always has been", to make it easier for him to "forget" this unfortunate episode in his life. Grete, however, who has artistic talents of her own, attempts to reorganise his room in line with his new, half-understanding the dizzy pleasure he finds in crawling upside down across the ceiling. But:

> Did he really want his warm room, so comfortably fitted with old family furniture, to be turned into a naked den in which he would certainly be able to crawl unhampered in all directions but at the price of shedding simultaneously all recollection of his human background? (p. 38)

It is the voice of his mother that brings to mind his old human existence, the memories that comprise his mental furnishings, although they somehow hinder his ecstatic transcendental meditations on the ceiling. But Grete has a realistic efficiency and she persists in clearing them all out, destroying the ambiguity: "In a room where Gregor lorded it all alone over empty walls no one except herself was likely ever to set foot." She is supposedly on his side, intuiting his needs, observing what food he can eat and his other bodily requirements, but her very closeness to him pushes him towards ejection from the family space.

Unlike Gregor, Grete is musical and can play the violin beautifully and it has been Gregor"s "dearest wish" to send her to study at the Conservatory. It is seductive however, a siren-song. It draws Gregor unthinkingly out of his cave, where he is allowed to listen to the family conversation beyond a safe boundary; and it is this mixing of boundaries that results in disaster.

> Was he an animal, when music had such an effect on him? He felt as if the way were opening before him to the unknown nourishment he craved. He was determined to push forward till he reached his sister, to pull at her skirt and so let her now that she should

96   THE ART OF PERSONALITY

come into his room with her violin, for no one here appreciated her
playing as he would appreciate it. (p. 53)

Gregor imagines how his very ugliness will become "for the first
time, useful to him; he would watch over all the doors of his room
at once and hiss like a dragon at any intruders", and finally, he will
"raise himself to [Grete's] shoulder and kiss her on the neck" (p.
54). It is a version of the fairytale of Beauty and the Beast, or of
Caliban's primitive sensual attraction to Miranda (Caliban, also a
cave-dweller, is likewise notable for his musical sensitivity). Kafka
wrote to Brod of his attitude to women: "I can love only what I
can place so high above that I cannot reach it." (Kafka, 1977, p.
273). Raised up to shoulder height, the lowly insect-child will be
the musical woman's true husband; he will protect the vision of
beauty from outside philistine intruders (such as the paying "lodgers") who have forced their vulgar presence into the heart of the
family or mind, taking over the sitting room but without appreciat-
ing its music. And whilst imagining his new heroic stature, Gregor
intrudes his own large insect-head steadily into the outside space
of the family sitting room, insisting yet again on being born and
getting closer to the source of knowledge.

However the caring aspect of Grete has turned into the new
"cleaning woman" who is fed up with this childish mess. "Strong
and bony", tough and impervious, she arrives towards the end of
the story, when the original housemaid and cook have deserted.
She is the only outside person who knows nothing of Gregor's
humanity; like the lodgers, who found Gregor more "entertaining"
than Grete's violin, she sees him just as "an old dung beetle", a
curiosity who holds no terror for her, just mild amusement which
is not even sufficiently involved to be sadistic. Grete had used to
clean his room, but as soon as this toilet-mummy aspect has been
delegated to the new cleaning woman, Grete treacherously seeks
her freedom. She tells the father:

> "He must go. You must just try to get rid of the idea that this is
> Gregor ... This creature persecutes us, drives away our lodgers,
> obviously wants the whole apartment to himself, and would have
> us all sleep in the gutter." (pp. 56--57)

By now his mother (the only one who really wants him to live)
is literally asleep, and Grete is entwined with his father, her arm
around his neck, united against him. The father caused the first
wound when he threw the apple (of original sin) that became

THE WOUND AND ITS TRANSFORMATIONS: KAFKA 97

embedded in the beetle's flesh – the rule of religious law. Now there is a new combined object. Without the use of any stick, Grete's gaze drives Gregor back into his room, then she turns the key in the lock and cries "At last!" It is the signal for him to drift quietly into death, his body dry, frail and flattened, deprived of life-juices: "Just see how thin he was." As he expressed this feeling in his diary the year before, "I lie here kicked out of the world ... my joints ache with fatigue, my dried-up body trembles towards its own destruction" (1988, vol. 1, p. 159). Meanwhile the life-force within Grete surges up, and the story ends with: "their daughter sprang to her feet and stretched her young body."

Kafka wrote that "He who keeps the idea of beauty never grows old" (Janouch, p. 30). Gregor feels that the idea of beauty has forsaken him, leaving him to wither, like the man who (in another story) grows old waiting "before the law" and ultimately dies, locked out from the visionary world, only at the last moment recognising that the gate was constructed and guarded solely for him. The dream has fled; his life has "atrophied" like the dried-up insect body; the gate shuts. Or, has the life of his work sprung into full-blooded being, at the expense of the life of his self, which has of necessity shrunk? The music has gone elsewhere, perhaps into the work itself; after death, as he said in one of his aphorisms, a work can find its independent life: "The state of death is to an individual what Saturday night is to the chimney sweep; he washes the soot off his body" (cited in Danta, p. 71). Filth, like his parents' bed, is associated with birth and the depths of being. The cleaning of the beetle's room releases the Gregor part from the Grete part of himself, allowing a type of development to proceed after a symbolic death, a catastrophic change. Has Grete's violin uncovered "the hidden sound of silence" as he called it, the "inaudible sounds felt in bodily tissues vibrating" (Janouch, p. 76). *The Metamorphosis* could be considered a fable about the price creativity exacts. The real metamorphosis is the musical Grete-part emerging from its chrysalis, the messy wreckage of his bodily existence.

A Country Doctor

It was during the course of his tortuous on-off relationship with Felice that Kafka was diagnosed with tuberculosis, and he always associated this "wound" with Felice herself, though the knife-attack was a characteristic feature of his dream-stories from the beginning. He told his later lover Milena: "You are the knife which

98   THE ART OF PERSONALITY

I turn within myself" (Kafka, 1953, p. 200) and earlier expressed his fantasy about the "joy" of twisting the knife in his own heart (1988, vol. 1, p. 129). And at the end of *The Trial*, which on one level narrates the abortive process of his engagement with Felice, Joseph K. almost, but not quite, manages to drive in the dagger himself: unless one takes the "executioners" – those who execute – to be his own hands.

Kafka said that in writing *A Country Doctor* (1917), he predicted his own tuberculosis. The story concerns the doctor's visit to a young man who at first seems perfectly healthy, merely malingering in bed, but then "on closer inspection" a gaping rose-coloured wound the size of a hand (or lung) is revealed on his thigh (Kafka, 2009, p. 49). The disease seems to be noticed, or perhaps created, in response to a "false ring on the night bell", resulting in a journey which is parallel to or co-extensive with the rape of the doctor's maid Rosa by his own groom. The two events are told as if they happen simultaneously, in two separate buildings or compartments of the mind. The fates of the two young people are inextricably intertwined, and it is essentially the fate of the doctor too: modelled on a favourite Löwy uncle, the doctor represents the helpless adult part of the personality with his useless skill of writing which, like psychoanalysis, seems unable to effect a cure.

"One doesn't know the sorts of things one has stored in one's own house", says Rosa to the doctor with a spirited sense of humour. She is referring to the fact that a pair of strong horses have just been discovered from within a disused pigsty in the courtyard, enabling the doctor to harness his carriage so that he can travel through the snowy winter's night to visit the patient. The horses (the animal energy) had appeared to be missing; but on a kick from his foot he notices "a warmth and smell as if from horses" and they rise out of the depths of the pigsty, led by the blue-eyed groom. In a story written ten years earlier, *Wedding Preparations in the Country,* the hero thinks he needn't go to the country himself for his wedding – he can "send his clothed body" instead, and remain lying in bed, assuming the shape of a beetle. It is Kafka's "black magic" picture of sex (1953, p. 136). The doctor's horses also suggest the lungs, which he termed "proud strong tormented imperturbable creatures" (Bamfield, 2000). While they whirl the doctor away in the snowstorm "like a piece of wood in a current", he helplessly hears the doors of his house "splitting apart" as the groom hunts for Rosa, who has "an accurate premonition of her fate".

Instantly he finds himself at the house of the patient. It is just another window in his own mind, as is the lumber-room in

THE WOUND AND ITS TRANSFORMATIONS: KAFKA   99

The Trial, which opens out from Joseph K's office to reveal two "warders" (his hands) being whipped by a punisher (the will). The doctor turns his back on one room only to enter another. He has lost his willpower, his "flourishing practice". The moment he thinks of Rosa lying under the groom, the uncontrollable horses push open the window and look in, observing the scene closely, and whinnying as if "from higher regions". They are the regions of Platonic "reason and desire" which, wrote Kafka, "first disclose the bare outlines of the future to me", and over which the "whip of the will" is permitted control (1988, vol. 1, p. 166). Are they also his internal parents, first carrying and then watching him? The thought-swift cross-country ride represents the "wild tempo of the inner process" that results from introspection. "It is easy to write prescriptions", Kafka pertinently observes on behalf of the doctor. The law sets down prescriptions; life is the wound that does not fit them.

Meanwhile the patient's sister draws the doctor's attention by flapping a bloody (virginal or menstrual) towel and this makes the doctor inspect the young man more closely, revealing the wound alive with rose-coloured wriggling worms. "Close up a complication is apparent. Who can look at that without whistling softly?" (Rose also being associated with the hectic flush of late tuberculosis, as in the "fading rose" of the knight in Keats' *Belle Dame Sans Merci*.) "You are dying from this flower on your side", the doctor tells the patient. "The blood is oozing away in the chinks between the great stones of the law", as Kafka put it in a diary entry (1988, vol. 2, p. 214). At the same time, in this case, it is a birthmark, integral to the young man's being; the rose of sensuality is killing him. The colony of wriggling worms, as a dream-image, becomes associated with the "nimble rabble of patients" who, clamorous with expectation, parasitise their doctor and "do nothing to help" him. They are "the people", demanding a new law of existence.

The doctor complains that now the "old faith" (the established religion) is dead, and its minister disrobed, the "people" (or parts of himself) are "always demanding the impossible from the doctor" – who is required to be in effect both physician and psychoanalyst, yet cannot control his own horses. The schoolchildren gathered outside the house chant their black magic incitement:

> "Take his clothes off, then he'll heal,
> and if he doesn't cure, then kill him.
> It's only a doctor; it's only a doctor." (p. 50)

100   THE ART OF PERSONALITY

Carried by the people, the doctor lies down naked on the bed next to the patient, in a parallel identification with him:

> "Enjoy yourselves, you patients,
> The doctor's laid in bed with you."

Their physical carrying is a mental urging, a powerful pressurising to play the role they have in mind for him now his nakedness is exposed. "I came into the world with a beautiful wound; that was all I was furnished with", says the young man. The doctor, lacking a prescription, interprets that the patient has "no perspective" and that plenty of other people have wounds from the "axe in the forest" that is perpetually cutting closer, though they may not even hear it – such is the human condition; life is a terminal illness, and all stories have closure. One of the horses (desire?) withdraws its head to allow him to escape through the window.

But his escape from the sinister vision is apparent rather than real: the dissatisfied rabble want a miracle so they are working up to violence. As Kafka saw: "Miracles and violence are simply the two extremes of a lack of faith" (Janouch, p. 113); the primitive chantings of populist movements such as nationalism always "begin with flags, songs and music and end in pillage and blood" (*ibid.*, p. 52). It is the same as the recoil against the truthful or artistic use of language, for (as Bion also insists) "A lie is often an expression of the fear that one may be crushed by the truth. It is a projection of one's own littleness" (Janouch, p. 168). In Kafka's view the destroyers of society and of language are the same thing, defending themselves against "the crude encroachments of civilisation" (Janouch, p. 173). For civilisation, like truth, is unwanted, and at the end of the *Country Doctor*, a new "ice age" seems to be on its way.

As Kafka once said of his writing, he was not trying to describe actual people: "These are only images" (Janouch, p. 31). Just as dreams are "only" dreams. Nonetheless the dream, the inner spectacle, has shaken his writer-doctor's perspective irrevocably, as he recognises his helplessness to rescue Rosa from the ravages of the groom in his own mind; his fur coat trails behind him in the snow as "Naked, abandoned to the frost of this unhappy age, with an earthly carriage and unearthly horses, I drive around by myself, an old man." His protective exoskeleton "lags behind" as Kafka said of outworn conceptions which have fallen behind the phenomena which unconscious intuition has brought to light (Janouch, pp. 32, 113). In political terms, "The revolution evaporates, and leaves behind only the slime of a new bureaucracy" (Janouch, p. 120). The

THE WOUND AND ITS TRANSFORMATIONS: KAFKA   101

doctor never gets home. The earthly carriage of his body is yoked to the unearthly animus of his spirit, a condition from which there is no escape, and it is all the result of inquiring too closely into the unconscious pictures that lie beneath conscious thought: responding to a "false alarm on the night bell", and discovering "the dream that reveals the reality".

A Report to an Academy

In *A Report to an Academy* Kafka reverses the transformation of man into animal that he used in *Metamorphosis*, and writes or rather speaks from the point of view of an ape who has been forced to convert into a man, or at least to learn his "language"; it is a complementary story. Instead of the incomprehensibility of the beetle's strange squeaking, the ape contrives to imitate the manners and speech of humans in a way that has the expertise of the colonised convert. His audience is one of learned academicians, perhaps those whom Kafka satirises in *Investigations of a Dog* as "hovering" well above ground level, or the connoisseurs of whom he writes: "A connoisseur, an expert, someone who knows his field – knowledge, to be sure, that cannot be imparted but that fortunately no one seems to stand in need of" (Kafka, 1988, vol. 2, p. 197). It is knowledge which has become disconnected from nature, from its animal roots in the heart of man.

Needless to say Kafka in *The Report* is interested in the gaps, the moments of interpenetration, when the genuine emotional situation breaks out or through the veneer of fake civilisation or knowledge and finds psyche-lodgement. It is when the primitive messages from the deep somatic depths of the personality manage to find a way through to consciousness. As the ape puts it: "I can take my trousers down before anyone if I like; you would find nothing but a well-groomed fur and the scar made … by a wanton shot" (Kafka, 2009, p. 54). What particularly disgusts the ape is not the smell of humans as such, but the way it has become mixed with his own native smell: "Smell for yourself! Put your nose deeper into the fur!"

The ape has been born into human society – or, the writer has been born into the public eye – against his will, and his Report essentially describes how the original loss of freedom when he was captured has been followed by an even greater loss, of identity:

> The storm which blew me out of my past eased off. Today it is only
> a gentle breeze which cools my heels. And the distant hole through

102   THE ART OF PERSONALITY

> which it comes and through which I once came has become so small
> that, even if I had sufficient power and will to run back there, I would
> have to scrape the fur off my body in order to get through. (p. 52)

In a similar way, Gregor was forced back through his doorway in
this way, scraping his sides, and his memory-furniture was removed
to allow him greater freedom of movement within his skeletal cell.
Society applies to the ape the carrot and stick method of education
– the stick being literally the stick, the whip, the cigarette burn; and
the carrot being alcohol and, later, fame. The fading of the ape's
memory is the inevitable consequence of not trying to force himself
back in to a lost haven, nature's cradle: Yet "I could never have
achieved what I have done had I been stubbornly set on clinging to
my origins, to the remembrances of my youth." Gregor's memories
attached him to his ordinary human family; the ape's memories
linked him to his place in nature's order; in each case the memories
have to be concretely removed like some kind of lobotomy.

The ape consciously abandons hopes of any genuine "freedom"
and seeks only for a "way out" of his cage: "I was pinned down
… I had to stop being an ape. A fine, clear train of thought, which
I must have constructed somehow with my belly, since apes think
with their bellies" (p. 55). His belly abhors the smell of alcohol,
yet his acquisition of language is inseparable from it. He describes
his "gradual enlightenment … first theory then practice." His
first word "Hello!" bursts out of him after much "squealing and
scratching" as he manages to imitate the behaviour of a "professional drinker, with rolling eyes and full throat", and then instantly
vomits. "I, enchanted with my gradual enlightenment, squealed
and scratched myself comprehensively wherever scratching was
called for… tilted the bottle, and took a drink"; while his teacher
"ended his theoretical exposition by rubbing his belly and grin-
ning" (p. 59). "A curse on you for teaching me your language" says
Caliban to his colonial master Prospero.

Kafka uses the ape to identify with not-fully-born forces in his own
nature which he felt had been forcibly repressed yet which periodically broke through in the guise of "the irrelevant" and found psyche-
lodgement, and which were essential to his creativity. As Kafka joked
to Milena Jesenská: to her father, both he and her husband looked
alike, since "for the European we both have the same Negro face".
"And so I learned things, gentlemen", explains the ape:

> Alas, one learns when one has to … one learns when one wants a
> way out. One learns ruthlessly. One supervises oneself with a whip

and tears oneself apart at the slightest resistance. My ape nature ran off, head over heels, out of me, so that in the process my first teacher almost himself became an ape and soon had to give up training and be carried off to a mental hospital. (p. 60)

His so far unparalleled achievement is that he has "managed to reach the cultural level of an average European" which has "helped me out of my cage and opened a special way out for me, the way of humanity." But, he stresses again, this is not "freedom" – meaning, of course, that it is not humanity either.

True freedom, Kafka always insists, comes from individual evolution, not from cultural pressures and training: "growing outward from within" not "upwards from below". The ape story is not only about colonising modes of cultural training; it is about the individual's own willing dependence on "regulations, prescriptives, directives" – the basic assumptions of the internal group and its bureaucratic organisation: "Men are afraid of freedom and responsibility. So they prefer to hide behind the prison bars which they build around themselves" (Janouch, p. 23). Kafka was interested in how value systems may be constructed outside religious codes or "bars" such as the patriarchal Jewish Law. But he did not underestimate the stress involved: how man was intolerant of his "transitional position" and always seeking to "rest a moment" – a moment that, like the villager in *The Great Wall of China*, might expand to infinity as he waits in a state both hopeful and hopeless for the messenger from the emperor of ultimate truth to finally arrive, fighting his way through the thickets of mental debris in a kind of reversal of the story of the Sleeping Beauty.

Investigations of a Dog

In his last stories, Kafka brings the narrative focus of his animal stories more completely within the bounds of the animal mind, placing the human mind at a distance as if to represent the unknown. The dog, the mouse of *Josephine*, and the mole-like creature of *The Burrow* are not hybrids or conversions of humans; for them the idea of a race of more knowledgeable or powerful beings is mysterious, unthinkable: although towards the end of *The Burrow*, in response to the sinister whistling that has begun to penetrate his earthly security, the mole formulates the possibility of "some animal unknown to me" – "the beast" which brings, or is, death itself.

104   THE ART OF PERSONALITY

In *Investigations of a Dog*, Kafka pursues further the implications of Gregor Samsa listening to the violin and being beaten out of life, his body dried up – the dangers entailed in aesthetic experience – and the limitations in knowledge of both the religious and scientific vertices when they are not linked together. Kafka felt himself to be unmusical (like Gregor) and that this was associated with his neurotic worrying: since "unmusical people lose sleep by unreal worries" (1953, p. 141); just as writers temperamentally "feel sorry for themselves" and cannot harmonise their ruminations musically. A musical temperament can cope with the anxieties aroused by the unreal.

In this story, the hero-dog has been stimulated to commence his philosophical investigations regarding the place of dogs in the universe as a result of an aesthetic musical experience in his youth. He recognises that from the very beginning he has been prey to nameless, irrational apprehensions, but had nevertheless manage to lead an apparently normal life as "a dog among dogs", thanks to acquiring "a certain melancholy and lethargy" which allowed him to carry on as "a somewhat cold, reserved, shy and calculating, but, all things considered, normal enough dog" (Kafka, 1961, p. 85). Now in old age he resolves to inquire a little deeper into these repressed feelings of apprehension, not so much on his own behalf as in order to understand the state of "dogdom" in general.

No sooner has he opened his mind to this inquiry, after years of closure, than a memory surges up from when he was a puppy and ran around "filled with a premonition of great things". The memory is of a troupe of seven dogs (said to represent the Yiddish actors who made an impression on the young Kafka) who "conjured music from the empty air", that is, they did not create it as much as call it into existence in the traditional mode of inspired artists. The puppy therefore finds he is "less surprised by the artistry of the seven dogs ... than by their courage in facing so openly the music of their own making, and their power to endure it calmly without collapsing"; the "blasts of music ... seize the listener by the middle, overwhelming him, crushing him" (p. 89). It is like the snowstorm of the Country Doctor, or the "storm" that he said Milena created in his room (1953, p. 59). The puppy, in between the musical storms that sweep him away, is horrified by the indecorous way the dancing dogs stand on two legs; has "the world turned upside down?" It is "against the law" of dogdom, and the puppy perceives that on closer inspection, the dancers too are feeling the stress, the tension. But the dance troupe are in touch with both somatic nature (as in the ape story) and also have a dreamlike intuition of the human master species (the parents) whose presence is never imagined by the hero-dog, or indeed, by any ordinary infant-dogs in this story.

The picture is reminiscent of a fantasy expressed by Keats:

> May there not be superior beings, amused with any graceful, though instinctive, attitude my mind may fall into as I am entertained with the alertness of the stoat or the anxiety of a deer? Though a quarrel in the streets is a thing to be hated, the energies displayed in it are fine; the commonest man shows a grace in his quarrel. By a superior Being our reasonings may take the same tone – though erroneous they may be fine. This is the very thing in which consists poetry, and if so it is not so fine a thing as philosophy – for the same reason that an eagle is not so fine a thing as a truth. (Keats, 1970, p. 230).

Man may be entertained by an animal's way of expressing itself without drawing the logical conclusion that a higher being than himself may be correspondingly entertained by his own movements and their "grace". This is also the situation of the investigating dog who is trying to pursue poetry into philosophy, eagle into truth – to translate emotional impact into understanding.

Inspired however by this poetic memory, the old dog first investigates the scientific foundations of dogdom in the form of a treatise on where the dogs' food comes from: that is, what nourishes their body. Kafka's satire on single-vertex science is:

> My personal observation tells me that the earth, when it is watered and scratched according to the rules of science, extrudes nourishment, and moreover in such quality, in such abundance, in such ways, in such places, at such hours, as the laws partially or completely established by science demand. (Kafka, 1961, p. 95)

But the old dog who has had an aesthetic experience as a puppy is not completely satisfied. He is aware of the efficacy of ritual and incantation, and now his heightened curiosity leads him one step further to ask, "Whence does the earth procure this food?" For a long time he bases his researches on the premise that "All knowledge, the totality of all questions and answers, is contained in the dog … For what is there actually except our own species?" (p. 97). And that only by mobilising the totality of "dog knowledge" through "the great choir of dogdom" can the ultimate truth be attained: "The roof of this wretched life … will burst open, and all of us, shoulder to shoulder, will ascend into the lofty realm of freedom." This idealist goal of an impossible freedom, an ascent into true being, is contrasted with the spurious knowledge of the "hovering

106   THE ART OF PERSONALITY

dogs" who are simply carried around in the air (by humans, that is), leading an "empty life on cushions up there": such a dog is "a feeble creature, an artificial, weedy, brushed and curled fop by all accounts, incapable of making an honest jump." These pampered debaters are "perpetually talking", yet their philosophical reflections are "as worthless as their observations" (p. 103).

So neither the hovering dogs nor the solid earth-scratching dogs who obey dog law can help the hero-dog in his investigations, which try to reach beyond the "law of religious codes" and construct "a new value system" based on instinctive religiosity. He believes that the chance was lost ages ago, in the earliest days of dogdom, when "the true Word could still have intervened", being "on the tip of everybody's tongue" in those heady pioneering or fundamentalist religious times. But "today one may pluck out one's very heart and not find it", and the only ambition of young dogs is to "become old dogs" (p. 109).

Unlike the ape or the beetle, the dog is not overtly hindered by his society; he constantly reiterates that he is not in conflict with other dogs. They do not use the stick or the whip; rather they rely on the power of what Bion would describe as basic assumptions, that is, the sense of comfort that belongs to unassuming dogdom and its law. When the old dog goes beyond what is decorous in his quest for knowledge, he is faced with "vacant stares, averted glances, troubled and veiled eyes" (p. 98). A dog's dual nature is that he instinctively wants both to know and not to know: "Every dog has like me the impulse to question, and I have like every dog the impulse not to answer" (p. 101); for "agreement is the best means of defence" – defence, that is, against the encroaches of the unknown.

If the body is nourished by watering the earth, what nourishes the spirit? It is already acknowledged that the provision of food may be "hastened by certain spells, songs, and ritual movements". So the dog turns his attention to these "auxiliary perfecting processes", which explain why it is that "the people in all their ceremonies gaze upwards" (p. 113), in line with the observed scientific fact that food often seems to come from above rather than from out of the ground, finding its way into a dog's jaws even at a slant. To penetrate this mystery the hero-dog resolves to fast: this "most potent weapon of research" being the most transcendental to a dog's nature and (though he is not quite sure whether it is forbidden by law) the most likely to open his vision to freedom. He isolates himself in the forest in order to fast, recognising that he is in a "border region" here

THE WOUND AND ITS TRANSFORMATIONS: KAFKA 107

in his studies, outside the received laws of dogdom. "Writing",
Kafka told Janouch, "is after all, a kind of invocation of spirits"
(Janouch, p. 42). And indeed the fasting proves an effective type
of incantation: the "greed" for spiritual food supplants the greed
for earthly food; he pursues the fasting process "as greedily as if
it were a strange dog" until the point at which, lying in a pool of
his own bloody vomit, he raises his eyes to see "a strange hound
standing before me" (p. 121).

The strange and beautiful hound is a hunter (a soul-hunter) who
uses the power of music to resurrect the fasting dog and restore him
to life in the world:

> I thought I saw that the hound was already singing without
> knowing it, nay, more, that the melody, separated from him, was
> floating on the air in accordance with its own laws, and, as though
> he had no part in it, was moving towards me, towards me alone.
> (p. 123)

The music links the investigating dog with his puppyhood when
he saw the seven dancing dogs but was too young to understand
the significance. It has its own laws (like that of Shakesepeare's
Ariel – "where is that music? in the earth or the air?"): not the
possession of the strange dog, but deriving from realms beyond
him; and yet it seems directed specifically towards the investigating dog, "me alone". Magically the old dog recovers from his self-
imposed illness. And from that point on he directs his research into
the "science of music" which now seems to him to be even more
"comprehensive" than that of food. He knows very little about this
field, but the "voice in the forest" has awoken him to what he calls
his "instinct" – a different level of investigation, perhaps hardly
scientific at all.

In another story of this last period, *Josephine the Singer*, Kafka
describes a mouse-singer who is not better at singing than her
fellow mice but nonetheless has a capacity to use her voice artistically for entertainment; this is "the real nature of the business".
Like the middle-class, middle-sized dog who is the hero of the
Investigations, such animal transformations represent a humorous
reflection on his entire writing career; he was well aware that his
stories were entertaining, not merely tortuous psychological or
metaphysical puzzles, and that this was what would make them
endure. Like the dancing dog troupe, they could capture the attention of the audience, without which no scientific "scratching and
watering" could take effect.

108   THE ART OF PERSONALITY

Like his earlier story *Before the Law* (incorporated subsequently into *The Trial*), the small degree of enlightenment achieved by the dog investigator occurs when he understands that the message from above, or the law beyond the Gate, is created not for society in general, but for the individual alone. It is the religion of the inner world, not of the outer system – even if it is limited in its truth:

> It was this instinct that made me – and perhaps for the sake of science itself, but a different science from that of today, an ultimate science – prize freedom higher than everything else. Freedom! Certainly such freedom as is possible today is a wretched business. But nevertheless freedom, nevertheless a possession.

The dog, by contrast with the man waiting "before the law", passes through to another stage of life – even if it has taken most of a lifetime, and even if it has not resulted in perfect, complete or ideal knowledge, but merely in the kind of "freedom" that is possible for him. Yet he now has a different picture of his place in dogdom, and of the contribution of his own experience to the totality of the dog-knowledge. He imagines that in the future there could be a different kind of science that incorporates music, religion and instinct and that has a special definition of "freedom" (like the ape's or Kafka's own).

Kafka's writings, naturally, are often seen in their contemporary context of early Freud; all would agree that "Kafka's imagination is a 'psychoanalytic' one. Not because he studied Freud but because he grasped intuitively the split in the self and the struggle of the unacknowledged part against the public part" (Greenberg, 1971, p. 26). I would like to conclude therefore with Kafka's remarks on the new science of psychoanalysis:

> I consider the therapeutic part of psychoanalysis to be a hopeless error. All these so-called illnesses, sad as they may appear, are matters of faith, efforts of souls in distress to find moorings in some maternal soil ... Such moorings, however, which really take hold of solid ground, are after all not an isolated, interchangeable property of man, rather they are pre-existing in his nature and continue to form his nature (as well as his body) in this direction. And it's here they hope to cure? (Kafka, 1953, p. 217)

What is even more psychoanalytic in the modern sense, is the goal to acquire mental conditions that nourish the search for truth and that therefore "free" man's nature rather than "cure" it. Bion (1974) insists on a creative tension between the three

THE WOUND AND ITS TRANSFORMATIONS: KAFKA 109

epistemological vertices of religion, science, and art (Bion, 1974, vol. 1, p. 39; discussed in Williams, 2005a), as does Kafka: "Prayer, art and scientific research are three different flames that leap up from the same hearth ... so that to sink into oneself is not to fall into the unconscious, but to raise what is only dimly divined into the bright surface of consciousness" (Janouch, p. 113). Writing is "a form of prayer" that brings the depths to light. And man's incurable disease is a problem of faith in the value of living – its "faith-value" as Kafka called it.

A prescribed religion is of no use, since "God can only be comprehended personally" (Janouch, p. 166). The hunt, the quest, the giddy horsedrawn carriage, is searching not just for a replacement of the law of the father but for the solid ground of "a new maternal soil", a new combined object that has slipped from the doctor's grasp as he abandons his prescriptions, trailing behind him in the snow. The quest is for the kind of freedom in which man's nourishment comes neither from the ground below nor from the unseen gods above, but grows outwards from within. "Truth is what every man needs in order to live, but can obtain or purchase from no one. Each man must reproduce it for himself from within" (Janouch, p. 167). Man needs to make use of the instinctual qualities that pre-exist in his nature and that continuously shape his existence. For his freedom will come not by being pulled upwards towards dizzy heights by some psychological prescription or moral law, but by growing outwards from within.

CHAPTER SIX

The valley and the mountain: Ibsen's inner landscapes

I bsen once said that he had always been more of a poet and less of a social commentator than the social dramas of his middle period might suggest. In later life indeed he regretted having stopped writing poetry: poetry being the language of the inner world, the place where the dialogue of conscious and unconscious, valley and mountain, is played out.

In this chapter I would like to focus on two plays rich in poetic or even allegorical meaning, *Peer Gynt* and *The Wild Duck*: plays that in addition deal with particular developmental phases in life: adolescence and puberty. Peer Gynt's confused, hedonistic anti-quest for his "self" makes an interesting contrast with the quietly determined Hedvig of *The Wild Duck*, misguided in their different ways. Ibsen wrote that "I do not believe any of us can do anything other or anything better than realise ourselves in truth and in spirit" (cited in McFarlane, p. xvi). He was well aware that this is a heroic struggle full of temptations and pitfalls or, as his mountain back-drops suggest, the chasms and avalanches of catastrophic change. Such chasms open up even in the drawing room or the attic, spaces in which everyday life interacts with a wild and tragicomic dream-world. The adolescent's attempt to become himself or herself alternates with the attempt to evade oneself, and as in real life, interacts with chance combinations of circumstance or family environment

112 THE ART OF PERSONALITY

to either win through, or succumb to despair or delusion. A brief postscript on *The Master Builder* and *When We Dead Awaken* considers how Ibsen applies these perennial themes of adolescence specifically to the condition of the artist, trapped in a social role.

Peer Gynt: *The life-lie in adolescence*

The "life-lie" is a phrase coined by the pragmatic Dr Relling in *The Wild Duck* to express his belief that the personality, whether young or old, needs to be protected from the truth in order to survive. The question is, of course, what constitutes truth, what does it mean to possess it, and in what mode should it be delivered. It is the subject of all Ibsen's work. In his middle period the lie is a social one; in his early and late plays it is the lie in the soul that he is concerned with, or the lie that looks like truth: just as his characters appear to be human beings but in reality they have a disguised animal mentality (like the collection of farmyard animals he kept on his writing desk as models). The animal mentality is similar to Bion's (1970) "basic assumption" mentality, the nonthinking level of existence represented by social conformity or conformities like that of the mayor or schoolteacher in *Brand*. The creative soul, by contrast, is shaped in relation to its internal object or objects, which often in Ibsen take the form of a muse-like woman, sometimes genuine and sometimes dangerously caricatured.

In *Brand* for example, written shortly before *Peer Gynt* and Ibsen's first major success in finding his own voice, there is a split between the idealised Agnes who becomes an object of sacrifice – prey to Gerd, the wild gypsy girl of the mountains – and the denigrated mother who offers worldly riches yet hopes her son will save her soul. The befouled mother with soiled values appears in a kind of dream:

> Her body in its rags
> As if it were a hoard
> Of precious, secret greed;
> Who looks like a crow or
> Hawk nailed to a barn door. (Ibsen, 1996, p. 39)

She "strips the corpse" of his dead father like a "swooping hawk":

> She tears open a purse
> As a hawk rips a mouse. (p. 45)

THE VALLEY AND THE MOUNTAIN: IBSEN   113

Brand cannot face the aesthetic conflict evoked by this split-off anti-mother who ravages the gold contents that he considers belong to his father-god, like Hamlet's Ghost, the "Hyperion" to his soiled "satyr" uncle-father Claudius:

> God's image, that you've marred,
> Shall shine again, purified;
> Resurrected by my will;
> Transfigured in my soul. (p. 47)

This splitting of the idea of woman results in a type of internal revenge, in the form of the loss of Agnes and their child. Agnes is acquired and in a sense stolen from his adolescent naïve but more joyful self, the artist named Einar. Obsessed with purifying his mother by transfiguring her ugly elements, Brand actively neglects his child in the context of an idealised picture of Agnes:

> Watch over our child,
> Agnes. In a radiant dream
> His spirit lies so calm,
> Like water that is stilled,
> Like a mountain tarn
> Silent under the sun.
> Sometimes his mother's face
> Hovers over that hushed place,
> Is received, is given back,
> As beautifully as a bird
> Hovers, and hovering, is mirror'd
> In the depths of the lake. (p. 67)

It is a beautiful Wordsworthian reflection, or rather illusion of his own making: "the depth and not the tumult of the soul" as Wordsworth famously put it (*Laodamia*). The calm is the calm of death; the mother's face watching the drowning child is as much a death-warrant as a lullaby, the aesthetics of perfection, in retreat from aesthetic conflict. Brand's fanaticism, obedient to the *lex talionis* of his possessive god, is ultimately based on self-idealisation, something as destructive of development as the monetary values of his own mother or the town mayor. "Let me be the martyr/ Not her", he pleads, but inevitably goes unheard, for that his the nature of his inner god. The wild troll-girl, crazy Gerd with her piercing eyesight, extracts his "idol" (the child) from its insecure cradle-nest and flings it to the winds like the ice-dove that embodies the mountain's superegoish response:

114   THE ART OF PERSONALITY

> GERD: Silver-white ice-dove, do you cry
> With terror now? Ah, the beauty!
> He's plunging down, he's scattering
> Whirlwinds of feathers from each wing;
> A mountain whirling like a swarm
> Of feathery snow. (p. 160)

Thus Einar and Brand, as two facets of the adolescent artist at a crossroads in life, lose their inspiration in complementary ways: mother, wife, and child succumb to the hawk and the avalanche.

Yet the artist or adolescent who has no fanaticism – no sense of developmental mission to change "the world" – traverses an equally fruitless pathway. Ibsen explored this alternative type of "selfhood" in Brand's sister-play *Peer Gynt* (originally more of an epic poem or Viking saga, that he then adapted for the stage). Peer's refrain throughout is an insistence on "being himself"; and yet like Lear, he is a child who has "never truly known himself" but has always evaded the commitment this involves. Where Brand is a fanatic, Peer is an escapee; they embody the "messianic" and the "fight-flight" personalities (Bion, 1970). It becomes apparent that being oneself is as great a problem as knowing the truth, indeed, they are the same problem.

The trajectory of Peer's story is fuelled by his garbled misquotations from the Scriptures and follows the wavering line of his relationship to women, or the idea of woman in various guises. The play opens with Peer and his mother Åse in their neglected family farm, and closes with Peer and Solveig his "mother-wife" (or ideal female object) outside the hut which he built with his own hands to house his memory of her, but has never lived in, being always chased out by his internal demons. The first home has suffered from his father's drunkenness and profligacy, which was coupled however with a naïve pride in his son's talents, though he had no idea how to promote these constructively (they are represented primarily by the button-moulding game). Peer's inability to commit himself to a true developmental path is associated with this debilitated, collapsible and misguided father, yet his inherited potential is also imaged by the wealth and prosperity of his grandfather who ran the family farm as a thriving business. The father's fault has become embedded in the son in the typical way of one of Ibsen's "ghosts": the carrier of both talent and insecurity.

The way that mother and son circumvent the father's absence is via an escapist but imaginative fantasy life of storytelling: they exchange positions, alternating between rider and ridden. Åse

THE VALLEY AND THE MOUNTAIN: IBSEN   115

would love to believe Peer's boastful stories, and veers between indulgence and scolding. In a standard childlike way he embroiders on stories he has heard in the past, making himself the hero, and asks (quite logically) why they couldn't have happened to him too. When Peer, to his mother's comical mixed reaction of delight and disapproval, takes Åse on a "reindeer ride" in Act One saying "I'm the reindeer – you be Peer!" and "Darling ugly little mother ... wait till I've done something really marvellous!", he is re-enacting a well-established scenario between the two of them. This is only fully explained in Act Two, when Åse tells Solveig's family how she and the child reacted to the father's dissoluteness:

> ÅSE: What could we do but try to forget?
> I was too weak to face the truth ...
> You do your best to keep from thinking;
> Some try lies, and some try brandy,
> But ah, we took to fairy tales
> Of princes, trolls, enchanted bears,
> And stolen brides ... (Ibsen, 1966, p. 98)

By this point of course Peer has literally stolen a bride from a wedding in the village. He has been fantasising being Emperor Gynt, or a knight in armour, with his mother riding behind on her broomstick. It is a mask for his personal insecurity. Uninvited, and conscious that he looks "like a tramp", he lies in the heather outside the wedding gathering (the adolescent group), staring into the sky, saying (like Hamlet to Polonius): "That's a funny shaped cloud – why it's just like a horse!" and ruminating on his exclusion by girls whose imagined thoughts "pierce me like gimlets". He believes that a strong drink would defend him against the laughter of the group, and the troll-like youths know that a "drunken hog" Peer would provide them with plenty of entertainment. Only Solveig, a newcomer therefore outside the group, has a different way of seeing, and is able to tolerate her own disturbance aroused by his sexual greed and baby-like desperate pleading:

> Oh yes, let me tell you, at night I'm a werewolf –
> I'll bite you all over your sides and your back!
> *(changing his tone and begging her desperately)*
> Dance with me, Solveig! (p. 52)

But the moment Solveig withdraws because Peer is "too wild", he slips into the role into which the group has goaded him, and runs away "like a mountain goat" with the bride slung over his

116   THE ART OF PERSONALITY

shoulders: "Mother! He's carrying her – like a pig!" shouts the
groom; later, in the mountain claustrum, a pig is the mount of
the troll-bride. He fulfils his animal reputation, according to the
expectations of the group, and succumbs to a trollish sexual union,
gathered into the troll kingdom of the Dovre-fell by the whirling
dance of three lonely herd-girls on the high pastures. As they lead
him on he imagines he is flying over the family farm as it was in the
prosperous days of his grandfather – the days when it had "glittering windows" of shining glass rather than bundles of rags stuffed
in the holes:

> Peer Gynt, you have sprung from greatness,
> And to greatness shall you attain! (p. 65)

It is a fantasy ride that ends with hitting his head on a rock and
falling unconscious, propelled by drink, sexual excitement, and
romantic illusions about himself. He has entered the cavern of
the trolls.

The dream or nightmare that follows this flight recapitulates
his experience of the village wedding, and by means of satire,
highlights its psychological dangers. The bride reappears in the
form of the ugly Woman in Green, with her witchlike reversal of
values: "Is it true?" she asks, as he sniffs around her, and he replies,
"As true as that you are a beautiful woman." As in Macbeth, "Fair
is foul, and foul is fair." It is a caricature of the idea of waking
up with vision changed by a love-juice dropped on mortal eyes
by fairies. He has forgotten the "vision of pure light" that was
Solveig: she has become an idealised and therefore unattainable
figure who could only reject him, and therefore, he has cast her out
of his mind and substituted her with a "negative" picture (as in
the photography simile that appears toward the end of the story) .
The new trollish couple agree on the "doubleness" of standards of
truth or beauty:

> WOMAN IN GREEN: Black looks like white, and ugly fair.
> PEER: Big looks like little, and dirty like clean.
> WOMAN IN GREEN: Oh Peer, I can see we shall get on
>   together! (pp. 66–67)

Where beauty lies entirely in the eye of the beholder, all that's
needed is a minor adjustment to vision that can be effected
by scratching and cutting of the eyeball. The Old Man of the
Dovre, father of the Woman in Green, offers to convert Peer into
a total troll:

THE VALLEY AND THE MOUNTAIN: IBSEN   117

> OLD MAN: I'll simply scratch your left eye
> A little bit, so that you'll see askew,
> Yet you'll think what you see is exactly right;
> Next I'll cut out your right-hand window-pane ...(p. 73)

This is not "nonsense", he insists, but "Dovre-sense" – it has reasons of its own, that are not arguable. As Irene Freeden has put it, it is a perfect description of projective identification (Freeden, 2002). Trolldom does not constitute a community but a narcissistic gang. In this psychological condition, far removed from the genuine aesthetic conflict of ambivalence toward the love-object, there is no remorse, no pain, no longing – just the negative state of frenzied excitement, whether pleasurable or punitive.

Peer was willing to accept the "battle-cry" of the troll, "To thyself be sufficient", since he could not really distinguish between this and the stamp of a human – "To thyself be true" – or the various biblical mottos which he has garbled. With his eyes and thoughts clouded by troll-juice he found it easy enough to join in the dance, to "adapt" to the demands of the group by tying on a tail with a silken ribbon (a token borrowed from the civilised valleys below). He can wear the badge of adolescent fashion. Yet some faint unconscious memory of his mother (representing true love) does however save him from doing what is catastrophically irreversible. He accepts that the window-panes of his grandfather's house (his human inheritance) may now be "stuffed with rags" but he recoils from having his own window-panes cut and scratched. As the little trolls – the mob – surround Peer and try to lynch him, echoing the group at the wedding feast, he calls "Help, mother!" and instantly the church bells ring and disperse the nightmare; the mountain cavern collapses like the "strange hollow and confused noise" of one of Prospero's masques. When he is not pretending to be Emperor Gynt he does have a genuine, if diminutive, sense of self-preservation that recognises his dependence on his internal object.

In the next phase too it is the idea of women that saves him from complete disaster. On ejection from the mountain hall he encounters the very spirit that makes him unable to confront anything: the Boyg – the slimy, misty shape-changer. The Boyg is the spirit of compromise that was anathema to Brand, and represents the complementary temptation or mindset: the temptation to avoidance rather than to fanaticism. Where Brand pursues the demands of his own will, Peer evades all choices that are demanded of him by life. This time he calls on Solveig for rescue: "Girl, be quick if

118   THE ART OF PERSONALITY

you mean to save me! Don't just look down, but pitch your silver prayerbook in his eye!" He is picked up by birds and the Boyg retires, saying his prey is "too strong. There were women behind him" (p. 81).

At the end of Act Two Solveig is known to be present, but hidden behind a wall; instead she is represented by her younger sister Helga who acts as a messenger, bringing food to Peer and returning to Solveig with Peer's silver button (his soul) and the words: "Ask her not to forget me." It is the first hint of the idea of the Button Moulder, the mysterious catcher of souls who appears in the final act, who seems conjured up by Peer's childhood game of melting buttons in a ladle (a game he played with his father who indeed encouraged him to melt silver not just tin); silver being a material too good to waste, and now associated with Solveig herself, with her silver book and clasp (the link with the bright untarnished object).

As always however the link made by Peer with the object is a momentary and fleeting one. At the beginning of Act Three we see Peer building his own mountain hut and (Quixote-like) imagining himself to be a knight in armour fighting with a pine tree; like Lear he is an outlaw with "no mother to bring him food", left to fend the elements of the world beyond his family home. It is a place of self-defence, with a strong door to "keep out spiteful goblin-thoughts". A little episode occurs at this point which only makes sense later on: while building his hut, Peer silently observes a boy (of about his own age) chop off his own finger in order to avoid conscription. "A finger won't grow again", he thinks, amazed at his irreversible action. The boy has to run the gamut of society's contempt and ostracisation when he is summoned to the recruiting office and they spit and sneer like trolls. Only at the end of the play do we realise his girlfriend was pregnant at the time, and that his purpose was not mere cowardice. The boy also built his own mountain hut, but he housed his family, and survived a series of natural disasters, each time rebuilding his life rather than running away – although Peer outlives him and sees his funeral. The amputated finger makes a parallel but also a contrast with the damaged eyes that Peer avoided when he was with the trolls. There, it would have represented a parody of the gouging out of Gloucester's eyes in *King Lear* to enable him to "see feelingly". Peer's method is always to maintain an escape route, a reversible perspective: to avoid the uncompromising demands of seeing the truth feelingly.

Nonetheless the very idea of commitment – even though prevented by the Boyg – seems to conjure up Solveig again. She

THE VALLEY AND THE MOUNTAIN: IBSEN   119

appears in response to a counter-dream of her own, saying she has received the messages from his mother and from Helga, and indeed "messages came in the wind and the silence"; they "swarm" in her mind (as it were in opposition to the swarm of trolls) and make links with his own thoughts. "Down in the valley", she says, "I could not know what thoughts you were thinking". Peer says:

> I shall need no bars against goblin-thoughts
> If you dare to go in and live with me here,
> This hunter's hut will be holy ground. (p. 89)

The mountain hunter's hut thus becomes a chamber in his mind where, even in his own absence, he keeps a good object who knows his goblin-thoughts yet is no longer afraid of them as Solveig had been, slightly, before she got the courage to "leave for ever" her own father and mother and come up to the mountains. She does not regard this as imprisonment but the opposite: she can breathe freely "up here in the buffering wind" but "down there was airless ... here pine trees whisper such song, such silence – I am at home". She is content with the hut that Peer fears is "cramped and ugly": "Ugly or splendid, I'm happy here." By contrast with Peer's Boyg-driven motto of "go round about", Solveig can declare that there is "no way back on the road I have taken".

She waits there until the end of his playing at life (like any patient analyst). She waits alone, since Peer is almost instantly chased away by the reappearance of the ugly green troll-woman, the negative side of woman, who grows alongside the beautiful one, bringing with her the lame troll-boy (an image of Peer, the offspring of their ugly alliance), "lame in shanks as you are lame in mind". Here clearly the troll-woman embodies what Bion calls "envy of the growth-promoting objects". As they grow, so does their dark shadow: "As your hut grew, mine rose beside it." The troll-woman will be forever voyeuristically intruding into the rela-tionship between him and his ideal Solveig: "I shall peep through the door and watch you both." The troll-woman's power derives from Peer's own weakness, his sense of being "shamefaced and ugly", and his belief that the way to Solveig would require him to be pure and rid of his own ugly thoughts so as not to contaminate her. As always, his solution is to run away:

> "Go round about", said the Boyg. So I must.
> My royal palace has crashed to the ground!
> A wall has grown round her – and I was so near;
> Now everything's ugly ... my joy has grown old.

120   THE ART OF PERSONALITY

> Go round about, lad; there's no way now
> That passes straight from you to her ... (p. 93)

He has a confused notion of a way of repentance, but feels it would all require too much steady work, that "might take years" of patching "fragments and shreds" of old memories: "you might patch a fiddle but never a bell"; and unlike the fingerless boy with his capacity for work, Peer needs instant gratification, whether of heavenly bliss or diabolical excitement.

Nonetheless this momentary intimacy with Solveig, even "at arm's length", enables him to attend to his mother on her deathbed. At this crucial point he appears to inwardly hear her call: "Oh God, is he never coming? ... I cannot send him a message", and at her bedside he movingly re-enacts their lifelong storytelling partnership. This time he is the parent and she the child, as expressed by Åse lying in the child's short bed while Peer sends her to sleep with his story of their ride together to Soria Moria Castle and heaven's gates:

> PEER: The castle is towering above us –
>   And the journey will soon be over.
> ÅSE: Then I'll just lie back with my eyes shut
>   And trust to your skill, my son. (p. 101)

There are echoes of Lear's fantasy of regaining Cordelia ("The two of us together will sing like two birds in a cage"):

> Well now, let's gossip together
> about everything under the sun ...
> I wonder if you can remember –
> Our team of beautiful horses! (p. 98)

The homely furniture reminds them of the everyday objects that formed the springboard of their mutual imaginative fantasies: the bed a sleigh, the blanket a sleigh-rug, the floor an ice-bound fjord, the cat a horse. Peer, watching closely, keeps asking her if she is cold. Judging astutely the moment of approaching death, he introduces her to St Peter, his namesake:

> I've called my old mother a hen, too,
> At the way she cackled and clucked;
> But *you* must respect her and honour her,
> And make her feel really at home.
> You won't find they come any better
> From these parts nowadays.
> Aha! Here comes God the Father! (p. 101)

THE VALLEY AND THE MOUNTAIN: IBSEN 121

God the Father is the masculine figure whom both he and she lacked in their picture of home, and whose presence he imaginatively evokes by way of reparation. For a moment he becomes that male presence and although it is a kind of fiction, it is a truthful fiction that for his mother, finally there is a good man in her life. Momentarily Peer has grown up. He tells his horses they can rest: "we've reached the end of the journey" and thanks his mother for all she gave him, "both beatings and lullabies" – they were both well-intended despite the confusion the contradictory messages that occupied his infant mind.

Åse's parting wish was to link Peer up with Solveig, "the girl who is longing to go to the mountains ... don't you want to know her name?" but he is not yet ready to explore the "mountains" of self-knowledge; he has a lifetime of worldly travel to undergo, during which he relies on the little homemade hut to contain her image even whilst he appears to forget all about her. When Ibsen first tried to adapt *Peer Gynt* for the stage he thought of omitting most of Act Four but was persuaded to change his mind. In theatre terms, it is the most colourful and burlesque section, Quixotic in its flow. All the same, this act tells a different kind of story from the rest of the play: it is the satirical basis for his future social dramas, with a series of bourgeois characters dressed up in various exotic roles, all committed to opportunistic capitalism, yet whose values are masked by a pastiche of spiritual and philosophical explorations – the fashionable, sophisticated form of Peer's misquotations from the Scriptures:

> VON EBERKOPF: But this for-and-within-one's-self existence
>   Has, I daresay, entailed a struggle?
> PEER: It has indeed – when I was younger;
>   But always I came out the winner ...
> VON EBERKOPF: You have a view of Life's conditions
>   That puts you in the ranks of Thinkers.
>   A commonplace philosopher
>   Sees every detail separately
>   And never grasps things as a whole,
>   But you see comprehensively. (p. 106)

Peer complacently explains his mode of self-education, achieved by means of reading about all subjects "in snatches ... choosing what is useful", whilst trading in slaves and warfare. Plied with drink, he elaborates on his successful philosophy of the Gyntish Self, and how "by force of money" he has become Emperor of all the world. In a caricature of Richard II's "hollow crown that rounds

122   THE ART OF PERSONALITY

the temples of a king" he describes "that world inside my vaulted skull which makes me *Me* and no one else ... just as a god can't be a devil", and his friends applaud his "poetic conception" of reversed values. Yet it is not so different from the rationale that lies behind many modern notions of psychotherapy that promote the external principles of self-worth and self-confidence rather than the internal principle of self-development. "I am *myself* – Sir Peter Gynt!" Only at the very end of the play does the meaningless of this statement become questioned by the protagonist.

Meanwhile Peer enters into a variety of "self" guises, increasing in their sophistication: he moves from pirate and financier to prophet, wandering scientist, and autobiographer. Echoing Rousseau's *Confessions* he declares:

> Should I write my life, without any concealment –
> A book that would serve as guide and example?
> Or wait – I have plenty of time on my hands,
> Suppose I turned into a wandering scientist,
> Laying bare the excesses of ages long past?...
> I shall follow the path of the human race,
> And float like a feather on History's tide,
> Re-living it all, as if in a dream. (p. 146)

It is of course all fake experience, repeating the compulsive storytelling of his youth when he re-lived in his fantasy the local legends of his valley and village, and claimed the adventures as his own. He is still trying to reincarnate himself in a new guise, as "master of all the Past", posing as a teacher of life's lessons – such as the deceitfulness of mankind, "and women – well, they are the weaker sex!" Clearly Ibsen enjoyed the opportunity of inhabiting his adolescent anti-hero to give free rein to every conceivable prejudice and misconception; there is a delight in Peer's very existence, absurdly muddled as it is, that rarely reappears in his later works.

There is just one point in Act Four – at the height of Peer's conclusion about women – at which his manic career pauses for the introduction of a brief vignette in which Solveig appears, spinning and singing:

> Here, until you come, I shall be waiting alone,
> And if you wait on high, I shall meet you there, my own. (p. 148)

The light of reason in his mind has not been totally quenched, although he is oblivious of its presence: for there is no sensuous link, no communication; Solveig is waiting alone. She is seen by the audience but not by Peer, since she is still too deeply buried below

THE VALLEY AND THE MOUNTAIN: IBSEN   123

his consciousness. Indeed when Peer related his romantic past to Von Eberkopf and co, he omitted all mention of Solveig and only told of the "girl of royal blood", namely the troll-woman, whose father demanded "equivocal conditions" that, he explains, he had to renounce. It is not possible to talk about Solveig, an internal object, in the setting of the worldly adventures of Act Four.

Peer therefore continues his pseudo-explorations in the history of culture. Regarding himself as a martyr to the quest for truth, he passes through Egypt where (in parody of Oedipus) he encounters the Sphinx, who reminds him of the Boyg, just as the statue of Memnon bears a remarkable resemblance to the Old Man of the Dovre:

> So that's it Boyg – you look like a lion
> When seen in daylight and from behind!
> Do you still talk in riddles? (p. 151)

Unlike Oedipus, he is not digesting his experiences but mindlessly repeating them; symbol-formation cannot occur without the link with the object. The Boyg turns out to be the statue or outward mask of Begriffenfeldt, the director of a madhouse in which "Absolute Reason dropped dead last night at 11 pm." It is the ultimate and inevitable conclusion to Peer's adventures into the delusional world, the furthest reaches of the claustrum. Peer discovers he has been long expected, as a messianic legend, parodying the Second Coming of Christ:

> BEGRIFFENFELDT: Peer Gynt! Allegorical! What I expected …
>   Peer Gynt! Yes, that is to say: The Unknown!
>   "He that should come", as the prophecy told me. …
>   Peer Gynt! Enigmatic! Profound and incisive!
>   Every word in itself is a marvel of learning!
>   What are you?
> PEER (*modestly*): I've always attempted to be
>   Myself. The rest you can find from my passport. (p. 153)

In addition to the socio-political features of identity noted in his passport, he embodies that favourite religious-philosophical category The Unknown; and his academic mastery of Romantic philosophy has resulted in his being dubbed "Interpretation's Emperor – based upon Self!"

This apparently integrated (but satirical) combination of assets worldly and spiritual leads him straight into the madhouse of delusory identity. Here he is hailed as the new ruler and tries to wriggle his way out of it, since "in here it's a question of being one's Self

124   THE ART OF PERSONALITY

beside one's self." But this, says Begriffenfeldt, is precisely what being one's self means:

> BEGRIFFENFELDT: As himself, he progresses full steam ahead;
> He encloses himself in a barrel of self;
> In self-fermentation he steeps himself,
> Hermetically sealed with the bung of self ...
> No one sheds tears for another's sorrows,
> No one considers another's ideas. (p. 157)

Peer has been driven almost mad by this portrait of himself in the troll-tinted mirror. Meanwhile a jihadist who believes he is a pen begs to be sharpened so that his suicide can purify the world:

> HUSSEIN: A knife! I am blunt! Make haste, someone, and slit me –
> The world will be ruined if nobody sharpens me!
> PEER: What a shame for the world, which – like most home-
> made things –
> The Creator believed was especially good. (pp. 163–4)

We remember Peer's intention a little earlier to write his autobiography. In the religious-artistic caricature, the pen desires to be "held" and "guided" by a master writer, and tries to inflict this role on Peer, who has approached close to deity in his manic fantasy world. Indeed all the characters in the madhouse, and in the world of his travels, represent aspects of Peer himself that ultimately evoke terror in him. As Hussein starts to "sharpen" himself, again Peer cries for help, remembering dimly that once he was not a pen but "the silver-clasped book of a lady" – the lost link with Solveig. Now he feels he has become "a printer's error", crying "Help me! My mind's giving way!" as he sinks into the mud of unconsciousness, "beside himself", and is crowned with the straw wreath of selfishness:

> BEGRIFFENFELDT: Ha! See how he triumphs in the mud –
> Beside himself! A Coronation!
> Long live ... the Emperor of Self! (p. 164)

What is it that saves Peer from the jihadism that is essentially the same as Brand's – the fanaticism of selfhood (in Blake's sense of tyranny over the object)? It is the fact that unlike Brand, the movement of the play is somehow controlled by the invisible, absent presence of Solveig, silently dominant even when the situation appears hopeless, owing to her capacity for patience, whereas Agnes loses ground from the moment she commits her own life to that of Brand (the patient), and more importantly, that of their child (the analysis).

THE VALLEY AND THE MOUNTAIN: IBSEN 125

In Act Five an elderly Peer approaches his homeland once again. The beautiful, individuated feature of the mountains and fjords of Norway, in which, somewhere, his object remains housed, gradually reveal themselves from the sea:

> There's the Hallingskarv in his winter dress,
> Showing off, the old rogue in the evening light.
> And there's his brother the Jokel, behind him,
> With his ice-green mantle still on his back.
> And the Folgefann – how fine she looks,
> Like a maiden dressed in shining white. (p. 165)

For the first time since he left Solveig we sense a movement of recognition, of returning to find his real self in the home where he left it years ago. Norway is the home of his memories that need to be re-lived and re-formed.

But as in Shakespeare's *Tempest*, there is a storm brewing, that tests the inner strength of the men on board. Peer's fake generosity, based on his entrepreneurial self-image, contrasts with the sailors' sense of reality that is based on their experience at sea and their responsibility to their families at home; they do not attempt a hopeless rescue of another sinking ship. As soon as Peer realises they all have families he withdraws his offer of a tip for the crew, overcome by envy: "There's no one waiting for old Peer Gynt/ Who's ever given a thought to me?" Yet his envy is real perhaps for the first time, on the verge of being acknowledged and thus becoming useful for development: in fact bringing closer the one who is waiting for him at the top of the mountain, giving him thought.

The storm brings to light a Strange Passenger from the depths of the ship (of his mind) who says he has no interest in Peer's money, but would like instead to have the gift of his "excellent corpse ... for the purpose of Science". The Strange Passenger, like Hamlet's ghost, is seen only by Peer, not by the ship's crew who are busy with their work task. When he asks who was that "lunatic", they eerily reply that he is the only passenger – in other words, the stranger is a part of himself. Peer's debilitated internal father has now become a scientist, a positivistic Freudian who is interested in the forensic dissection of his idiosyncratic dreamworld:

> STRANGE PASSENGER: You'd be opened right up, and have
>   daylight let in.
>   What I'm trying to find is the place where dreams lurk ...
>   I'd go carefully into each one of your crannies – (p. 163)

126   THE ART OF PERSONALITY

This type of psychological investigation can only reveal the truth of a "lunatic" brain when the subject is dead, incapable of a transference relationship. Ibsen was himself puzzled by the Strange Passenger; he said he inserted him as a caprice. Traditionally the figure of the dark stranger would represent death, and he seems to be a macabre, Gothic precursor to the Button Moulder, who is a more developed analyst-figure tailored more individually to Peer's particular story. The Strange Passenger is a tomb-robber (as in Bion's [1973–74] use of the Ur excavations to differentiate the religious from the scientific state of mind); his interest is in performing autopsies and dissecting cadavres. He surfaces twice – just before and just after the ship founders – and in between is the episode in which Peer fights off the Cook for control of the upturned dinghy which can only rescue one of them:

> COOK: Remember that I have children at home!
> PEER: I need my life much more than you –
> I haven't any children yet. (p. 175)

As the Cook sinks, Peer swings himself up onto the keel of the boat, with the pronouncement "Amen, lad. You were yourself right to the end." Yet there is a kind of genuine logic in his determination to hold onto life at the cost of anyone else's –"I *won't* die! I shall reach the shore!" – that impresses on us that he does indeed have work to do before he can close his story. He still has no idea what it is to "be yourself"; only then might he be ready to die. Indeed when the Strange Passenger asks him if he has ever "honestly known what terror means", and the achievement of conquering genuine fear, a window is opened on the depths of Peer's self-ignorance. Developmental terror is different from his usual childish panic in the face of the Boyg, and for a moment Peer glimpses it, only to deny the Stranger's message as that of a "wretched Moralist" – that is, not somebody from whom he can learn any lessons. That will be left to the Button Moulder; as Ibsen jokes, the hero cannot die in the middle of Act Five.

Once on dry land, Peer's first encounter takes the form of the funeral of the boy who years ago had cut off his own finger in order to farm and to raise his family. "Here's somebody going the way of all flesh; thanks be to heaven it isn't me!" The boy's story is one of humility, loyalty and endurance; he was never cast down by society's contempt or life's natural disasters (avalanches) but remained steadfastly "true to himself" within his own horizons, which he knew were not those of glory and patriotism:

THE VALLEY AND THE MOUNTAIN: IBSEN   127

> But on that upland slope
> In the small circle where he saw his duty,
> There he was great, because he was himself –
> The metal he was forged from there rang true. (p. 182)

His work of love required no reward – not even from his own sons, who emigrated to America and forgot their Norwegian father's heroic efforts to get them educated, clambering over the cliffs to school. The peasant lad whose soul-button is forged of true metal stands as a complete foil and contrast to Peer who has all his life, eddying in roundaboutness, evaded work and internal struggle. Yet Peer is impressed by the priest's tribute and its rhetoric – he has always loved a good story, and his way of loving it has always been to instantly introject and appropriate it as his own. In an adhesive identification with the fallen hero he feel as though it were himself "lying asleep/ Hearing my praises sung in a dream". So in the priest's story he finds "nothing to make one's mind uneasy":

> The theme the Parson's discourse hinged on –
> Being inflexibly one's Self –
> Was, in the main, most edifying. (p. 183)

Yet again he has evaded seeing the moral or message of the story; instead he goes round about as usual and re-invents himself as a "poor but virtuous" man who, like the peasant, has been dogged by fate but still "goes his own way" despite all obstacles: "Now for home! … 'Go round' said the Boyg … and so I must."

His memory-route now brings him to an auction taking place at the farm after the funeral of the bride whom he abducted from the wedding feast years ago. Amongst the "rubbish" items is the casting ladle in which as a child, "Peer Gynt cast his silver buttons" – a joke amongst his old acquaintances and the new generation, to both of whom he is a stranger. He declares that the most real thing he possesses is a "dream" of a prayerbook with a silver clasp, at which they all laugh. He attempts to tell his real story but still they do not recognise him, saying that Peer Gynt hanged himself years ago: he is an unreal person, a mere legend. Yet in the story he tells them about a pig (himself) housed under the cloak of a ventriloquist Devil at a "trickster's freak-show" (themselves), he allegorises his own feelings rather than slipping himself inside someone else's story and taking it over. There is a hint of emotional reality in the very distance between himself and his audience, the uncomprehending adolescent gang: he is not known amongst them, but perhaps somewhere, somebody knows him.

128   THE ART OF PERSONALITY

This gap in knowledge brings him once again to the terrain in front of Solveig's hut. He has left the valleys now for good. He is seen scrabbling about in the earth searching for wild onions, for basic food and water, head down, like Nebuchadnezzar:

> Now the greybeard comes back to his mother again ...
> And then when I die – as I probably shall,
> I can crawl in under a fallen tree
> And pull the leaves over me, just like a bear ... (p. 190)

He catches himself in the delusion of being an "Emperor of animals" (sensuality), and laughs, "You're only an onion", or a crawling baby, like Lear in search of Cordelia:

> Once you start thinking, you trip yourself up.
> Well, *I* at least can laugh at that danger
> As long as I'm safely set down on all fours! (p. 192)

At this point he looks up and notices the hut on the hillside where Solveig lives: the reindeer horns over the porch, and the bars made "to shut out goblin-thoughts". His new attentiveness releases Solveig's singing into the air: she makes it clear from inside the hut that she is still waiting, and Peer realises:

> There's one who remembered, and one who forgot; ...
> O sorrow! *Here* was my Empire set!

Unable to bear his own remorse, he instinctively, as always, runs away. He is now on the wild barren moor, strewn with "ashes and mist and wind-blown dust" and blackened by forest fires, like the landscape where Macbeth met the witches. Here he encounters "thoughts he should have formed, words he should have spoken, songs he should have sung, tears he should have shed, deeds he should have done". Instead of digesting his own feelings he has built a scaffolding of lies over them, in a metaphor prefiguring *The Master Builder*:

> Tales and dreams and still-born knowledge
> Form my pyramid's foundation;
> On them shall the work rise upwards
> With a scaffolding of lies.
> From the roof-top flaunt the motto:
> "Flee from truth and shun repentance." (p. 193)

He understands that his very life has been a "whited sepulchre" built on knowledge that has been denied, still-born, like the wisps of dust and mist (Bion's beta-elements).

THE VALLEY AND THE MOUNTAIN: IBSEN   129

Of the "unformed thoughts", the one that has most impact on him is the notion that he could be accused of deeds he *hasn't* done – that is, of not committing himself sufficiently to do anything at all, in his life of roundaboutness. At that moment he hears his mother's voice in the distance, as in a dream, accusing him of being a poor coachman and upsetting her in the snow (recalling his last ride with her to heaven's gates). A new scheme of values is forming which includes the idea of wasted potential, and this leads to the appearance of the Button Moulder. He has specific instructions to seek out Peer Gynt and melt down his raw material for reuse – something which Peer should understand from his childhood hobby:

> BUTTON MOULDER: Now, you know the trade – how it
> sometimes occurs
> That a casting turns out, as they say, with a flaw ...
> If a button occasionally hadn't a loop,
> What did you do with it?
> PEER: Threw it away. (p. 199)

The loop is the link with his good object: the object exists but the link is not attached; hence his thoughts remain unformed, unsymbolised. His spendthrift father had a habit of throwing out loopless buttons, but, says the Moulder, his own Master would never waste good material since "the mere fact of your having a soul gives you a certain value as metal":

> BUTTON MOULDER: Now *you* were designed as a shining
> button
> On the coat of the world ... but your loop was missing.

Peer is told he has "*never* been himself", so may as well "die completely". Yet Peer's heroism consists in his tenacity; like Barnadine in *Measure for Measure* he knows he is simply not ready to die and so refuses to go along with it:

> Dear fellow, just *lend* me myself – on parole:
> I'll be back soon. Since we only live once,
> We do tend to cling to the Self we were born with. (p. 202)

His urgency somehow suggests his unconscious hidden quest to make contact again with Solveig, as he gradually spirals further up the mountain slopes. But before he can allow himself to do this he has to increase his understanding of what his "self" actually consists of.

130   THE ART OF PERSONALITY

In between the three meetings with the Button Moulder, at different crossroads, Peer encounters first the Old Man of the Dovre, then the Devil, both of whom contribute to the "negative" picture of his self that (as in the photography metaphor) is gradually defining the positive. Peer is astonished to hear from the Old Man that he counts as a genuine troll since he has always followed the troll's motto "To thyself be enough": "You've lived as a troll, but you kept it a secret." It turns out it is not the horns or tail, nor even the eye operation, that is the ineradicable stamp of a troll, but the spirit beneath the skin. Is that where the self lies? At the next crossroads, Peer puts this key question for the first time:

> I've just one question first:
> What, after all, is this "being one's self"? (p. 209)

It is a phrase which has been repeated like an endless refrain throughout all his adventures, yet it has never occurred to him to question what it may mean. The Button Moulder informs him that it means reliance on his object rather than on his ego:

> BUTTON MOULDER: Being one's self means slaying one's Self.
> But that answer's presumably wasted on you,
> And therefore let's say: "Above everything else
> It's observing the Master's intentions in all things."

Peer objects that he does not know what the object intends; to which the Moulder replies he has to rely on intuition: "One just has to guess".

> PEER: But a man's intuitions so often prove wrong,
> And then one is sunk, as it were, in mid-ocean!
> BUTTON MOULDER: Exactly, Peer Gynt, it's when insight is lacking
> That the lad with the hoof makes the best of his captures. (p. 210)

The Button Moulder, who is a kind of angel – an emissary from God – has given Peer a hint of the danger. The idea of insight is a new one for Peer, who has always projected his fantasies into action and imagined that he was thereby "being himself". He has never had a conception of observing the intentions of an internal object and thereby strengthening himself. This is what makes him vulnerable to the Devil, "the lad with the hoof" – whom he meets on his way to the next crossroads, and who informs him that "a man may quite well be himself in two different ways", like a photographic image that exists in two chemical states – either "faithful to life"

THE VALLEY AND THE MOUNTAIN: IBSEN   131

or a trollish negative. This time, trusting to intuition, Peer evades capture by asserting that Peer Gynt is to be found at the "Cape of Good Hope", a Bunyanesque state of mind beyond the Devil's reach, even though this means he has to finally accept that he has been "expelled from the self-owning nobility". He has to accept his state of unknowing and of lostness in the hope that he may be found by his object and restored in a positive sense.

For a moment, therefore, having shed his illusions and the cloak of a fake identity, on the verge of Bion's "catastrophic change", he experiences the terror that the Strange Passenger spoke of: the fear of being "lost in the void", of being no one because he has no one:

> Is there no one? No one in all creation?
> No one on earth and no one in heaven? ...
> So unspeakably poor can the soul return
> Through the sombre mists into nothingness. (p. 219)

He feels on the pulses the absence of a soul-holder, forgetting that long ago he gave a silver button to Solveig via her sister, with the message not to forget him. Now, he returns to the original aesthetic conflict of the newborn baby or soul, with a hymn to the beauty of the earth, the mountains of his homeland:

> Do not be angry, oh lovely earth,
> If to no purpose I trampled your grass.
> Oh lovely sun, your glowing rays
> Have squandered themselves on an empty house
> Where no one within might be warmed and gladdened –
> The owner, they say, was never at home.

The hymn reminds us of the description of the Norwegian coast at the beginning of this act. But what he envisions now is self-erasement:

> I will climb up high to the steepest peak
> And watch the sun rise once again:
> I will stare till I tire, at the promised land,
> Then let the snow drift over me ...
> And there they may write: "Here lies – No One."

Only when he is thus spiritually prepared, can he face meeting Solveig again. Solveig is blind, but in a sense so is Peer; he has to ask the Button Moulder what is that light, that sound of sighing? "Only a woman's song." By long-established habit, he instinctively

132 THE ART OF PERSONALITY

tries to run away as usual, citing his "roundabout" litany. Then he
stops, and for the first time commits himself to go in one direction:

> Something bids me go in … go back – go home.
> *(He goes a few paces, then stops.)*
> "Round about" said the Boyg!
> *(He hears the song in the hut.)*
> No! Now for once
> The way runs straight, though it's never so narrow. (p. 221)

Only once he has erased his selfhood (in the Blakeian egocentric
sense) can he find himself, that is, in relation to his internal object:

> PEER: Where has Peer Gynt been since last we met?
> … Since he sprang from the mind of God? …
> SOLVEIG: Oh, your riddle is easy.
> PEER: Then say, if you know!
> Where was I? Myself – complete and whole?
> Where? With God's seal upon my brow?
> SOLVEIG: In my faith, in my hope, and in my love. (p. 222)

The "father" is not one who keeps a list of sins and punishes them
but who "forgives when a mother prays", as it were continuously,
not at a single reckoning; Solveig is the woman, both mother and
wife, who has been singing for him all along.

The Button Moulder, having performed his re-introduction,
slips into the background and his voice is heard from behind the
hut: "Peer, we shall meet at the last cross-roads." As in the classic
aesthetic conflict, death is part of the picture for the newborn; yet
for the time being, the space of a life-span, the casting ladle has
been replaced by the cradle:

> I will cradle you, I will guard you;
> Sleep and dream, dearest son of mine.

Åse has been reborn as Solveig, as she hoped long ago, on her deathbed, when she tried to tell Peer the name of the girl who longed to
leave the valley and go to the mountains.

The Wild Duck: *The life-lie in puberty*

Hedvig, the young heroine of *The Wild Duck* (with the same name
as Ibsen's sister), is Solveig as she might have been had she not
been able to wait – that is, to refrain from acting out her fantasy
world. Hedvig in her attic is threatened with blindness; Solveig

THE VALLEY AND THE MOUNTAIN: IBSEN 133

in her hut accepts or achieves it. This is a play from Ibsen's mid-career, and stands apart from those before and those after it, almost in a category of its own: neither a social drama, nor an allegorical drama, yet with both a realistic and a fantasy level, and like *Peer Gynt*, a strong sense of a particular phase in personality development – namely puberty – but this time from a female perspective. Fourteen-year-old Hedvig is at the centre of the play and the other characters swivel around her, all claiming identity with the wild duck in some form, at various times. The portrait of Hedvig is reminiscent of Munch's painting *Puberty*, with the huge and resonant shadow (full of dark thoughts) emanating from the shy girl who is about to bloom. There is a sense in which Hedvig is the only real person in the play, with the possible exception of her mother Gina (and her alias Mrs Sorby); all the men, despite the dramatist's skilled and realistic portraiture, seem like features of her fantasy world: a collection of naughty, messy or opinionated child-dolls, ignorant of the fact that she alone is the real mother of the wild duck, the poetic spirit of development. She is, according to the adults, in the process of losing her sight, which she is supposed not to know, but which is a good excuse for not going to school, although she slips out at dusk for a daily walk – a time when she is not clearly visible to others. Meanwhile at home she can concentrate on the puppet-show of her inner fantasy world and on "touching up" photographs of outside people. Behind her, at the back of the stage, is the loft which mirrors her picture of the outside world with its bourgeois salons and – beyond those – its distant woods and "works" where people retreat to do their hunting, sulking, or plotting, before returning to the valley of everyday routine. Hedvig is prey to her own artistic imagination, which wells up like Munch's shadow beyond the photographs that she can work on so meticulously, and she has already been experimenting in the kitchen with the exciting game of "houses on fire". In this play more than Ibsen's others, we have the sense that "all the world's a stage/ And all the men and women, merely players." They are all personages in Hedvig's puppet theatre.

It is Relling, the realistic but cynical doctor, who points out that Hedvig is at a difficult stage of life named puberty, and who talks about the "life-lie" that is necessary to maintain a stable foundation for the fragile self (Ibsen, 1988, p. 204). In his view, the Ekdal family needs to be cocooned in fantasy, which is the equivalent of his own drunkenness. His enemy or rather counterpart is Gregers Werle, a Brand-like man with a mission, who believes that the only way to build a secure foundation is by forcing everyone to see what he

134   THE ART OF PERSONALITY

calls the "truth" – meaning the two-dimensional truth of facts. It is the kind of truth that surfaces in the social dramas, like syphilis running through the generations, or poisonous chemicals in the town's water-pipes. Yet the real psychological or emotional truth of the Wild Duck corresponds to neither of these vertices, and the play shows how the understanding of puberty is consistently evaded by the characters surrounding Hedvig.

Ibsen thought of *The Wild Duck* as a new departure that would encourage younger dramatists. It is autobiographical in a way different from his many other explorations of the artist's dilemma: retaining the atmosphere of his own childhood and its loft, puppet theatre, father's bankruptcy, etc. Yet it also contains key figures, or aspects of himself, that are found throughout his oeuvre and that now congregate around Hedvig as living ghosts: the fanatic Gregers Werle; his father, the crooked entrepreneur whose success is founded on the disgrace of his less intelligent onetime colleagues (the Ekdals) to whom he is bound by his guilt; the humane but comfortable doctor; the pragmatic "housekeeper" style woman whose capabilities outmanoeuvre the neuroses of the bourgeois mistress; and now the young girl whose vitality has stirred calm waters into turbulence all around her, focusing on the metaphor of the rescue of the wild duck from the depths where it dived after having been winged by old Werle. And in so far as *The Wild Duck* is a dreamplay, Hedvig is not a simple victim, since the characters of her world are internal figures and hence she bears some responsibility for their existence and interaction.

Of the five acts of the play, the last four have the same setting: namely the studio of the Ekdals' house opening to the loft at the rear. This is where the real action takes place. The first act has the obvious purpose of sketching the background to the family "ghost story" so that the mission of Greger Werle to reveal the "truth" can be set in context and established, as when Brand declared "Now I know my task." It also has the effect of creating two worlds: a social world and a heightened world of inner reality. Behind the veneer of the lunch party skilfully presided over by Mrs Sorby, and presented with Ibsen's characteristic social satire, parts of the personality are meeting again after a long separation: father Werle meets his son, and Gregers meets his "best and only friend" Hjalmar Edkal with whom he has had no contact for sixteen years (approximately the lifetime of Hedvig). He sees himself as the "clever dog" who will expose the family and social lies that have sustained this period, in particular the guilt of his father – a quest that is metaphorically represented by finding the wounded wild duck who has gone down

THE VALLEY AND THE MOUNTAIN: IBSEN   135

to the depths to die. At the same time he dredges up the ghost of his dead mother whose inner unexplained sickness haunts the cheerful efficiency of the housekeeper-type mother represented by both Mrs Sorby and Gina Ekdal. The two types of mother-wife are brought into conflict; the two male "best friends" also have parallels and contrasts, both being romancers and missionaries in their way.

The Ekdals are the Werles' alter-egos – their hidden weakness and vulnerability, but also artistry, behind the bourgeois sophistication and success. They link the distant wild heights of the Hoidal "works" (an area on the fringes of civilization) with its artificial representation in the attic of fantasy: a world or worlds that contrast with respectable valley life. Old Ekdal is indeed the first to be identified with the wild duck, "plunging to the depths" when he was pronounced guilty of illegally felling government timber up at the Hoidal works (p. 123). Old Werle, however, though equally guilty, survived the experience and profited from the result; as often in Ibsen's plays, one man's success is built on overturning someone else, as when Peer Gynt straddled the boat in the storm and pushed away the Cook to drown. Gregers is surprised to find that his father "may almost have a conscience", which takes the form of appeasement in relation to the Ekdals and to his dead wife with her "clouded" eyes that are said to derive from her disapproval of his sexual infidelities; these haunt him and now seem to surface in his own failing sight. His eyes have always been weak, according to his son; now this becomes the reason he feels the need to retire to the other world (Hoidal) and relax his hold on the business in the town: "I have to watch my eyes, Gregers, they have started getting a bit weak" (p. 125). His own clouding eyes are an indication also of an internal change – which according to Hjalmar later is the result of "retribution" from some superegoish power. It is reminiscent of the old religious superstition that masturbation makes people blind. In this play, as possibly in *Peer Gynt*, eyesight represents the route for sexual fantasies and "deviations" (in Gina's term), where Hedvig too in her dark shadow-life is possibly infected.

On the occasion of the engagement party of Act One, Werle in effect renounces sexual relations and allies himself with a housekeeping-wife, like the arrangement he made for Hjalmar and Gina, his cast-off mistress (who is nonetheless very similar to Berta Solby). The party is marked by an absurd but significant game of "blind man's buff". Gregers however, allergic to all forms of play, suspects he is being "used" by his father in this game of blinding and seduction, of secret cover-up. Werle accuses him of "seeing with your mother's eyes", complaining and condemnatory: "and he says he's

136   THE ART OF PERSONALITY

not neurotic!" Werle understands that Gregers' own sexuality has been sublimated into the "claims of the ideal" for which he is seeking a new object (having failed with the workers' families up at Hoidal). The smooth social veneer is also scratched by the appearance of old Ekdal, who is only allowed to use the back stairs, but on this occasion totters across the drawing room with his minder (Graaberg), muttering in an uncomfortable, humiliated manner that he has come the wrong way because "the gate's locked". It is essential to Werle's "blindness" that these maimed features of his repressed life remain in the depths and are not dragged into open view: the gate must remain locked. He can admit finally that he is "lonely" but, like the wild duck, such emotions must be kept out of sight. And Hjalmar goes along with it, denying that he recognises his father in the pathetic old man who spoils the complacency of the party. He is a ready victim for Gregers' messianic urges:

> GREGERS: There he sits, so tremendously trusting and innocent, in the midst of deceit, living under the same roof with a woman like that and not knowing that what he calls his home is built on a lie … Now at last I see an objective I can live for. (p. 128)

He sees Gina-Berta as a seductress who undermined his mother's rightful position, accounting for her "sickly conscience" (an unexplained psychosomatic condition which made her an invalid). His search for a mission is really a search for an opportunity to take revenge on his father, if not socially with the workers, then sexually by rescuing or seducing the wild duck within his family.

The second act of the play transports us into the studio in whose inner recesses (the loft) the wild duck is housed. It is described as a fine bird with just one fatal flaw – it has been winged, and thus its inner nature is destroyed and it can only survive in captivity, in a basket. As the studio set opens we are immediately introduced to the matter of Hedvig's eyesight – her reaction against wild pubertal growth – and by implication, to Hjalmar's lack of intelligence, his own type of blindness:

> GINA: You must put the book away now. Your father doesn't like it; he never reads himself in the evenings.
> HEDVIG: No, Daddy isn't such a great one for reading.
> GINA: Can you remember what we paid for the butter today?
> HEDVIG: It was one crown sixty-five. (p. 129)

In the family dynamics, with comical reiteration, Hjalmar proves incapable of doing anything either practical or intellectual,

THE VALLEY AND THE MOUNTAIN: IBSEN   137

including holding Hedvig in the basket of his mind. The impression is that Hjalmar and Gina do not have sexual relations; she is his carer, and there are no other children. Clearly Werle is the real father, and Hjalmar Ekdal a kind of doll-sibling for Hedvig to play with, indulge, entertain, and feed, just as she is the "little wild duck mother" (as Relling calls her). Hjalmar represents what Gregers calls the "trusting and innocent" superficial face of puberty, innocent only in denial of the turbulence in the depths. Yet the ability to read, to count the housekeeping expenses, and to take and retouch photographs (which is supposed to be his trade) are all beyond him. Instead Hedvig is the one we see doing the retouching, her own form of sublimation. All Hjalmar can do is eat; and his constant feeding is a major feature of the household business; it fuels both his tenuous happy moments and the underlying whinge which expresses his insecurity: "*I* don't need any of life's little pleasures!"

Hedvig, in collusion with Gina, ingratiatingly pampers this pretend child-father, telling him how nice he looks in evening dress "with your moustache and your curly hair" – he is her duck-in-a-basket. This is the life-lie: not the fact that Hedvig has more than one type of father, or Werle more than one type of wife. Ibsen thought of puberty, the boundary between childhood and adulthood, as defined by losing the ability to play with dolls. Yet Ibsen's characters never stop playing with dolls, in the form of other people. Hedvig is at the centre of the "web of deceit" in which all are involved, in a sort of wilful blindness which contrasts with the evidence of her penetrating intelligence (such as, "Perhaps I'm not really Daddy's!"). The moments of apparent family harmony are achieved by the life-lie in which everyone plays a part. One such moment is when Hjalmar, guilty of petulance (on realising he'd forgotten to bring Hedvig anything from the party), at last agrees to have his flute handed to him:

> HJALMAR: You mustn't forget I'm a man beset by a whole host of troubles. Well, now! (*Dries his eyes.*) This is not the moment for beer. Bring me my flute.
> (*Hedvig runs to the shelves and gets it.*)
> HJALMAR: Thanks! There we are. With flute in hand, and both of you close to me ... ah! ... What though we have to pinch and scrape in this place, Gina! It's still our home. And this I will say: it is good to be here. (p. 139)

His expression of satisfaction is accompanied by some sporadic flute-playing, of an amateur and undeveloped nature, designed to project a romantic self-image: a Bohemian folk dance is travestied

138 THE ART OF PERSONALITY

by being delivered inappropriately "in a slow elegiac tempo with much 'feeling'." Hjalmar has artistic pretensions and just a miniscule degree of talent. The women constantly need to flatter him in order to make things more "cheerful", something which overrides any of their own needs or comforts.

At this very moment of tenuous, brittle happiness, Gregers Werle knocks on the door with his mission of revenge: he has come to "open Hjalmar Ekdal's eyes". "Oh!" says Gina, shrinking back from the figure in the doorway. It is reminiscent of Keats's *Lamia*, whose love-retreat is punctured by the philosopher Apollonius with his "demon vision". (This "Oh!" is echoed later as old Werle arrives to precipitate the catastrophe; and by Molvik's "Ugh!" as old Ekdar emerges from the loft with a bloody skinned rabbit.) The victim of this piercing eyesight is Hedvig, caught between Gregers' determination to root out her nascent sexuality, and Hjalmar's determination to prolong his picture of a prepubertal, carefree "singing bird":

> HJALMAR: Oh, can't you see we haven't the heart to tell her [about her blindness]. She doesn't suspect anything. Happy and carefree, just like a little singing-bird, there she goes fluttering into a life of eternal night. (*Overcome.*) Oh, it's quite heartbreaking for me, Gregers! (p. 141)

The emotion that overcomes him derives from his own heartbreak rather than concern for Hedvig. As he says later, "in my house nobody talks to me about unpleasant things"; and Hedvig's development beyond him is one of them.

Gregers enters with a preconception of his role as the "clever dog" (p. 149), really an attribute of his father, intended to penetrate the Ekdals' fantasy existence but really projecting onto them a fantasy of his own. The metaphor is that of rescuing the wild duck, bringing it to light. The wild duck has in fact become a pet, a captive, rescued from Werle's ruthless hunting gun and tamed in so far as it has come to accept its basket. The "open-air life in the forest and on the moors, among the beasts and birds" of which Gregers reminds old Ekdal, is his own romance. Ekdal the one-time bear-hunter is terrified of the wild outside, keeping to the back corridors in Werle's house, and avoiding going out of doors in his discredited army uniform. It is similar to the way Hedvig avoids going out of the house except in the evening half-light when she will not be seen, though supposedly it is because it will not strain her eyes. She does not want to fly away into the "wide world" any more

THE VALLEY AND THE MOUNTAIN: IBSEN   139

than does her grandfather. Both Ekdal and Gregers image aspects of Hedvig, or of her internal objects with opposite qualities: the avenger and the escapee. She alone seems to intuit the true nature of the drama going on when she says of Gregers and his heavily symbolic story of the dog: "All the time it was just as though he meant something different from what he was saying." But then, it is really her inner drama, just as (she insists) it is *her* wild duck: "*My* wild duck. Because it belongs to *me*" (p. 146).

Meanwhile Hjalmar has reinvented himself in unconscious imitation of Gregers, his intelligent alter-ego or "best friend": saying (as he helps himself to another sandwich): "As truly as I have a mission in life, so shall I fulfil it!" The little studio society is constructing its revenge upon itself and its pretensions.

Hedvig's fourteenth birthday the next day gives shape to the action of the play: the action being the distorted knowledge of art and fantasy which provides the basis for the tragic outcome. There is a sense of covert excitement which Gina, whose intelligence is veiled by her lower-class speech, attempts to deflate through her (deliberate) malapropisms:

> GINA: Funny creatures, men! Always have to have something to deviate themselves with.
> HJALMAR (*angrily*): That's right, yes. We always have to have something to divert ourselves with.
> GINA:Yes, *that's* what I said. (p. 163)

Hjalmar addresses Hedvig in the tone of a naughty boy being watched by his schoolteacher, who has been sent by mother Gina "to keep an eye on him" and check he is not avoiding his homework and masturbating instead: "What to you want to come sniffing round like this for? Are you supposed to be keeping an eye on me, or something?" Hedvig is only too glad to do his homework for him – "Let *me* have the brush, Daddy" – and he willingly hands over the brush whilst insisting he is "not taking responsibility" for her eyesight. Hedvig's supposed blindness relates to her constant placation of this indolent boy-daddy, whom she "just wants to be near" whilst pretending not to look at the mess he makes of the touching-up work she knows she can do better (in conjunction with her mother who is the real photographer).

In this context appears for the first time the comical matter of Hjalmar's "invention", something dredged up by clever-dog Gregers with his apparently genuine delusions about Hjalmar's talents. Hjalmar is not just a fake father and a fake photographer

140   THE ART OF PERSONALITY

but a fake artist waiting for his inspiration – the "great work" he sees before him:

> HJALMAR: An invention is something you can never be completely master of. It's largely a matter of inspiration ... of intuition ... and it's pretty nearly impossible to predict when that will come ... Inspiration, revelation, you know – when it comes, it comes, that's all. (p. 166)

Gregers concludes that Hjalmar has "a bit of the wild duck" in him, an artistic soul needing to be rescued. Their joint fantasy is that the invention would rescue the House of Ekdal from its social humiliation and at the same time make Hedvig's blighted future "secure" ("I shall insist on your having ... something or other" declares Hjalmar: "That shall be the humble inventor's only reward"). But for Gregers, Hjalmar's talent suffers from "some insidious disease" owing to his father's machinations and he has "gone down to die in the dark"; his mission is to pull him out of the "poison swamp" (p. 167).

At the heart of the central act is the strange rapport established between Gregers and Hedvig, around whom the neuroses and obsessions of the other characters revolve. On his arrival Gregers was described as "following Hedvig closely" with his eyes; and this is succeeded by an opportunity to interrogate her while Hjalmar and old Ekdal are playing in the loft, behind the new screen. Gregers is a type of intellectual investigator who is incompetent in all other aspects of life, and narcissistic in his failure to appreciate the feeding and cleaning done on his behalf. The way he establishes his presence in the household is by creating an "awful mess" in his room by his inability to light the stove, despite his insistence on "doing for himself" and causing mummy no trouble. In the dialogue with Hedvig we become aware of a hidden but problematic identification between them: that she is, in fact, his half-sister, not just biologically but mentally. Hedvig has inherited their father's weak eyes (flawed sexuality), while Gregers has inherited a "sickly conscience" from his mother (contrasting with Gina's robust one) and he is determined to reform these family characteristics.

Gregers' probing into Hedvig's inner world and the life of the loft is a kind of seduction. They quickly come to a intimacy of smiles and glances, focusing on the wild duck whose "mysterious origins", like themselves, derive from old Werle himself. Hedvig tells Gregers about her mode of self-education, given that Hjalmar is too busy to help with lessons, and Mr Molvik the parson is usually drunk – a state which "comes over him like a sort of revelation" – the equivalent of

THE VALLEY AND THE MOUNTAIN: IBSEN   141

Hjalmar's waiting for inspiration and revelation and the opposite of a work ethic. As becomes increasingly evident, Hedvig doesn't want to leave the studio-loft and go out to school, the real world: she has a world of her own, seeing more in it than pigeons and rabbits. When Gregers asks if she doesn't ever feel she wants to "get out into the big wide world itself and see something of it?" she replies, "Not me! I'm always going to stay at home and help my father and mother", touching up photographs or learning to engrave pictures like those in the books in the loft, which include "a picture of Death with an hour glass, and a girl" – the contents of her Gothic imagination. Hedvig is happier in her make-believe latency world, a place where "time stands still", than in the "wide world": identified with the disabled wild duck which belongs to her and in a sense *is* her, and likewise, doesn't belong to the adolescent group:

> HEDVIG: She's completely cut off from her friends. And then everything about the wild duck is so mysterious. Nobody really knows her; and nobody knows where she's from either.
> GREGERS: And the fact that she's been down in the briny deep. (p. 160)

Hedvig is startled that Gregers uses the precise expression "briny deep" with which she had always privately described the loft. The precise expression, not just the fantasy content, is important and shows the nature of their kinship, a mental sibling-link. Despite the contrast in character and experience the impression grows of a common focus, a secret conversation between them that desires to investigate the briny deep.

Thus the scene is partly set for her suicide, as a means of enacting Gregers' mode of truth-seeking, with his searching eyes dedicated to rescuing the House of Ekdal from his father's wound. There is a difference nonetheless between Gregers' rigid obsessive mode of symbolism, and Hedvig's more flexible imaginative mode. When Hedvig says the loft is "just a loft" he says:

> GREGERS (*looking hard at her):* Are you so certain?
> HEDVIG (*astonished):* That it's a loft?
> GREGERS:Yes. Do you know for sure? (p. 161)

He wants Hedvig to become a tool in his mission to "claim the ideal" and clean out the polluted family-fantasy world, regardless of the stink he has made in his own room. "Don't tell your mother – she doesn't understand us" he says, of his idea that she should shoot the wild duck to prove her "spirit of self-sacrifice";

142   THE ART OF PERSONALITY

but by now the duck and Hedvig are becoming confused with one another. Overstepping the proprieties of playing and reality, he insinuates his own concretely symbolic mode of thinking and establishes a kind of incestuous secret siblingship, though Hedvig is not as committed to his idea as he imagines and next morning says his proposition didn't seem "much of an idea" after all.

Meanwhile Hjalmar also prepares unconsciously for Hedvig's "self-sacrifice". Whereas old Ekdal's hunting gun no longer works and has become a toy or relic, the pistol is a live weapon, associated with suicides, and is highlighted as the solution to "the tragedy of the House of Ekdal". Hjalmar has not only left it on the shelf but brought it to Hedvig's notice: "Don't touch the pistol, Hedvig! One of the barrels is loaded, don't forget." The pistol is laid ready as a result of his ruminations on the demands of "the ideal" made on an artistic temperament such as his own: "claims that a man can't disregard without doing violence to his own soul" (p. 179). Between her identifications with the two egotistical romancers, Gregers and Hjalmar (each corresponding to facets of Hedvig's bookish imagination), and her own practical skills (she finds out from Ekdal how to use the weapon), the scene is set for her suicide and its psychological and physical facilitation. Gina, suspicious without entirely comprehending the nature of the danger, says Gregers Werle has always been "a queer fish", and when he wonders where is the "radiant light of understanding" now that the truth has been revealed, he fails to understand why Gina removes the shade from the lamp, demonstrating his concrete thinking. "You're not trying to understand me, Mrs Ekdal", he complains (p. 184). He is obsessed by the notion that his "close friend" Hjalmar, his protégé, must be "no ordinary man" but some kind of misunderstood visionary, if only the cover could be removed from the life-lie.

Yet Gina too is guilty of trying to keep the household running too smoothly, according to her own life-lie in which past mistakes become irrelevant, unmemorable – "I'd pretty nearly forgotten all that old business" as she tells Hjalmar. She and Berta Sorby are intimate (and in a sense the same person); so when Gina hears that Werle is finally going to marry Berta she exclaims with satisfaction, "At last!" At last there will be a marriage on a "secure foundation" without deception, as Gregers sanctimoniously intended for Gina and Hjalmar. In fact it only seems to take place because old Werle recognises he is becoming debilitated, but it is part of the same movement as his formal recognition of Hedvig (via the birthday letter declaring her inheritance). Gina however is insufficiently alert to what Dr Relling calls "a difficult age" with "all sorts

THE VALLEY AND THE MOUNTAIN: IBSEN   143

of funny ideas" (p. 186), and only now begins to connect this with Hedvig's dangerous game of houses on fire.

In Relling's view "pretty nearly everybody's sick" and the "life-lie" has therapeutic value. But in a sense this is his own missionary statement, no better than that of his enemy Gregers Werle with his "inflamed scruples" – the "national disease"; as often happens, a pair of contrary characters represent sides of one coin. Reliance on the life-lie for therapy is undermined by Hjalmar's pretence of being a creative artist or inventor who has not had time to complete (or begin) his masterpiece. Hedvig's conclusion that "I'm not really Daddy's" (p. 197) is a standard pubertal fantasy that in fact comprehends her two split fathers – the real but weak-sighted one beginning to impinge on her mind (as imaged in the inheritance) as the false one withdraws from her "eyes": "Those eyes ... I can't bear to look at you ... I have no child" says Hjalmar. Despite his romanticisation of the "darker things in life" that have now found their way into his consciousness, he is approaching a more truthful relationship to Hedvig, connected with a glimmer of understanding about his worthlessness: his "invention" had value not in itself but because Hedvig believed in it "with all the passion of a child" (p. 213). There is genuine pain in his "terrible uncertainty" that "perhaps Hedvig never loved me at all". The haunting doubt is not that she was not his genetically, but that she didn't love him: she may belong in spirit to the other, real parents – the ones who have things to give "with full hands beckoning to her" (the significance of her "inheritance"). He understands, at last, that his hands are empty: "They can take her away from me any time they like." On the threshold of the depressive position, as his life-lie deflates, he realises that he has no child because he is not a father, nor a husband, nor is he an inventor because "practically everything's been invented already". Reality is penetrating his life-lie, even though he is unsure whether his panic derives from having a knife twisted in his heart, missing his supper, or being unable to find his hat which means he would be "risking his life" out in the snow. He has finally realised his inability to give anything worthwhile to his love object, and at that moment, therefore, she does become his love object for the first time.

But the moment of approaching knowledge is always a dangerous one. The shot goes off in response to Hjalmar's loud wail, "Hedvig, are you willing to give up this life for my sake?" (p. 215). It is an operatic conversation between the two of them, as if she were listening for the cue, on either side of the new screen that he and old Ekdal erected the previous day. It is a tragic-comic interpretation of

144   THE ART OF PERSONALITY

Gregers' conviction that "I knew redemption would come through the child" – though not in the way he predicted and attempted to stage-manage. There is a sense in which the truth for Hedvig and Hjalmar occurs simultaneously as they relax their life-lies in unison, like brother and sister. She does not belong to him: not merely genetically, but because she is an independent or wild creature who belongs to nature; and he does not belong to her, as a doll to dress and feed. She has begun to be aware of a new "strangeness" in everything, puzzling and disorienting her, as when she told her mother that everything Gregers said seemed strangely to mean something else – where does the real meaning lie?

Her suicide, although impeccably executed, is the result of a momentary intention or identification. It does not have tragic inevitability, but something perhaps more characteristic of puberty – a sense that it could go either way, depending on a chance combination of encounters between those around her, or inside her. "I just feel I want to die", she says, like so many just-fourteen-year-olds, collapsed on the sofa (p. 197). Who is to say they don't mean it? Her Gina-like practicality and Werle-like determination make her shot effective; yet it is not the result of a fixed ideology like that of Gregers' "claim of the ideal". Indeed as she said earlier, after a night's sleep she found on reflection that "strangely", his idea of shooting the wild duck was "not much of an idea" after all – not very imaginative. She came up with a better one. Her shot is like a photographic touch-up, a dramatic image like those in the picture books of the loft, as if death were not a real thing, just one of those "funny ideas" children get in puberty. In some ways she prefigures Hedda Gabler's perverse vision of the pistol shot as an "act of beauty" – whether it is used on herself or someone else. Hedvig treats the pistol like a pen: just as old Ekdal, the great bear-hunter in his second childhood, can't tell the difference between "an attic full of dead branches" and "the great living forest of Hoidal". "The forest's revenge", he says, as Hedvig is laid down on the sofa, clutching the pistol so tightly in her fingers that it cannot be removed. It is the instrument of her art.

Postscript: the late artist

The theme of the artist and his muse is central in Ibsen's late works; plays such as *The Master Builder* and *When We Dead Awaken* entail an almost desperate, hypercritical self-dissection in which he castigates his own over-sharp vision, which appears self-destructive in

THE VALLEY AND THE MOUNTAIN: IBSEN   145

its impact on both the man and the artist in society. Master Builder Solness (whose name suggests some kind of sun-god) appears to have neither talent, qualifications, nor competence – merely worldly success which is founded on parasitising those qualities in other people, whom he uses like the "airy servitors" of his fantasy, in identification with Shakespeare's Prospero.

By the time of *The Master Builder*, Ibsen had perfected the mutual enhancement of symbolism and realism. In the earlier play *Ghosts* ("those who walk again") the idea of the sun is in fact connected with madness, a softening of the brain resulting from syphilis; in *The Master Builder* the madness is not biologically explicable. It is a nightmarish dreamplay based on internal dialogue between those parts of himself which devour one another in the scramble to get to the top – whatever the top may mean: the elusive castle in the air is perhaps the presumed house of thought, in psychoanalytic terms the claustrum of the head-breast (Meltzer, 1992). He is, according to the doctor and everyone, "on top of his profession" – but what is the top and what, he asks, has that to do with "happiness"? The play opens with the approaching death of an old practitioner, Brovik, on whose skills Solness has relied throughout his career, together (more lately) with the design flair of his son Ragnar, who is also held in servitude, using his young fiancée Kaja as hostage – her thoughts and desires have been commandeered by Solness. They are the true internal parents, degraded into the position of child-servants. When a young couple appear with a request for a villa (really representing Ragnar and Kaja themselves) he becomes confused as to what a "home" is – whether he knows these people, and whether they know what they mean by a home; he says he can't get the plans straight in his mind yet he is reluctant to allow Ragnar to do them for him. Solness is aware that despite his many churches and homes he has no "foundation", that his personality has never been built – hence his fear of madness imposed by a retributive superego. He has never known what it is to make a "home" as indeed his wife accuses him: can building his own new home with a tower on top really rectify such a situation, or is it just another example of his phallic competition with God: "a master builder free in his own field, as you are in yours"? (Ibsen, 1981, p. 349).

Into his anxious state a false muse intrudes, in the form of troll-like Hilde from the mountains, a doctor's daughter from Lysanger (meaning sword of light). She has abandoned the "cage" of her father's house and arrives with only a knapsack of dirty underwear which Aline Solness deems it is her "duty" to service. Like Kaja, Hilde seems to know the master builder's thoughts, or rather to be

146   THE ART OF PERSONALITY

one of them, summoned by his desires. She appears to be an alternative to Aline who, like Solness himself, has a rigid internal superego that imposes duty and guilt rather than creativity and nurture; she, not he, is responsible for the death of her babies owing to her "duty" to breastfeed even when her milk had dried up. The false sword of light, however, is essentially an instrument of masturbatory or egotistical mania, as shown in Hilde's half-veiled gaze and continual refrain "How exciting!"

> SOLNESS: I'd got an idea; through that little black crack in the chimney I might perhaps make my way to success – as a master builder.
> HILDE: (*staring into space*): That must have been exciting.
> SOLNESS: Irresistible almost. (p. 320)

Solness explains that to be a master builder it is necessary to have "helpers and servants" who have to be "summoned imperiously, inwardly" (like Prospero's masquers or Ariel); it cannot be done "alone". But he is really summoning a bird of prey, like Brand, for this is how the mountain girl secures her "kingdom": "And why shouldn't I go hunting too? Take the prey I want? If I can get my claws into it." To which Solness replies, she is his "sunrise" (his false high-rise [p. 325]). In a sort of demonic transference she inveigles his fantasies out of him (the worldly success based on his "black crack", an internal faultline) and engineers his downfall in front of the public before whom he had been posing all his life. The "firm foundation" she provides to build "our castle in the air" is a contradiction in terms: it is in fact a treacherous quicksand, a net like that set by Clytemnestra for Agamemnon. Ultimately it is Hilde and Aline together who bring him down – as imaged in the way that Hilde, watching with the "enigmatic expression in her eyes", seizes Aline's white shawl and in effect waves Solness into dizzy self-destruction: "My … my … master builder!"

In a sense Solness has always been "dead", never been himself. In his last play, *When We Dead Awaken*, Ibsen explores the possibilities of bringing the hero to life. Peer Gynt, despite appearing to have a complete life-cycle, is rather like Peter Pan in remaining a perpetual adolescent or naughty boy; really he never grows up, never grows old. But when this avatar of Ibsen becomes the sculptor Rubek, there is a real sense of a lifetime having passed, and of self-reckoning before the Day of Judgement. It is internal judgement of course: a savage, almost grotesque critique of the artist's failures in both personal and vocational terms. And as always in

THE VALLEY AND THE MOUNTAIN: IBSEN   147

creative literature, in a sense the artist is Everyman – no different in his inner composition, just more closely observed. The play took Ibsen longer than usual (three years) and was perhaps never finished; he kept rewriting the last act in particular. It was his last work, since he then had a series of strokes that prevented him from putting words together. With hindsight we are liable to read this catastrophic disintegration into the final avalanche that whirls Rubek and his muse away and off the stage. Perhaps we should not do so but as with many artists' last works, *The Dead* has a quality of overview, and a premonition of another more devastating change – like Bion's *Memoir of the Future* (1991) with its ending "I have a date to meet fate."

Yet some type of date to meet fate occurs on the frontier of every major move forward. Experience allows writers to become more daringly experimental with time, and this always seems to involve a more piercing focus on the nature of their art – what they are doing with it, what they are doing in it, and what it is all for. The function of the artist is both explicit and allegorical in this context. We no longer have the feeling that it might mean something else, as we do in Ibsen's late-middle period where, from *The Wild Duck* on, characters are both realistic and serving a purpose beyond themselves, in terms of the play's total meaning. In *The Dead*, we are conscious of the bare bones of a schematic mental landscape of madness-and-creativity: of the spiritual and the bestial, the maiden and the troll, the ego and the id; and somewhere hidden in the eagle-eyed high peaks, an ambivalent superego flashing lightning and thunderbolts, ever watchful of the artist's hubris. The play has no everyday meaning: it is not about the best kind of holiday to take (cruise or climb?) when you return to the bleak north after years of living in Mediterranean climes; it is *only* about the artist's creativity – or its loss and potential return in some new work. Ibsen was 71 when he wrote it and was on the verge of seeking a return to the poetic dramas of his early career: regretting that long ago, following the spirit of the age (as any successful writer must), he had renounced "Shakespearean" modes as unrealistic dinosaur-language and committed himself to "the language of everyday life" and to portraits of everyday people: people whom he now regarded with revulsion as masked farmyard animals, ignoble species of neither one kind nor the other.

When We Dead Awaken has a wonderful title that perhaps isn't quite lived up to by the fabric of play itself, like many an experiment on the verge of breakthrough. Originally Ibsen was going to ironically entitle the play *Resurrection Day* after the statue which

148   THE ART OF PERSONALITY

is Rubek's masterpiece, as modelled by Irena, who is now seeking revenge on his troll-like usurpation of stony forms. The play goes back to the landscapes of *Brand* and *Peer Gynt*, with their poetic attempts to integrate the everyday valley world with that of the dangerous but beautiful mountain peaks that irradiate sun and avalanches. What can be the intentions of the mountain-god (or goddess) that dispenses both illumination and catastrophe, and whose inner bowels house the caverns of the trolls? In the three acts of the play we move further and further up the mountain: from the lazy bourgeois comforts of the champagne-serving spa on the fjord estuary, up through the healthy mountain air of the still-horizontal *vidda* where children play, to the dangerous, vertiginous boundary between forest and glacier where the bear-territory merges into that of eagles and hawks. We are particularly aware of the stage furniture, the painted scenery at a further remove of reality, and the illusion of internal reality behind all these levels of representation.

Here the female muse takes three forms: Irena the vengeful, lost spirit of creativity; bored Maia with her youthful sensuous vitality; and the Dark Sister who shadows Irena through close observation like an analyst-figure, yet ultimately fails to save her or her sculptor. The play opens with Rubek and Maja discussing their sense of deadness, and mutual desire to come north in search of the spirit that is lacking in their own relationship and in the comfortable valley of their lives. Indeed the characters are all "dead" in various senses: they have betrayed their soul through false memories (Rubek), become enslaved to an illusion (Maja), had their soul torn out and made into a statue (Irena), or never had a soul and gorge only on bodily appetites (Wolfheim). Yet between them a soul could be constructed and "awoken", stirred into life. Or such, we believe, is the author's hope, through the underlying pattern of their formal dance-like encounter with its interchange of two couples under the supervision of the dark observer.

Rubek has had enough of the people whose "hidden meaning" he has imitated and indeed caricatured in his life of image-production, and satirises the "domestic circus" of his animal-like human portraits (Ibsen, 2006, p. 203). His head is full of meaningless rumblings which, like the talk of the railwaymen at the frontier, is "murmuring, muted, meaningless, out there in the dark" (p. 201). Maja has vitality but no interest in his work (epitomised by the last sculpture created with Irena, *Resurrection* Day), and merely accepts society's basic-assumption verdict that Rubek is a great artist: "Why, the whole world knows it". He had promised to take Maja "up a high mountain" and show her "all the glory of the world" but

THE VALLEY AND THE MOUNTAIN: IBSEN   149

instead, she is shown merely the "ecstasies" of the ignorant public, which she regards with indifference, and Rubek condescendingly blames this on her: "You weren't made for mountain-climbing, Maja my pet" (p. 205) – she has not performed her prescribed role of injecting her youth into his jaded personality, of being a muse. They have disappointed one another's expectations.

Into this sterile partnership emerge from the past the visceral hunter Wolfheim (home of wolflike instincts) and Irena the mad ex-muse, clothed in white like a ghost, and accompanied by her deathly shadow the Sister in Black, who is both guardian and persecutor. In the dance, partners are exchanged. Wolfheim knew Rubek in the old days when he was not famous: "In those days, even a filthy bear-hunter could venture to approach you" – that is, in the past, Rubek recognised his own bear-hunting instincts, whether in life or art; and even now, despite the expanded difference in social class, they can agree on certain similarities between hunting and sculpting. For stone also has to fight: "It is dead and withstands, with all its weight and power, its own hammering into life. The bear is exactly the same, when someone comes poking at him in his lair" (p. 211). To make a sculpture vital it has to be hunted and chiselled, in a life-and-death struggle between the material and the sculptor – attack being the road to reparation (in Kleinian terms, as Adrian Stokes and others would put it). Now there is no real attack, just a surreptitious two-faced sneering, clothed in fancy dress. The artist in Rubek is suffocated and frustrated by his own hostility to the public yet his dependence on their approbation. The dead part prefers it that way and does not want to be hammered into life.

Irena is introduced as if she were a dream of Rubek's. She nurses her dangerous impulses close to the naked body which she feels has been abused: the hidden knife of her madness lies within the folds of her flowing white dress and at key moments is withdrawn from her breast, then stealthily replaced, usually owing to her consciousness of the gaze of the Sister in Black, keeping her madness within bounds. Maja is convinced Rubek was dreaming when he had a night-time vision of a white figure walking amongst the trees in the garden; and confirmation of her real-life existence has to be extracted from the reluctant hotel Supervisor (the conscious respectable ego). "You mean the Professor wasn't dreaming?" asks Maja at the same time. But in a sense, he is dreaming; Irena is one of his ghosts, returning as two people rather than one. And Wolfheim (another guest whom the Supervisor would prefer to ignore) responds to a dream of Maja's, being Rubek as she had imagined him – someone who would show her the mountain

150   THE ART OF PERSONALITY

heights of sexual adventure. Their union is simpler than that of Rubek and Irena which is characterised by miscommunication about the nature of their work together and the "child" it produced.

Rubek's guilt concerns the additions he made to the sculpture after Irena left him, when he enlarged the group to encompass his further knowledge of life – the swarm of human figures with secret animal faces "just as I knew them in life" (Ibsen's social dramas); while the figure of Irena herself is "back, subdued", no longer the sole object of the viewer's gaze. Irena's guilt took the sadomasochistic form of deserting Rubek without explanation, deciding he would have no further "use" for her:

> RUBEK: Where did you go to, Irena? For all my seeking, you were as one vanished from the earth.
> IRENA: I passed into the dark: while there the child stood in transfiguring light. (p. 214)

As if envious of the child's glory, she debased herself in prostitution, "posing as a naked statue in living tableaux", "pulling money", and driving men mad, including her last two husbands. One husband is literally dead, the other metaphorically so, since she "killed him with a fine sharp dagger I have always with me in my bed", along with her "many children". Rubek guesses there is "hidden meaning in all this"; we imagine her children may be hidden or aborted talents, perverted into madness as if by ancient Greek furies. Her knife seems a counterpart to his chisel, guarding her soul from impure hands. (Indeed the play has many overtones of the Oresteian trilogy; although this time the woman seeking revenge is herself the absent one, and the sacrifice of the child – unlike Iphigeneia – is equivocal and may be revokable, brought to life again.) Rubek's hidden fear of Irena's needle or knife (whose existence he only senses unconsciously) takes the form of a reciprocal fantasy, an egotistical idea of the purity of his own vision: "You became for me a hallowed being, never to be touched but in adoring thought alone" – hence he never touched her sensually, lest his "creative purpose" be defiled by ugly Wolfheim tendencies. It is as though physical meaningful contact only exists for him in the form of struggling with his art materials, the stone "catacombs", and must be kept separate from the transcendent idea of the work – or is it illusion? His entire earthly or sensual existence is split off into his work with the stone. What kind of sacrifices does art entail for the playwright as a person, as someone desiring a life on earth? These are the questions adumbrated by the play with its dialogues of "hidden meaning" and its mountainscape background. And as the play progresses the dancers gradually climb higher up the mountain: first to the *vidda*, the open field where children play, then up to the dilapidated mountain shelter on the scree, placed precariously between the precipice with its narrow path and the high peaks and chasms beyond.

The Wolfheim-Maja couple complicate any form of simple revenge on the artist, and Irena's knife is always replaced in her flowing robes. While Irena is shrouded in white, cloudy intimations of madness, Maja like Wolfheim has a positive disinterest in both art and mind:

> RUBEK: You've not any real clear notion, how it feels to be an artist.
> MAJA: Lord above, I've not the first notion how it feels to be myself.
>   (p. 229)

She has come up the mountain not to ascend the high peaks and vaporise into spirituality but to penetrate the forests and hunt the bear – her idea of "the glory of the world" is a sexual earthy one of blood and gore. Her attitude undermines Rubek's narcissistic talk about needing someone to "complete" and "be one with" him in his artistic aspirations. His picture of the Platonic nature of his relationship with Irena in the past is for her a fake: hypocritically or stupidly denying what it meant for a woman to "strip herself naked" for him. "For an artist that means nothing" he says, pompously. When he tries to talk to her about his hidden fear of madness, she tells him he is just boring and his real fear is that of old age. Her dismissive attitude does however enable him to formulate his belief that his art has tyrannised over his life (on the lines of Keats's "Life to Milton would be death to me ... I wish to devote myself to another sensation" [Keats, 1970, p. 325]; Keats indeed wrote an "Ode to Maia"). Rubek's soul has become identified with his inanimate material: "Isn't it of altogether greater worth to live amid beauty in the life of the sun? Than go on and on till the end of one's days, in a chill damp catacomb, slogging away until exhausted unto death, at lumps of clay and blocks of stone?" As the stone, rather than the chiseller, he implicitly desires the knife to release him.

Meanwhile, throughout, the Sister in Black watches the various manoeuvres of the two couples, always half-hidden in the landscape as if she were an organic part of it, and only partly revealing her presence at certain points to draw Irena back into her orbit – as when at the end of Act One she opens the pavilion door ajar and Irena slips obediently inside, or when at the end of Act Two she

152   THE ART OF PERSONALITY

silently draws Irena down the hill as if by magnetism. The knife and the gaze seem invisibly connected. Irena says she will kill her eventually; but until the very end, the Sister manages to telepathically hold her emotional strings.

We know Ibsen was never satisfied with the final movement of the play, whose first draft was in fact just an extended conversation between the four protagonists by the mountain hut (in stagecraft terms, the same as the pavilion-consulting room of Act One which housed Irena and her nurse). The action opens with Wolfheim's attempted rape of Maja but she proves herself "quite the she-wolf when aroused", a fitting match for him; and instead, the earthy couple get to know each other a bit better: Wolfheim's satyr-horns have their origin in an early rejection by a woman whom he once rescued from the streets and "wanted to carry life long, lest she should dash her foot against a stone". Maja explains her disappointment in the "mountaineer" Rubek who confined her youth in a "chill damp cage ... with colossal ghosts of men and women turned to stone" (p. 248).

Suddenly "the storm is on us" as Rubek and Irena arrive, toiling up the narrow path: "Aren't you hearing the shocks of the wind?" Wolfheim admires the way Maja braces herself to confront the other two – "the hawk and his strange lady" – since there is no way to "slip past them". Nor can Irena slip past the dark Sister. But neither couple, in this version, are prepared to take shelter in the mountain hut and have a merely verbal dance. Instead Ibsen indicates their conversation via the directions of their crossing paths on the face of the mountain. Wolfheim can only rescue one person at a time: anyone else must wait for the men with ropes to come up from the valley. The valley-ropes are the straitjacket that terrifies Irena (an everyday or ordinary sexual life). Bent on avoiding the valley's restrictions, the other couple are pushed further up the mountain to the transcendent peaks, the heart of the catastrophic storm that will be their destruction. For the first time Rubek notices that Irena has a knife; he is told it was intended to kill him, but then she realised, during their talk the previous day by the stream, that he was "already dead".

> IRENA: There we sat, before Lake Taunitz, the two of us, clammy corpses, playing a children's game with one another.
> RUBEK: I wouldn't call that being dead ... that love between us is assuredly not dead. (p. 253)

Their outlived childhood has become a "dead" game. If it is really alive, there is only one (dubious) way to prove it is authentic (or so they believe) – to fling themselves into the oncoming avalanche: this is their "freedom", with the storm representing the nature of their relationship: "The life within us and around us is in a ferment and raging as ever it was!" They leave the "half-darkness" and "wet gravecloths" of their previous existence (the mindset in which clay or clammy sculptures are formed) and head up through the gathering mists to "the light, the splendour and the glory ... the mountain peaks above!" Their freedom lies in their self-destruction. Our viewpoint now is the same as that of the Sister in Black who has emerged on the scene in time to see them swirled away in the avalanche, like Brand; and meanwhile Maja's song of freedom is heard from the valleys below. With grotesque satire the Sister speaks the last words – and her only words: "Pax vobiscum".

Perhaps it is a play that would only have worked in poetry. Unlike *Brand* or *Peer Gynt*, it does not suspend our disbelief in the way of Peer Gynt's rediscovery of Solveig in the mountain hut, which we somehow have faith in, even when he is captured by the claustrum of the troll kingdom, the capitalistic and sensual aridities of the world-as-desert, or the absurdities of academia. *The Dead* seems more of an intellectual exercise; we appreciate the inevitability of the cross-pairing of the two couples, and the way it is imaged on the stage landscape in a kind of dance; yet the ultimate picture of two paths taken simultaneously perhaps does not sustain the required emotional weight of integration, of developmental catastrophic change. Nonetheless is it is of great psychoanalytic interest, in terms of the silent transferential interaction between the helpless observing analyst (a figure of great ambivalence) and the various parts of the personality which are seeking and avoiding integration. Together with the other plays about the adolescent and the artist – those key exponents of catastrophe – it brings into question the very nature of truth-seeking and whether it is enough to rely on the straitjackets of scientific inquiry, bourgeois expectations, good intentions, and messianic hopes. Or is some other kind of communication required in the attic of fantasy, the consulting room, that can guide the multi-facetted personality between the valley and the mountain?

CHAPTER SEVEN

Dostoevsky and the education of a man of faith:
The Brothers Karamazov

Dostoevsky was preoccupied throughout his major novels with the problem of how to picture, define, become a man of faith, in a sense that was neither the "simple faith" of the child or peasant, nor the dry doctrine of the official believer: how to achieve a state of mind that was neither unquestionable nor arguable. However the novels, especially *The Brothers Karamazov*, suggest that he saw faith not as a given but as an achievement of spiritual education, the result of life in the real world. His own faith, he famously said, was "forged in the crucible of doubt" and he was contemptuous of the "thickheads" who accused him of ignoring sophisticated nineteenth-century metaphysical developments and returning to a primitive religious notion.

Despite being indeed a "tragedian of ideas", as he is known, Dostoevsky all his life was suspicious of disembodied ideas. He said he would rather have Christ than truth even if Christ turned out to be wrong. For him, truth could not be considered in the abstract, but only through confronting the virtually impossible task of creating a picture of the "perfect man" – a picture which must embody the essential conflicts and qualities of humanity, not a "fugitive and cloistered virtue" (as Milton called it). Milton had been unsuccessful in his own attempt to create a realistic, empathic picture of his hero Christ, in *Paradise Regained* (which turned into a dry treatise); Dostoevsky had been similarly unsuccessful in loading virtues onto Prince Myshkin in *The Idiot*, splitting his undesirable features into his epilepsy and his alter-ego Roghozhin, both of whom end up side by side on the floor beside the murdered heroine – losing the truth in the process. Indeed splitting had been Dostoevsky's primary mode of character-analysis, of depicting the internal wars between good and evil: with every male protagonist having his "double" in a traditional gothic sense; the very name of Raskolnikov in *Crime and Punishment* means "splitting". And generally the split hero is engaged in a drama with heroines who are either outcast (but innocent) prostitutes, or wellbred hysterics.

His characterisation in *The Brothers Karamazov* draws on all these prototypes but is different in certain essential respects. He names his hero as Alyosha (Aleksei) but at the same time we know it is not only Alyosha but the brothers as a trio, distinct and yet united, each representing essential aspects of the complete man to be found not only in the author but in humanity as a whole. The name Karamazov implies the innateness of the "black smear" of original sin, and without his brothers Alyosha would be another idealised figure rather than, as is often emphasised, a genuine Karamazov. It was a felicitous stroke to spread the life-instinct between three brothers rather than simply a hero and his double – all of them trying hard *not* to murder the father who brought them up motherless. As it is, the brothers are not hollow allegorical types but realistic individuals with their different, characteristic modes of experiencing conflict; yet at the same time, owing to Dostoevsky's "prophetic tone" (as Forster [1927] described it), when taken together they embody ideas beyond themselves, a prescience of future states of mind. Several times Alyosha learns about his Karamazov nature through identifying with Dmitri and Ivan; correspondingly, those two absorb aspects of Alyosha as it were by osmosis in the course of their trials. In Freudian terms, the death instinct is embodied in the illegitimate, accidental, unacknowledged half-brother Smerdyakov (the "stinker"), a figure whose power comes not from within himself but from the degree of others' susceptibility to him. Despite his intelligence he has a parasitic, shadowy identity that contrasts with the vibrant individuality of the "good" or "legitimate" brothers and that is ultimately expressed in his suicide. The odds are stacked therefore in the favour of the three brothers who have substantial inner worlds, and our interest lies in their turbulent attempts to develop their capacity for love, to realise their passionate natures.

DOSTOEVSKY AND THE EDUCATION OF A MAN OF FAITH   157

The underground man

By way of introduction to the novel I would like to say a few words about the satirical tract *Notes from Underground,* which Dostoevsky wrote when he was poised on the threshold of the great novels that followed. Dostoevsky is a master of tragi-comedy on a Shakespearean scale, and the tonal complexity of the major novels has its roots in the dilemma pictured by the mouse-like "anti-hero" whom Dostoevsky imagines as situated beneath the floorboards, peering out at life through a crack yet unable to participate in it. The Underground Man sees himself as a "man of heightened consciousness", the antithesis of a "normal" uncomplicated, healthy man of action. He is familiar with all the latest ideas, and one of his problems (he points out) is being more intelligent than anyone else. His soul has been driven underground into existential torment as a result of the influence of contemporary ideas or rather ideologies: first those of romantic liberalism (corresponding to the men of the 1840s, known in Russia as the "fathers") and then those of the rational utilitarians of the 1860s (known as the "sons", as in Turgenev's *Fathers and Sons*). At 40 years old he finds himself neither wicked nor good, "neither a hero nor an insect. And now I am living out my life in my corner, taunting myself with the spiteful and utterly futile consolation that it is even impossible for an intelligent man seriously to become anything, and only fools become something" (Dostoevsky, 1993, p. 5). He is educated in traditional notions of the "good and the beautiful" but found that the greater his awareness, the more liable he was to do "ugly" things, contaminating his idealism (in psychoanalytic terms, an intolerance of frustration and aesthetic conflict that leads to splitting rather than integration). Even if he had "time and faith" to turn into something different, there seems no way out, "perhaps nothing to change into". He has no aspiration of "becoming", no mental picture of a "perfect man" to spur him on.

Then we learn that he slipped into this nihilistic malaise after his liberal romantic phase had reached a dead end. He recounts this phase in the second part of the story: it was a time when he envisioned himself as the redeemer of a young innocent prostitute (a popular motif), but instead, as soon as she discerned his own inner angst, despite himself, he drove her away. The story ends with his recollection of the slamming door as she leaves the building – something which he says he will never forget. The prostitute, Liza, leaves for ever, but the reluctant bond with his sneering

158   THE ART OF PERSONALITY

Smerdyakov-like servant Apollon remains: "I was unable to throw him out, as though he had combined chemically with my existence … my apartment was my shell, my mansion, my case, in which I hid from all mankind, and Apollon belonged to that apartment" (p. 113). He is confined in his claustrum or exoskeleton together with his personal devil, the "lackey" who controls him. As such the Underground Man is the comic precursor to Ivan Karamazov, and also, in his romantic phase, to Dmitri.

But there is also an Alyosha in him trying to get out. Liza was able to differentiate between the Underground Man's hidden torments and his self-romanticisation which she says is "all from a book" – that is, inauthentic expression. The authentic emotions are mouse-like, hidden, deducible but not expressible. As he remembers the long-past episode with Liza, which has suddenly become vivid in his mind, the Man himself seems to finally take in this distinction, and makes a plea for "living life" instead of the kind of conventional "book" that satisfies men's desire for slavery. Everyone loathes "living life" – they feel it's "better from a book" and can't cope with independence but "beg to be taken back under tutelage" (as Ivan will say, through "miracle, mystery and authority"). They want the protection of rules and basic assumptions, whether religious or revolutionary. He ends: "We don't even know where the living lives now, or what it is, or what it's called … We're stillborn … Soon we'll contrive to be born somehow from an idea. But enough; I don't want to write any more from Underground" (pp. 129–130). He has at last understood what's wrong with him but has no idea how to make it right. Interestingly a passage in which the Man comes to the conclusion for the need for faith was excised by Dostoevsky's censors. He complained, but never later reinstated it; perhaps because it could only have been another theoretical statement, not a living demonstration, which would require a wider drama, namely the scope of a full novel with its multiple perspectives and persons.

The *Underground Man* is Dostoevsky's statement of an educational need: how can the living mind be brought out from underground, become e-ducated, led out of itself? In *The Brothers* the universal man is set free from his floorboards to roam the town of Skotoprigonesk (meaning Pigsty or Cattlepen), and his soul migrates between the three brothers. The farmyard-town with its bestial inhabitants, welltrodden "back ways" and high fences, is a mental landscape, the unpicturesque equivalent of Keats' "wreathed trellis of a working brain" or Emily Bronte's moor. As the paths are criss-crossed, most frequently by Alyosha who

DOSTOEVSKY AND THE EDUCATION OF A MAN OF FAITH   159

tries to weave everyone together, the interdependence of all the mental impulses becomes reinforced. Memories, conversations, disquisitions, eavesdroppings, accidental and violent encounters, are condensed within a tight space-time scheme more typical of a classical tragedy than a nineteenth century novel (the main action takes place within three days). Another structural feature, adding to the complexity of "living life", is the voice of the narrator who speaks "now", precisely thirteen years after the events of what we are told is only the first part of the Karamazov story; he makes a special plea for the reader to like his hero Alyosha, who would by now be 33 years old, hence (on the Christological model) may be dead; a suspicion reinforced by his use of tenses when he tells us that Alyosha's key memory of his mother lasted "all his life", implying that his life is over. The main action of the hero's life would have constituted a second novel had Dostoevsky's own life not been cut short. Alyosha was the name of Dostoevsky's three-year-old son who died of epilepsy shortly before he began writing the novel; and also the name of the dead child of the peasant "woman of faith" who comes before Father Zosima not to be "comforted", but to be heard: she is Rachel weeping for her children, and this needs to be acknowledged. Probably Alyosha is the corn of wheat that (in the biblical citation that prefaces the novel) must die in order to "bring forth fruit" – the fruit being the growing children (ourselves) who read his story and at the end cry "Hurrah for Karamazov!" The educative model is founded on nourishing memories as distinct from nursing grievances, and sets up an identificatory process with the reader – something which the narrator tries to establish early on.

Accidental parentage

In the first part of the novel it is made clear that a family "catastrophe" is about to happen, focusing on the "old buffoon" to whom Dostoevsky slyly gives his own name, Fyodor. As in *King Lear* the old man in his confusion about women (money and the breast), infantile greed and oedipal possessiveness, is required to end his reign so that the Karamazov spirit may be transformed and set on a new developmental route. The problem is how he should be "killed", and this will have something to do with the way the brothers come together, getting to know one another for the first time in their history: that is, attempting to integrate the various aspects and talents that they represent. It is given as something

160   THE ART OF PERSONALITY

of a mystery why the brothers have come together at this point in time – except that it is associated with the idea of womanhood. Thus Alyosha suddenly quits his studies to come and look for his mother's grave, resurrecting his vivid early memory of her; Dmitri wants the money-woman of whom the greedy Fyodor has been trying to deprive him, in the form of Grushenka; and Ivan is there purportedly as intercessor for Dmitri but subconsciously in order to experience the full torment of Katerina Ivanovna and the devil, and already she is vacillating, switching her attention over to him. Up to now he has financed his own high-powered philosophical studies through signing himself "Eyewitness" to a regular newspaper column (p. 10): in other words by peering at the world like the Underground Man, rather than living in it. The fact that he has arrived in his father's town indicates his need for a new perspective. Alyosha never gave a thought to financing his studies; he knew that someone would pay for him. He, however, is targeted by Liza, a girl heading towards an adolescent crisis. Liza was once a pubertal companion but has now grown "naughty" and become a "little demon". Thus all three brothers are entangled with potential partners and with the idea of "ruined reputations", along with a bag of roubles that takes on the variable significance of a badge of honour or disgrace, virtue or bondage, freedom or possession (being confused with "the woman", whether the internal mother or the female genital.)

Fyodor, like his alter-ego Zosima (the alternative father), has a special insight into the nature of the sons. Despite his play-acting, he can intuit through an alcoholic haze that Ivan's civiLizad hostility is more dangerous to him than Dmitri's violent temper and physical assaults. It is observed that Ivan is the son who is most like him; Ivan indeed lives with him, whereas the other brothers have found their own lodgings; and Fyodor, like Ivan, makes a pet of Smerdyakov, the son who will destroy him (associated with a "dragon-baby" who died, son of Martha and Grigory, and for whom Smerdyakov becomes a replacement). In particular Fyodor tries to contribute to his education; but the falseness or uselessness of this education, which appears so benevolent, is imaged in Smerdyakov's vanity, his fancy clothes and culinary concoctions, and strumming on the guitar to perfect his self-image. His rationalist sneer at the biblical myth of creation enrages Grigory but makes a link with Ivan. Ivan's own vanity takes the form of educational dialectic with Smerdyakov, believing he has directable potential. Smerdyakov is thus enabled to attach a literal interpretation to Ivan's suppressed murderous rage toward his father and translate it into action. When

DOSTOEVSKY AND THE EDUCATION OF A MAN OF FAITH   161

Ivan offers up the argument that "all is permitted", he is unaware of his own projection. Smerdyakov outwits him, murdering his father on his behalf, as if this were the logical outcome of their being two "clever men" together. He seems to believe himself in some type of special homosexual relationship to his teacher, on whom he takes revenge by hanging himself, thereby making himself unavailable as a witness at Dmitri's trial. Smerdyakov's statement "It's always good to talk to a clever man" echoes in Ivan's ears and drives him to delirium (Dostoevsky, 1976, p. 259). The Smerdyakov aspect of the Karamazovs is thus most closely assimilated to Ivan the "clever man" of ideas, in his attempt to found a morality free from identification with internal objects.

Ivan, like the Underground Man, knows all the arguments but cannot believe in any of them except in an intellectual and behavioural sense. While Fyodor fears Ivan, Zosima is the first to perceive Ivan's inner anguish and lack of faith. The twin father figures Fyodor and Zosima are both on the verge of death in their respective ways. Dostoevsky brings them together in one of his favourite scandal settings, supposedly to settle a family quarrel but really as opposite poles through which to confront and picture the tensions of family relations. Here at this seminal gathering, Zosima carefully considers the arguments in Ivan's controversial publication, which concludes that religiousness needs to pervade and educate the state – something with which the monks naturally agree; Zosima then penetrates beneath the surface argument to question the true beliefs of the author, and makes contact with the "fretting" inner Ivan who cannot answer the question of the immortality of the soul, that is, of the soul's reality as something distinct from either the body or the mechanical intellect.

Dmitri's ordeal is also intuited by Zosima when he bows to the ground before him, acknowledging his future suffering; while Alyosha he sees as a kind of son, who reminds him of his brother Markel, the person instrumental to Zosima's own conversion from a violent rakish Dmitri-like officer to a saintly elder. Conscious of his impending death, he charges Alyosha with remaining close to his brothers – not just one but both of them: "Be near your brothers – and not near one only, but near both" (p. 68). This psychic proximity is part of his education, as he is sent out of the monastery into the world, so he can begin to recognise parts of his true Karamazov self via his brothers (sensuality and suffering). A childish faith is no longer sufficient. Alyosha had been seeking refuge from aspects of his own nature in the monastic life, as Liza had perceived when she teased him with her attentions, leaning out of

162   THE ART OF PERSONALITY

her bathchair during the audience with Zosima, and demanding why Alyosha had forgotten her and their childhood games. Later Alyosha muses, "Why had [Zosima] sent him into the world? Here was peace. Here was holiness. But there there was confusion, there was gloom in which one lost one's way and went astray at once" (p. 144). His instinct at school was to cover his ears when vulgar stories were told about women; Zosima implies that not listening is not good enough. It is not possible to educate without first being educated. As Alyosha says to Dmitri, regarding his education in women: "I am the same as you are ... the ladder's the same. I'm at the bottom step and you're above, somewhere about the thirteenth ... the ladder's the same" (p. 98).

As with Zosima, Alyosha is taken as a true son by Fyodor, revivifying his capacity for feeling. Until this moment he has in a sense never met any of his sons, and has only the haziest notion of how they came to exist, as if surprised that any of his sexual encounters could result in procreation. (And once having arrived, the changing of their "little shirts" is immediately left to Grigory and Marta's backyard nursery, and then to their respective boarding schools.) But by contrast with his distrust of Ivan and Dmitri, a fondness for Alyosha arises instinctively in him, associated with a resurrected memory of his long-forgotten second wife Sophia, the holy hysteric whose eyes "slit his soul" and whom he had tormented with his debaucheries. He forgets that Ivan had the same mother – it seems psychically impossible to him, and it is implied that for a moment his fantasy was that Ivan was born in the same way as Smerdyakov, by the rape of someone like Stinking Lizaveta, a woman who is literally dumb and unable to argue her case. But then, the whole point of bringing the family together in one "town" is to investigate the internal or psychic linkages, both opposing and complementary. The devil and "angel" sons (as he calls Alyosha) derive from the same mother. Fyodor even acquires, through his "angel" or good part of himself, a type of respect for Zosima, the holy elder whose monastery-school he had ignored or despised till then. He rescinds his command that Alyosha leave the monastery (as Alyosha knows he will), despite his jealousy of the chosen alternative father and his own need for "angelic" protection through this loved son. At their last meeting Alyosha gives his father a kiss on the shoulder; neither understand why, but it is sensed by both as a final farewell.

The gathering of the Karamazovs in Zosima's cell, that sets the action in motion, also includes some outsiders whose natures contrast with those of elemental passion. Primary among these are Miusov and Rakitin. Miusov, brother of Dmitri's mother Adelaida,

DOSTOEVSKY AND THE EDUCATION OF A MAN OF FAITH   163

is a man of the forties: a liberal romantic touched by western influences (which for Dostoevsky represent spiritual contamination). He "almost" (but not quite) joined in the fighting at the French barricades; and his only concern after the family row at Zosima's is to ensure that the monks know it was not his fault but solely Fyodor's. As a result, congratulating himself on his decency (in an Underground Man style), he decides to drop his lawsuit against the monastery about fishing rights, though as the narrator points out, he hadn't the faintest idea where the river and woods were anyway. That is, everything he does is a type of civilised or respectable posing, which is partly why Fyodor relentlessly teases him with his unrespectable buffoonery. Nonetheless the posing of Miusov tells us something about the origins of Dmitri's own juvenile bad behaviour, deriving partly from his mother's line: Adelaida had married Fyodor on a whim to call attention to herself, and is compared to a girl who drowned herself in order to look like Ophelia – all self-deceptive displays of false passion. The childish side of Dmitri appears when he jumps out into the roadway that night to surprise Alyosha, shouting "Your money or your life!" (p. 140). He is still playing army games and needs to be educated out of them, which will happen through the Snegiryov story that later plays an important part in the educational theme, in which Alyosha does his best to rescue the family whose father Dmitri had humiliated. It is not the sensuality in his parental make-up but its absence (senselessness) that leads Dmitri astray: indeed the narrator remarks on how Adelaida, despite her beauty, was the only woman for whom Fyodor felt no sensual attraction.

The other man in the gathering who is without passion is the novice Rakitin, "a seminarian bent on a career" who is described as a friend of Alyosha's whose heart Alyosha can see into. Miusov has no illusions about careers – he is too lazy, old and comfortable. But Rakitin of the "lowered eyes" is ambitious and this dominates the picture of the type of anti-education he embodies. He has a chip on the shoulder over his humble background, and is determined to rise by whatever social networking comes his way, even making use of the irregular (but noble) Karamazovs if possible. He waits for Alyosha "at a turning of the path" on his way to the fateful seminary dinner; his role is to intercept, to distract, divert into the wrong direction (a feature also of Smerdyakov). When, on the path, Alyosha surmises that perhaps Ivan is "seeking suffering", Rakitin's response is: "Oh, you – aristocrats!" (p. 72). Education through suffering seems to him to indicate an aristocracy of feeling, more than literally of birth; it is an indulgent super-refinement

164   THE ART OF PERSONALITY

that gets in the way of the career ladder. He is envious of Alyosha for not being envious of him, for accepting his careerism and still seeing him as a friend (for example, when he laughs at the accuracy of his prophesied picture of Rakitin's future imposing house on the Neva). Later Rakitin discovers Alyosha prostrate on the ground, grieving for Zosima or rather for his own disillusion that the elder's body has not been miraculously preserved but stinks with corruption; it is his first personal crisis of faith, forcing him to distinguish between the body which corrupts and the soul which may be immortal – and thus to internalise his parental object. Alyosha, says the narrator, fell to the ground a weak youth, but arose transformed into a "resolute champion ... for ever" (p. 341).

At this crisis point, Rakitin attempts to betray Alyosha by taking him to Grushenka in return for payment. Rakitin's angry hiss that "You're no Christ and I'm no Judas!" simply reinforces the biblical parallel (p. 336). But the meeting of souls that then takes place instead of the intended seduction is beyond Rakitin's rationalist imagination. Instead of the money metaphor, the onion of love (and not "that type of love" – that is, the sensual) is given and received to their mutual benefit; each revives in the other his faith in the goodness of their internal object. Rakitin's cynicism contrasts with both the romanticism of Dmitri (for whom his bag of money takes on a metaphorical significance) and with the literalism of both Ivan and Fyodor, who also believe in the power of money to save or manipulate.

Virtuous women

To turn now to the young women who partner the brothers in their sensual search for suffering. Grushenka is initially, through rumour, portrayed as a she-devil, despite the protestations of both Fyodor and Dmitri who know her to be "virtuous", at least in their (deep) sense. It transpires indeed that she is not a harlot but a businesswoman, educated by her elderly protector Samsonov who tells her she is "a wench with brains [who] must look after herself" when he is gone, rather than expecting any inherited gratuities (p. 323). And in the scene of the "onion" – the failed seduction stage-managed by Rakitin – she shows another type of virtue, namely a compassionate heart and sisterliness toward Alyosha, whose presence has the power to draw souls out of the burning lake with only an onion, but not to create a soul where there was none. But it is Katerina Ivanovna rather than Grushenka who evokes fearful premonitions in Alyosha when Dmitri commands him to go to her to relay his

DOSTOEVSKY AND THE EDUCATION OF A MAN OF FAITH   165

"bowing out" of their engagement (p. 135); for a beautiful exterior may house a more frightening devil than mere sensuality – namely the devil of "virtue". Dostoevsky insists on the double sense of the "bow", each respectful of the other, and retiring from engagement. The original "bow" marks Katerina's torment, her humiliation that the young officer did not take her virginity (his payment) but gave her the money anyway that she would have earned by "selling her beauty" as Grushenka bluntly puts it. Even at that stage it was a "bowing out"; he had enough experience to know that this haughty messianic maiden was not his type; it is she who insists on their betrothal, and he who breaks it, rejecting her yet again. His rejection is not spiteful but a feature of his increasing wisdom: he is impressed by the mixture of love and hate aroused in him by Katerina, and this encounter becomes a turning-point in his wish to become a gentleman. "I will be a god to whom he can pray", she says (p. 172). Katerina does not understand she has already saved him; her pride is severely dented and she becomes obsessed by Dmitri's bow, which festers in her heart as a spur to revenge, even though it forms an introduction to Ivan who is far better suited to her (and who has the same name as her father).

Having heard Dmitri's account of Katerina's "virtue", in the sense of noble self-sacrifice, Alyosha is at a loss to explain his own forebodings when he knocks on her door. Here Dmitri understands more than he does, since he knows the power of jealousy and therefore also, the distinction between jealousy and self-love. He knows that Katerina's sacrifice for her father (or potential sacrifice) is a function of her being "in love with her virtue", not with himself (p. 105) – and possibly not of her father either but rather his reputation (indeed, various hints suggest that the father was probably, like all that political family, embroiled in shady transactions, no better than Fyodor). Dostoevsky in one of his notebooks considers Katerina Ivanovna an example of "self-invention", in the sense that "a person fails to live throughout his life but invents himself" (Dostoevsky, 1976, p. 769). Her invented persona is only penetrated near the very end, when the lie that she loves Dmitri "becomes truth" but this is only momentary as it is intolerable and unsustainable, so again she seeks refuge from life's aesthetic conflict, in hysterics and romantic escapades.

This distinction between true and false feeling is played out in front of Alyosha during the masterly theatrical scene entitled "Both together", in which Grushenka emerges from behind the curtains, displayed by Katerina as a prize possession of her own, only to reverse the directorship and prove herself a "tigress", much to

166   THE ART OF PERSONALITY

Dmitri's admiration when he hears about it: she should be "hung on a scaffold". It is the beginning of the *Antony and Cleopatra* theme. The whole business is designed to initiate Alyosha into the wiles of femininity. Grushenka, in sugary tones, knows how to act the romantic role of the rescued prostitute that Katerina demands of her, centred on the money-virtue (female genital) and its powers of manipulation; but she has real feelings and so upturns Katerina's fake romantic tableau. Katerina does not learn much from this charade, nor does Alyosha at the time, but he is an intimate witness to Dmitri's interpretation of it. Dmitri's hopes have been enhanced as a result of his account, understanding that it is Grushenka's way of sending him a love-letter via Alyosha. He sees the appropriateness of a match between Katerina and Ivan, not merely as a way out for himself. But she is obsessed with "saving" men rather than loving them. The main obstacle to her turning to Ivan is her obsession with saving Dmitri's soul, which is precisely what ruins him. Later she explains to Ivan at length why (sacrificing her own desires) she will never renounce Dmitri but continue to save him even from a distance: she turns her rejection into a campaign. In addition to torturing Ivan, her vanity in not committing herself to him – except to enlist him in "saving Dmitri" – leads to her betrayal of Dmitri in the trial scene and possibly to much of Ivan's psychological trouble.

Following on from this dramatic scene, "another reputation is ruined" – as Dostoevsky humorously entitles the section in which Liza sends Alyosha a love-letter of his own, in a pink envelope (p. 140). Alyosha cherishes it with a "soft, sweet laugh" spiced by a touch of the "sinful". But he does not instantly respond to, or recognise, Liza's desperate desire to lose her virginity, imaged in shutting her finger in the door, saying "I am wicked" – after which she throws herself at Ivan in another letter which is a parody of that to Alyosha. We remember she is the daughter of a progressive society lady of "little faith", and she herself has little faith in Alyosha who used to "carry her around" as a child but is (according to her teenage impatience) too slow in progressing to the next phase. We suspect there would have been much more of Liza in the next novel (and Dostoevsky's notes suggest as much). Alyosha, on leaving the monastery and shedding his cassock, is shown neatly dressed much as Liza wished him to look; but at present, his primary attention is elsewhere – on the one hand with his brothers, on the other hand, with the schoolboys. He is educating and being educated simultaneously.

The making of the generations

God and the devil are fighting and the battlefield is men's hearts, says Dmitri (p. 97). As does Milton, Dostoevsky gives the devil all the best lines and the most powerful arguments – his own favourites – whether from within the character the devil has entered into, or in the form of dreams or hallucinations. The heroic characters, both adults and children, are subject to this battle in their hearts; it is only the complacent characters, satisfied with their worldly and spiritual status, who undergo no struggle and have no sense of "other worlds" beyond themselves. Essentially it is the battle between the *pro* and *contra* of self- versus object-oriented values; and even within the self, there may be either cold or hot "devils", leading either to despair or to aspirational envy.

In effect Dostoevsky puts his own ideas and theories into the melting-pot, in order to see whether through art and inspiration they may be transcended by a picture of the "perfect man" which organically creates itself, rather than one which is deliberately drawn to measure like an icon. By "perfect man" he seems to mean something like: the essence of what it is to be a man – something whose "mystery" had interested him since the age of seventeen. At around the same time as conceiving *Karamazov*, Dostoevsky wrote *An Accidental Family*, the story of an adolescent youth, as an expression of his ambition to "guess at the innermost spiritual world of one on the eve of manhood ... since it is those from whom the generations are made". But he found that the picture of growing or "perfect" manhood needed greater dimensionality or complexity. The new picture is an inclusive one, requiring (as he wrote in a letter) a hero who would be "at times an atheist, a believer, a fanatic, a sectant ... a wolf-cub, a nihilist ... put into a monastery for instruction" (Dostoevsky, 1976, p. 742): in other words, a Karamazov. If Alyosha is the focal hero, it is not because he is perfect in the sense of idealised, but because he identifies with all his brothers and their struggles with nature and nurture and therefore comes to represent "the eve of manhood" as an existential state.

The legend of "The Grand Inquisitor" and the life of "The Russian Monk" are at the centre of the doctrinal debate, and Dostoevsky at one point insisted they were the most important parts of the novel. Yet he was aware that the life and precepts of Father Zosima, as recorded by Alyosha, could not carry sufficient weight to overcome the effect of the catalogue of crimes against humanity that Ivan has assembled. (We wonder more how the manuscript came to be in the hands of the narrator – another

168   THE ART OF PERSONALITY

indication that Alyosha is dead.) Dostoevsky therefore said that the only real answer to the Inquisitor lay in the novel itself and the way it developed as a whole polyphonic work.

Just as Smerdyakov wishes he had never been born, so Ivan wants to "return his entrance ticket" to God's unjust world (the suicidal tendency) because there can be no "yes but" excuses for the instances of cruelty to children that he lists – all real events recorded by Dostoevsky from the newspapers, for he like Ivan was an acute "eyewitness" of society's abominations. Ivan believes that his cruel, inquisitorial superego really wants to "make man happy" (as in the Underground Man's satire of a tyrant), but Alyosha observes there is "no great cleverness and no mysteries and secrets" in the inquisitorial position (p. 242), and at its core is his lack of faith in the possibility of spiritual redemption taking root in the earth, that is, within human nature. He does not answer his brother point by point but seeks for the deep meaning: "brother, what are you driving at?" Ivan feels he has only enough life-force to last him until age 30; he insists on the need to keep the world under control, but with the implication that he should be amongst the special class of "clever people" that maintain the stupid masses in happy servitude through "miracle, mystery and authority". Alyosha tells Ivan that since his love of life exists "regardless of logic", he has already done half the work to redeem his position; the "second half" of the task involves "raising your dead, who perhaps have not died after all" (internalisation, as Alyosha has himself done with their mother). His main answer is not through argument however but in the Christlike kiss on the lips that he has taken from Ivan's own story, as if to enliven that object-identification from within Ivan.

It does not work, of course. The brothers part and go different ways for most of the rest of the story – Alyosha observing how Ivan's shoulder droops irregularly as he walks, a sign of his spiritual imbalance ("disorder"). Ivan is becoming increasingly drawn into the world of the devil-like aspect of himself featured in Smerdyakov whom he believes he is educating, seeing him as a "prime candidate" for revolution. Smerdyakov embodies the death-instinct side of the wailing "idiot" mother, the holy fool who is herself split into Sophia and Stinking Lizaveta (confused at one point in Fyodor's mind). This particular struggle appertains only to Ivan and Alyosha, not to Dmitri who has inherited a simpler madness via Adelaida – that of the egocentric Byronic romantic. Dmitri's buried faith is simple and feeling-based, not intellectual, and rises to the surface during his trials; whereas the intellectual Ivan has a horror of becoming what Katerina calls "a little religious idiot" (as she hisses at Alyosha). Ivan describes himself as "awfully fond of children", but we never see this in action except in the perverted form of the alliance with Smerdyakov, whereas Alyosha is actively drawn into the world of the schoolboys, whose devilishness (calling names and throwing stones) is transformable, since their better nature is still reachable.

Something of Smerdyakov has got into Alyosha nonetheless. His crisis takes the form of wondering whether his internal object is indeed a "stinker", when Father Zosima's corpse succumbs to earthly decay: is Zosima a Sophia-type mother or a pathetic Lizaveta Smerdyashaya? Father Paissy gently rebukes him with being amongst those "of little faith", but knows he will somehow "return" (p. 316). Superstition over this "scandalous" matter of the sacred elder's "corruption" ranges from the triumph of the crazy ascetic Father Ferapont, high on forest mushrooms and hallucinating devils, to the disappointment of Madame Khokhlakova, who is obliged to relinquish her hope of miracles and to take up a new faith in "mathematical certainty ... I'm all for reason now" (p. 361). Despite the sense that some "catastrophe" is about to happen, Alyosha finds himself locked in conversation by Madame Khokhlakova, and is thus unable to fulfil Zosima's instruction to stay close to *both* his brothers, not just one. The Khokhlakovian comedy brilliantly offsets the Mityan tragedy. Owing to the pervading mental "stink", Dmitri is somehow "forgotten". Although Alyosha makes superficial attempts to trace him, he has actually lost emotional contact; his sense of obligation "did not reach his heart and instantly faded out of his mind and was forgotten"; this only strikes him later during the trial, when he keeps asking, "how could I have forgotten?" (p. 645).

It is Grushenka in the scene with the onion who pulls Alyosha out of the burning lake, "raising his soul from the depths" and enabling him to fight off Rakitin, his personal devil: he says to him that although he has "lost a treasure such as you never had" (Zosima) he has "found a sister" (p. 329). The conversation with Grushenka and Rakitin helps him to differentiate, and to lose interest in Rakitin's false friendship, though it is Rakitin who actually states it is finished – the final straw being Alyosha "forgetting" the bribe of 25 roubles, as if it were of no importance. Rakitin is only a petty devil, not a powerful one; there is no Judas-like glamour attached to his sins. Forgetting Rakitin thus contrasts with forgetting Mitya, which still represents confusion caused by Ivan and Smerdyakov. The clarification in Alyosha's mind as a result of Grushenka leads to the dream of Zosima's resurrection. Whilst listening to Father

170   THE ART OF PERSONALITY

Paissy reciting the story of Cana of Galilee, Alyosha becomes aware of a dual reality: he is aware that Zosima is in the coffin, but also that he is "here too", walking toward him. That is, the miracle consists in internalisation, not in the arrest of bodily decay. It is after this dream that Alyosha is internally strengthened and able to begin his work in the world, rising up from the ground a resolute fighter in the conviction that "someone visited my soul in that hour".

"I have a real grief", Alyosha tells Liza (p. 179). The key word is of course "real". Earlier he had interrupted her mother's chatter with the request for a piece of clean cloth to bind his injured finger – a rare occasion on which Alyosha asks attention for himself. Real feeling contrasts with the posturing that reigns in the Khokhlakova household, where the devil of idleness presides. "Yes you are not screaming, I am screaming ..." says Madame Khokhlakova to her daughter, in her confusion. The woman introduced to us as "of little faith" follows all the latest fashionable alternatives, not in dress but in ideas – anything to brush away her boredom. The subject of her lengthy monologues ranges from "miracles" through "reason" to the "reformed law courts" and the new idea of "aber-ration", which all seem connected in her mind: "They found out about aberration as soon as the law courts were reformed"; and Dmitri's case can now be seen as one of aberration – as can the behaviour of her difficult daughter.

The scene in which Khokhlakova tries to send Dmitri to the gold mines is one of Dostoevsky's comic masterpieces. Obsessed by the shame of the "spot on his breast" (namely Katerina's remaining 1500 roubles), which marks the difference between being a scoun-drel and a thief (a seducer and a rapist), Dmitri asks for the 3000 which symbolises for him the power to acquire Grushenka, to carry her off. Aping the role of an amateur psychologist, Khokhlakova declares: "I'm an experienced doctor of the soul ... I've studied your gait and come to the conclusion: that's a man who would find mines" (p. 363). Oblivious to his desperate if absurd request for money, she offers him a more elevated type of assistance: "I'll make you a present of *the idea*", insisting on a "mathematical" response to her elevated brainchild "the idea". This, her latest mission – besides being a sinister prediction of Dmitri's sentence to a convict's labour in the Siberian mines – is mixed up with fashionable themes such as "the woman question", ethics and aesthetics (the "moral beauty" to be found in "the word Mother"). The day before the trial, she confesses she is "ready to die of curiosity" (p. 541). Yet she is not heartless; she merely represents the ideological confusion or "disor-der" that reigns in the mind which is ever flitting from one god to another, or one suitor to another, without any emotional meaning (faith) to give it inner stability.

As the devil's influence spreads like a contagion, Liza Khokhlakova delves further into her adolescent crisis. It is not enough to be "carried about" by Alyosha in pubertal games. Regaining her physical mobility, she rises from her childish bath–chair and switches from the innocent liaison with Alyosha to sado-masochistic fantasies directed at Ivan (whom she "doesn't like" but this itself excites her curiosity). In the chapter "A little demon", she confesses she wants someone to "marry, torture, deceive and leave" her (p. 549), and senses Ivan is sufficiently tortured to be able to fulfil this desire (though he does not reciprocate, having trouble enough with Katerina Ivanovna). Her original engagement with Alyosha was not based on sexual love, but on trying to penetrate his mystifying preoccupation with "saving his soul" – as she said, she wanted to know how he "became an angel" (p. 178). On Alyosha's part, too, the engagement was more dutiful than real, carrying out Father Zosima's instructions to find a wife: he won't find anyone better than Liza, he says, and anyway, who else would have him? Liza's outbreak of perversity is associated with reading the "nasty" books her mother keeps under her pillow, and with devilish fanta-sies, such as that of watching a child being crucified, whilst eating pineapple compote to enhance the enjoyment. Alyosha admits he too has had the dream of being assailed by little devils; he accepts the transference. He observes that she has a capacity for "suffer-ing", and they are united over the Snegiryov affair; the potential exists for a more complex future relationship. However he tells her that her "luxurious life" is partly to blame for her "disorder" (confusion) and that it is better to be poor – a worker. (At the time of their childish engagement, they had planned to "care for people as we would for the sick".) He also assents to her analysis of their little society's enjoyment of the parricide drama. The townsfolk of Skotoprigyonesk are the ones eating pineapple compote whilst Dmitri is being crucified, the most exciting entertainment in years. (This is when, after Alyosha has left, Liza deliberately shuts her own finger in the door, saying "I hate everybody" [p. 554]).

Liza's blackened finger echoes the swollen foot of her mother, that somatises her own devilish-sexual fantasies; it results from her hand having been squeezed too hard by Rakitin. So Madame Khokhlakov swops with her daughter the role of invalid. With her swollen foot she becomes a spider in the midst of her web, tena-ciously controlling other people's movements from the sofa, refus-ing to let Alyosha move away until the next visitor has come to

172   THE ART OF PERSONALITY

entertain her. Liza's sadomasochistic injury, unlike her mother's foot, is a genuine expression of adolescent disturbance – it actually hurts. In that sense it makes a link (as well as a contrast) with the bite Alyosha sustains from Ilyusha, the child whose name echoes his own. The bite touches him to the quick – literally the bone. It contrasts with the fantasies somatised by Liza and her mother. The pain is not only physical: the plight of the boys is what stings Alyosha's heart, in a way that Liza does not. It is a depressive pain of identification. The sting arouses interest, rather than pity or reforming zeal, and proceeds towards creating a bond of love that is paralleled in power only by the love between Dmitri and Grushenka, in its final evolved form. Unlike his alter-ego Rakitin, Alyosha does not choose a career: rather, he finds a vocation, amongst the children whose reality contrasts with the newspaper cases that in principle cause his brother Ivan such existential torment. Liza Khokhlakova does not need him, but Kolya, Ilyusha, Smurov and the others do, and are indeed only a year or two younger than Liza herself.

Teaching methods

Alyosha's reparative role in the world of the schoolboys has links both with Ivan's predicament (where he feels powerless) and with Dmitri, owing to his role in the humiliation of Ilyusha's father Snegiryov. The bond with Ivan is stifled by the Smerdyakov-devil; the bond with Dmitri is also somehow lost (literally, he cannot find him), but both his brothers are present in the background as shadowy emotional links, during the building of the relationship with the boys. Alyosha's entry into the Snegiryovs' living-room marks the opening of his eyes to the world in a way that contrasts with Ivan's "eyewitness" journalistic viewpoint. As he takes in the family situation – humiliated father, searing poverty, sick wounded child, demented mother, two sisters (one a gentle cripple, the other scholarly and impatient to be off), he can only mutter: "I see and hear" (p. 185). He already knows the feeling of "real grief" but, outside the monastery and the ladies' drawing rooms, encounters grief greater than his own. Dostoevsky's chapter titles ("Lacerations in the drawing room", "Lacerations in a hut") emphasise the different nature of the pain in the different settings. The stone-missile flung by the boys has "entered into Ilyusha" (inflaming his tubercular lungs) in the sense of a metaphor for truth: "the truth entered into him and crushed him forever", that is, the truth about injustice; and Alyosha takes this insight personally, via his bitten finger. A

DOSTOEVSKY AND THE EDUCATION OF A MAN OF FAITH 173

real stone marks the place where father and son wept together over their helplessness, outcasts from society, a "beautiful and lonely spot" at the border between town and pasture, a place "where God alone saw us". Alyosha's task is to work from the basis of the dual nature of the schoolboys who, as Snegiryov says, may be "angels" individually but are "a merciless race" when together. He therefore takes them individually to the Snegiryovs' hut to make it up with Ilyusha, before reuniting them as a group. At the same time he is of course repairing Dmitri's "insult" or attack on the family; Snegiryov says satirically that this is not that insulting Karamazov but his brother, "radiant with modest virtues" – something which has yet to be proved.

The schoolboy scenes portray a tenderly ironical picture of the children's view of the adult world, whose prejudices the children keenly observe and imitate without, as yet, being deeply corrupted. Dostoevsky originally conceived the novel as being one about children; and the conversations between Alyosha and Kolya Krasotkin, the "wolf-cub" child-hero, are the most entertaining in the book in their humour, poignancy and realism. Kolya is a new Karamazov in the making, providing Alyosha with an opportunity to observe a "charming nature" when its "distortions" are still malleable (p. 526): a much more effective novelistic strategy than a straightforward narrative of the past. Believing that he can "think for [himself] without being taught" (p. 521), Kolya is full of manipulative tricks and belief in his own powers, even though his omnipotent games are comical and endearing rather than tragic; the core of sincerity is retained, but the potential for tragedy is also there. He has the precocious opinionatedness that Ivan also had as a child, believing that power consists in possessing secret knowledge (a distorted identification with his dead father, whose books he raids for this purpose). At present he is using the "secret" answer to the question "who founded Troy" in order to wield power over the others and their schoolteacher. He absorbs what he has gleaned of the latest political and educational ideologies, whilst convinced of his own originality, as in: "I am an incurable socialist, Karamazov"; "I know how to talk to the peasants ... I like to stir up fools in every class of society" (p. 501); or, "The study of the classics is simply a police measure, to stupefy the intellect" (p. 521). When his babysitting charges retort to a casual remark that their mother never whips them, he replies "I know, I only said it for stylistic reasons" (p. 494). Rhetoric is his outer shell, his persona, divorced from the inner identity which he fears is vulnerable and unprotected.

174   THE ART OF PERSONALITY

Dostoevsky knows that the most effective way to parody ideas, whether they are fashionable formulae or precious personal convictions, is to place them in the mouths of schoolboys. Even his own favourite aspiration to "realism" is humorously parodied through Kolya, as it was through Khokhlakova's sentimental froth (when she proclaimed "I'm all for realism now"). Dostoevsky insisted he was not a psychologist but a "higher realist" (cited in Freeborn, 2003, p. 133). Now he humorously allows Kolya to advise Alyosha to become a realist (p. 522). Kolya declares he has vowed to "abandon himself to real life"; but the context is his pubertal dissatisfaction with his physical appearance: feeling himself to be ugly and short, he takes refuge in what he calls real life. Emotional realism is precisely what is lacking in Kolya's secondhand ideas, based as they are on scavenging from authors such as Voltaire, Belinsky, Pushkin, etc., whom he has not properly read but rather rummaged through for quotations in order to mystify and gain authority over his listeners – peers, peasants, and schoolteachers. Thus when Kolya's secret about the founders of Troy is rumbled (his hidden history book is discovered by one of the younger boys) he defends his status by switching position, with a dazzling display of namedropping. The tactic, used also with the peasants, is to attain superiority by stirring confusion – though he doesn't always win his game. He has also had anti-educational discussions with the poseur Rakitin; but never any spiritual teacher to help him meaningfully evaluate ideas instead of testing them through playing tricks, as happened in the episode of the peasant and the goose.

It is significant that Kolya also sees himself as a type of teacher. He believed it was in his power to discipline Ilyusha when, persuaded by Smerdyakov, he fed the dog a piece of bread with a needle in it. The needle is in a sense the child's own sin, or is interpreted as such; everyone is convinced that if the dog could be brought back to life, so would Ilyusha be. But the dog cannot be found, and the lethal piece of bread turns into the stone that seems to strike him down for ever, crushing his already tubercular chest: the ingested devil is now breaking his heart. Kolya's misconceived cruelty in his educational methods reinforces Ilyusha's despair. Originally he had taken on the messianic role of Ilyusha's protector: "I am teaching him, developing him", which included meting out a degree of punishment designed to "form his character, lick him into shape, make a man of him" (p. 504); that is, he treats the younger boy in the same way as he treats the dog. It is a reasonable idea by the pedagogical standards of the time, but Alyosha's alternative methods demonstrate the inadequacy of the carrot-and-stick

DOSTOEVSKY AND THE EDUCATION OF A MAN OF FAITH

approach. A new pattern or image of the "perfect" teacher emerges out of his developing experience.

Kolya's redemption lies in his youthful flexibility; unlike Ivan, he is not committed to any particular ideological argument; he is still Dmitri, Ivan and Alyosha rolled into one. He has a "charming nature" and his good aspects have found reciprocation in real people – as in his closeness to his mother, and the babysitting scene where he takes seriously his duties toward the younger children. Moreover he openly confesses he has always wanted to get to know Alyosha, but wants to be in control of the opportunity, which means he delays his visit to the dying Ilyusha until it is almost too late: what appears to be a reparative gesture is spoilt by his obsession with being the theatre-director, playing god, insisting that his performance has transformed their sorrow and made them happy: "You are all happy now…" (the totalitarian view).

Outside the Snegiryovs' hut, he has a private conversation with Alyosha. The narrator in fact sees them as "two lads", younger and elder brothers; we remember that Alyosha himself is only twenty. By the end Kolya has acquired through Alyosha some of Dmitri's passion, when he says to Alyosha that their talk has been "a declaration of love", and asks if that is "ridiculous" (p. 527). Alyosha replies no, just as there is no shame in playing horses and other childish games: games are the first stage of dramatic art, with children being the actors, and so even more authentic than in theatrical expression. The fear of looking ridiculous is a "form of vanity" propagated by the "devil" and it has "entered into the whole generation". His hope that Kolya may be "like everyone else but not like everyone else" lies in Kolya's "impulse to self-criticism", which co-exists with his ordinary feelings. (This conversation contrasts with Khokhlakova's earlier spurious confession to Father Zosima regarding her lack of faith.) Play is the first form of art, the expression of fantastic reality; but as we see with Kolya's theatrical show, in which he uses the dog Perezvon as his chief actor and puppet, the directorial mentality (even in a child) can hinder its therapeutic efficacy.

Folies à deux

Two months pass between the murder of Fyodor in September and the trial of Dmitri in November. During this period Alyosha works to exorcise the devilish spirit of the schoolboys. His background educational efforts have emotional reverberations with the troubles of his brothers, which are narrated in tandem, but where

176   THE ART OF PERSONALITY

he has no direct influence other than trying to keep up communications. The foreground is taken up by the relationships of Dmitri and Grushenka on the one hand, and Ivan and Katerina on the other; and the trials of all the partners, taken together, represent an approach to the definition of true love and its self-sacrifice, on the lines of *Antony and Cleopatra*. True love is partly defined through misconceptions of it. While Dmitri and Grushenka are clarifying their own view of each other, Ivan and Katerina become more entrammelled in illusion. Unable to face the aesthetic conflict within themselves, they spend all their energies trying to manipulate the first couple. Ivan's relationship with Katerina is consolidated in their plot to arrange his escape – a sort of psychological *folie à deux*, whatever its defensibility in social and judicial terms. Katerina, as we know, is obsessed with becoming Dmitri's "god" and saviour, not only through providing money (in conjunction with Ivan) but by importing the celebrity doctor and lawyer from Petersburg, who turn out to be expert promulgators of "disorder".

Ivan's involvement in all this is fuelled by belief in Dmitri's guilt (which even Katerina does not share). It is a belief based on lack of faith in the possibility of an internal mother-god-saviour; Ivan has no such internal figure, only a hated father; or at least, his "angel" figure is represented by a young inexperienced brother whom he regards as naive. (Here we see the similarity between Ivan and Fyodor.) With all his cleverness, Ivan has difficulty in thinking. He has no power of self-scrutiny, no internal object with which to think: by contrast with Kolya who begins that way but then latches onto Alyosha to fill this psychic gap. The escape plot takes up so much of Ivan's attention that he is diverted from questioning his own feelings of guilt; hence he becomes increasingly the prey of Smerdyakov, equating him with the devil within, really a narcissistic projection. It is Alyosha who first intuits Ivan's sense of guilt when he declares "It was not you who killed father" (p. 569). As always with moments of intuition, this is spoken directly from the unconscious, as if "not of himself but obeying some irresistible command ... God has sent me to tell you", that is, to turn Ivan to introspection. Ivan is astonished by his brother's intuition which goes so far beyond his own. To him it is uncanny, and he can find only a concrete and crazy explanation: he is convinced that Alyosha must have "seen him" (the devil) in his room, that is, his mind. He repudiates Alyosha when he comes too close to perceiving his inner disease, insisting "I can't endure prophets and epileptics ... leave me at this crossing" (p. 570). His paranoid attitude is that his disease must be kept a secret. His superego-god has turned into

DOSTOEVSKY AND THE EDUCATION OF A MAN OF FAITH 177

a devil, as indicated by his terror when Smerdyakov refers to the "other" person in the room but (when pressed to explain) says he means God; for Ivan, God and the devil are fused. And the other person who confronts Ivan as a hallucination of his alter-ego is indeed very father- or Fyodor-like: a sort of caricature of a shabby, liberal, Herzen-like figure – a type whom Dostoevsky first viciously pilloried, but later viewed more gently (and very reminiscent of Hamlet's Ghost).

The "crossing", the parting of the Skotoprigonevsk backways, where Ivan diverges from Alyosha, in fact marks a spiritual turning-point: he begins to investigate his repulsive feelings, in particular, that of shame at eavesdropping on the stairs the night before the murder, which he feels to be the most despicable act of his life (a prying into his father's secrets). Through the three visits to Smerdyakov, Ivan gradually approaches the truth about himself. He can only take a small dose at a time of this antidote to his own "cleverness". It is a sadomasochistic investigation, like an addict returning to his despised but indispensable drug. The visits are recounted with sinister suspense, as if the chasm of hell were drawing him magnetically toward the abyss, glimpse by glimpse; and the slow speed of his comprehension is underlined by the refrain about the "clever man", emphasising how Ivan's cleverness has made him stupid in the area that most matters – that of self-knowledge. "You hit the mark indeed. And you will be clever, sir", repeats Smerdyakov; then points out how he has been acting as a denied aspect of Ivan himself: "following your words, I did it" (p. 590). Ivan, the man of clever words, irrefutable argument and dialectic, is both hunter and hunted (echoing Dmitri with his persecutors, in the "wolf hunt"). "We two clever people have something to say to each other", as Smerdyakov's screwed-up left eye seemed to say to Ivan. The hunt culminates in Ivan's sensation of "insane terror" when Smerdyakov takes off his garter and unrolls his white stocking; the fantasy here has suggestions of homosexuality, the action of a male prostitute revealing the false packet of money, which turns out to be useless evidence without Smerdyakov's personal confession (the intellectual Ivan has the stupidity to present the money in court as evidence, as if it were different from any other package of 3000 roubles.) When someone else enters the room, he hides the money under a religious book, just as earlier, it was hidden behind the icons in Fyodor's bedroom, a fact only known to Smerdyakov. The implication is that the revealing of "secrets" is itself a kind of perversion, a false view of knowledge; and it is associated with the attitude to femininity and the kind of "purse" within which it is

178   THE ART OF PERSONALITY

perceived to be contained (thus the white stocking contrasts with the home-sewn amulet which Dmitri wears around his neck and which represents both his femininity and his honour).

This is the rock-bottom moment at which Ivan acknowledges his unconscious bond with the devil. But the seeds of spiritual regeneration are indicated when, on the way home from Smerdyakov, he rescues the drunken peasant whom, on the way there, he had knocked over and left to die in the snow. The peasant had served to remind him of his complicity in the murder by singing "Vanka's gone to Petersburg" (p. 590) – reminding us of how Ivan turned his back and left for Moscow on the fatal day. Back at home, he encounters the hallucinatory father-devil who delivers "homeopathic doses" of "faith" (p. 612), tormenting Ivan by belief and disbelief in turns, insisting on his reality as the "indispensable minus" without which debate would not be possible and the "new man" of society able to overcome the old "slave-man": "Knowing that you are inclined to believe in me, I administered some disbelief". His clear logical dialectic becomes enveloped in the smog of his brainstorm, imaged by the snowstorm, which is then pierced by Alyosha's knocking at the window to tell him what he has already guessed about the suicide; the angel appears with the seed of self-knowledge. But in his vulnerable state this is dangerous: it marks the beginning of Ivan's delirium. He is too weak to tolerate this knowledge, now that his false shell of cleverness has been undermined. Yet again Smerdyakov has outwitted Ivan, who was hoping that Smerdyakov would be sent to Siberia, whilst he merely had to cope with "moral condemnation" for his passive non-intervention.

Ivan's brain "disorder" contrasts with Dmitri's increasing love of "order"; his nightmare contrasts with Dmitri's "good dream", the dream of the starving "babe" and the poor black peasant huts (p. 471), from which he wakes energised and desiring to do some good in the world. This dream is the culmination of his progression towards faith in Grushenka's reciprocated love. Before Mokroe, Dmitri had envisaged, with scientific curiosity, the passage of a bullet through his brain. This was associated with the image of a "high fence" entering his thoughts, referring supposedly to suicide at dawn, but in fact contributing to the sense of a more ambiguous impending catastrophe: "At dawn Mitya will leap over that fence ... you don't understand what fence Fenya ... I'll step aside ... live, my joy" (p. 374). He does not understand the nature of that fence either, nor how it will lead him to gaining Grushenka. In the process of "stepping aside" to make way for the first lover, there are a series of near-violent encounters with women as he moves towards the

DOSTOEVSKY AND THE EDUCATION OF A MAN OF FAITH   179

meeting at Mokroe. A sequence of exclamations of "Aie!" mark the steps with a kind of crescendo: first there is Khokhlakova's cry as he rushes out of her room, then an old woman whom he nearly knocks over, then Grushenka's servant Fenya, and finally Grushenka's own "Aie!" as he enters the blue room at the inn where she is sitting in the company of her old Polish lover, bored out of her mind. (It is like the story of Dmitri's life in flashback– one extravagant bodged fiasco after another.)

This is the moment, Grushenka afterwards explains, when her complacent old "gander" was replaced by a "falcon" flying in; discerning his fear, she realises at last: "Fool! That's the man you love ... it's me he's afraid of, only me" (p. 414). It is a revelation to herself. The earlier meeting with Alyosha had begun the process by loosening her woman-of-the-world carapace, putting her in contact with her own feelings of guilt and the egotistical clinging to her own resentment at being abandoned by her first lover: "Crawl back, little dog" (p. 335). She had looked on the Polish lover as a "schoolmaster, all grave and learned"; but he did not teach her anything; instead, "I was struck dumb" – another image of false education. Only now does she realise she had deceived herself in maintaining a false picture of this shoddy romance, whilst believing she was only "playing with Mitya" (as she put it in the onion scene). Now she can say: "Mitya, how could I be such a fool as to think I could love anyone after you?" (p. 414). Dmitri's love too takes a new turn at Mokroe: "a strange new thought flashed into his mind" – the possibility of reciprocation – something extraordinary and unforeseen, which turns all his omnipotent suicidal plans upside down. It is the "high fence" at which there is a meeting of minds, by contrast with the surreptitious scaling of fences that has paced the story hitherto. "I've taken her soul into my soul and through her I've become a man myself" (perhaps he can't see the passage of the bullet through his brain after all). Love is not about conquest and possessiveness but about reciprocation and mutual introjection of qualities.

Blows from heaven

The old, worn-out, selfish sensualist in Dmitri disappears with Fyodor's death. The "Fyodor" part of his nature had been projected out of himself into his "father" (a primitive psychic origin) but is now outgrown and repudiated. It has fathered a new attitude to sensuality. As his love develops he realises it is no longer only

180   THE ART OF PERSONALITY

Grushenka's "infernal curves" but her soul that captivates him (p. 563). Dmitri is the "new man" born out of the old Fyodor; the phrase "new man" is used in various ways, both ironically and as straight statement of fact. He rises up as a result of a "blow from heaven", a catastrophic change (p. 560). Usually we might expect an improvement in morale to manifest itself in an improvement in appearance. But in this case, Dostoevsky associates Dmitri's old self with clean linen and a dandyish style, like Fyodor when he was waiting in his bedroom for Grushenka with unruffled sheets. Instead, real love results in the revealing of Dmitri's dirty underwear which is exposed to view at the same time as his ugly toenail-penis; and there is a fine line between public humiliation and private humility. The toenail and stained shirt in particular suggest dependence, recalling the dirty smock he wore years ago when he was a small boy looked after by Grigory, and given a present of nuts by Doctor Herzenstube – temporary father figures who provided him with a precious memory that educated his soul. What torments him is the dirty (uncomprehending) eyes that attempt to scan his exposed inner soul. They misunderstand the nature of dirt – the fact that for him Grigory, despite his (unintentional but dogged) false witness at the trial, gains his worth from being "as faithful to his father as seven hundred poodles" (p. 632). Faithful to his father, whom Dmitri did not have the heart to kill; and a representation of the fatherly goodness which Dmitri nonetheless had the heart to introject, despite his intellectual realisation that Grigory's was an unthinking doglike devotion.

For as Alyosha tells the boys at the end of the novel, a good childhood memory, even from a bad home, can save the soul forever "if only the heart knows how to find what is precious". He was himself saved by such a memory of his mother, marking the beginning of his life's work, and echoing Father Zosima's memory of his own brother, whom in turn he identified spiritually with his adoptive son Alyosha (p. 264). Whilst not discounting the environment (he "sees and hears" full well the condition of the Snegiryovs), Alyosha sees no educational function in a blame culture, but only in the positive, personal, recognition of the "precious". Dmitri's early introjected good guardians are brought to light only during the trial, and weigh against his rage at Fyodor.

"God was watching over me", says Dmitri later, referring to the moment when he did not kill his father. Fyodor's death (even before Dmitri is aware of it) marks a change in Dmitri's understanding of the female character – a dawning knowledge which he tries to evade and run away from, as figured in his frantic

DOSTOEVSKY AND THE EDUCATION OF A MAN OF FAITH   181

attempts to obtain the "money" (i.e. the woman) by means other than direct apprehension – via Khokhlakova, Lyagavy, etc. Only when all these means are end-stopped does the possibility of the "other man" in Grushenka's life become real in his consciousness, making it inwardly clear that he needs to overcome his jealous rage and sacrifice his own possessiveness to the loved one's "joy". "The lad had all, now the lad has nought" – meaning, he says, not money but "the female character". Yet it never occurs to him that if Grushenka wished, she could herself provide the "money" to unite them: that is, give her love freely; she only tells him this later when he is able to believe it, having relinquished his pride. Only after "giving way" to a mythical lover can he abandon the concept of love as a conquest. Love entails giving the object freedom, even in the face of jealousy. Like Antony in Shakespeare's play he has to shed the soldier's mentality before becoming a lover, though his "noble heart" is never in doubt; and the same applies to Grushenka as to Cleopatra: she needs to shed the cruel, titillating "whoreish" aspect of her personality that had smothered her genuine jealousy, with which she has to struggle from now on, for the first time. Dostoevsky is clear that crucial thoughts only enter the mind when it is ready to receive them – at an appropriate point in its education, achieving through aesthetic conflict the "high fence" of catastrophic change.

The tragicomic trial scenes, and those leading up to it, represent a symphony on the theme of misconception, in the sense of Money-Kyrle's definition of a "concept", whose basis is always some fantasy of the parental intercourse – and almost every variation of a concept is fantasied "except the right one" (Money-Kyrle, 2014, p. 210). Grushenka imagines that even in prison, Dmitri is planning to "throw her over" for Katya, and this is the significance of his dream about "the babe" – "What is this babe?" (p. 538). Yet she now has her own baby in the shape of the homeless old man Maximov, who is a sort of replacement for her former protector Samsonov – one has died into the other in her lifespace: "Everyone is of use Maximushka, and how can we tell who's of most use?" This new caring relationship images her inner womanly transformation, and is of use to her self-knowledge. Dmitri's view of life has also undergone a transformation: within the "peeling walls" of the prison has sprung a new "thirst for existence and consciousness ... I exist" (p. 561). He is the Underground Man reformed, inspired by a vision, a vocation: "For all the babes, for there are big children as well as little children, all are babes, I go for all, because someone must go for all". It is his acceptance of his new Christlike role of harrower

182   THE ART OF PERSONALITY

of hell – but he can only accept it so long as he imagines Grushenka goes with him. Later, when it is clear she cannot, he asks Alyosha's "permission" to make use of Ivan and Katerina's escape plans, but again, only after Katerina has been pushed to the point of feeling some genuine love for him, for the first time: "For a moment the lie becomes truth" (p. 721). This is the confrontation that, uncharacteristically, Alyosha insisted on "mercilessly": that is, he has no mercy on Katerina's sadomasochism. For Alyosha, Dmitri's life is too important to be sacrificed to her self-indulgent fantasies; but Katerina cannot sustain this emotional realism for long, and at the trial she collapses.

Meanwhile Rakitin is engaged in producing spiteful and slanderous articles for his Petersburg journal: first about Khokhlakova who has rejected his advances, and after that, with the intention of proving "some theory" about Dmitri being corrupted by his environment "plus a tinge of socialism". He doesn't believe it of course; what he really believes is that Dmitri has been stupid in getting found out, because "a clever man can do what he likes" (echoing Smerdyakov). He is one of the plotters, like Ivan, contrasted with the truth-seekers: those for whom thoughts and images are composed by devilish "little tails" in the brain rather than by the "soul". In his account of the trial the narrator observes how Rakitin bustles around in the role of a lead witness, "appearing to know everything; his knowledge was amazing, he had been everywhere, seen everything, talked to everybody, knew every detail of the biography of Fyodor Pavlovich and all the Karamazovs" (p. 633). Except that of course he actually knows nothing at all in any real internal sense; and his authority is comically deflated when his personal petty avarice is exposed. Rakitin "knows a lot", says Dmitri, about the nerve-centres of his otherwise mechanical brain; yet he himself should be sorry to "lose God", meaning the life-spirit housed within (p. 557). For the modernists there is no distinction between mind and brain, making them susceptible to suicidal impulses, as when Dmitri himself examined curiously the bullet that he intended to send into his brain at dawn after reaching the "high fence" at Mokroe. The bullet is the anti-creative tool of internal inquisition, like Ivan's own Grand Inquisitor – as distinct from the exploratory curiosity aroused by the "mystery" of being "a man" (as Dostoevsky expressed his own vocation; cited in Freeborn, 2003, p. 18). Like Antony, Dmitri is simple but not stupid, hence is the first to be redeemed by love, and from his new philosophical position can affirm that "I exist" – this itself is the mystery, the existential "high fence".

DOSTOEVSKY AND THE EDUCATION OF A MAN OF FAITH

The internal object

The false logic displayed by both the prosecutor and the defence lawyer at the trial is the *reductio ad absurdum* of the misconceiving mind. Ippolit Kirillovich, the prosecutor, has a "passion for psychology" (p. 625), but his pseudo-psychological insight is undermined because he unconsciously builds his case on his jealousy of his virtuous wife's fascination with Mitya; this taints all his logic and characterisation. Fetyukovich, the defence lawyer, is more complicated since he gets the sequence of events right, but his reconstruction of the facts is ruined because he doesn't believe a word of it himself, and has decided on his conclusions before even meeting Dmitri. On fashionable lines similar to Rakitin, he proves Fyodor was not really a proper father in any case, and such fathers must expect to be murdered. That is, his case is designed to be a hymn to his own cleverness: he knows it is what the ladies want to hear, and they are rapturous; "frantic applause" comes from half the audience (p. 708). Psychology works both ways – as do the other buzzwords in the air such as mysticism, chauvinism, rationalism, and the "salvation" of the fallen man.

The jury of peasants, stubborn, poor and uneducated, but nonetheless sensing an attack on their values, refuse to be bullied by the lawyer's clever antics, and persist in upholding their own wrong preconceptions. Mysticism, chauvinism, and psychology wash over their heads. Given that opinion is wrong on both sides, the question arises, does it matter if people are telling the truth? Dostoevsky answers, it matters that they tell the truth to themselves; this is the only real meaning; a story can be recounted accurately in every literal detail and yet have not a word of truth in it. Even the "one fact" to emerge (the amulet with the money) carries no weight. The only truthful evidence given in the courtroom takes the form of "believing" in the innocence of the accused, or "seeing from his face" – evidence with no legal validity whatever, yet in Dostoevsky's view, far more significant than any argument since it is based on intuition, and each time, represents a small revelation to the witnesses themselves; only when they tell the story do they understand it. When Ivan enters the court and tells everyone about the Oedipus complex ("Who does not desire his father's death?") the audience deflect the impact away from themselves by insisting he is not in his "right mind", to which he reacts: "I should think I am in my right mind ... in the same nasty mind as you and all these ugly faces" (p. 651). It is not a popular declaration because it recommends that the audience look into their own hearts rather

184   THE ART OF PERSONALITY

than simply being titillated by the reality-show before them. They don't want the theatre of the courtroom to become a mirror to nature where they may learn about themselves. The same dilemma of course applies to all art forms and the nature of their communication – including the novel itself; like the children's prototypal games, it is all "playing horses".

Having played devil's advocate to all his own ideas, undermining them all in the same way – by demonstrating the absence of a vital internal link – Dostoevsky ends the novel on a note of hope for the future. We know it is only the first part of a story, one "moment" in the hero's past life. Two possible roads to the future are heralded: one being Mitya's escape at the staging-post on the way to Siberia, which we somehow doubt will be successful, owing to the lack of realism in Katerina Ivanovna who has masterminded the idea; it is another self-satisfying romance. The escape plan is another misconception, a failure to learn from experience. The other direction is pictured by the group of schoolboys (twelve in number, like both the jurors and Christ's disciples) at Ilyusha's funeral. The funeral takes place in parallel with Dmitri's condemnation and crucifixion. But the schoolboys have a life of experience ahead of them. Alyosha recognises this will be full of trials, for which Dmitri's is a model: trials from both outside and inside, when "wickedness" rises to the fore in their minds. Indeed, we feel, Alyosha is speaking for himself as well as for the boys; they become the internal children who will keep him in touch with reality, even if he should (as Dostoevsky apparently planned [Freeborn, 2003, p. 122]) become a revolutionary and kill the Tsar.

When the little group of mourners stops at Ilyusha's stone on the way to the funeral dinner, Alyosha gives an alternative funeral oration to the official burial service provided by the Church. It reinforces the living inspirational link between himself and the boys. In this moving speech he describes the meaning of a true education:

> "People talk to you a great deal about your education, but some good, sacred memory, preserved from childhood, is perhaps the best education. If a man carries many such memories with him into life, he is safe to the end of his days, and if one has only one good memory left in one's heart, even that may sometime be the means of saving us." (p. 734)

Ilyusha's stone is both pagan and prophetic, in the sense that Forster meant when he said that Dostoevsky's characters have an existence beyond themselves: "to be a person in Dostoevsky is to join up with all the other people far back ... infinity attends them" (Forster, 1927,

DOSTOEVSKY AND THE EDUCATION OF A MAN OF FAITH   185

pp. 172–174). Here Alyosha deliberately tries to establish that link between the stone and infinity, to encourage the boys on that basis "not to be afraid of life".

The stone, with its echoes of Christ's sepulchre yet free from all dogma, is a symbol of the house for a good memory – the internalisation of the meaning of their time together which is now coming to an end, with their spontaneous cries of "Karamazov, we love you!" Alyosha's pause on the path to reinforce the spirit in the stone is a metaphor for the nature of conception itself, by contrast with the process of misconception which is founded on omnipotence. The memory is anchored in the stone which contains the spirit of Ilyusha, in contrast to the missile-stones of victimisation or the bread with the needle – the wound. It is the seed that (in the parable), firmly anchored in the ground, has to die before growing into new life. The new conception is reinforced by their going together to eat the pancakes that affirm life's mixture of joy and sorrow, lament and celebration: "'And always so, all our lives hand in hand! Hurrah for Karamazov!' Kolya cried once more rapturously and once more all the boys chimed in" (p. 735). They are the last words of the novel, and we know it is not "always so" at all – that there will be trouble ahead in the world and encounters with the devil within – but Alyosha has done his best to ensure the "good memory" takes root strongly enough to serve as internal object in those future trials, even when he may be absent, engaged in his own trials, or interred in his own sepulchre. As Dostoevsky said of himself: "I am a child of the age ... a child of disbelief and doubt ... till they put the lid on my coffin ... I would prefer to remain with Christ than with the truth" (cited in Freeborn, 2003, p. 40). In Bion's terms, the ineffable object "O" can only be known through its intersection with a life-object.

Note
Critical works to which I am particularly indebted are: L. Breger, *Dostoevsky: The Author as Psychoanalyst* (1989); D. Chizhevsky,"The theme of the double in Dostoevsky" (1962); E. M. Forster, "Aspects of the Novel" (1927); R. Freeborn, *Dostoevsky* (2003); W. J. Leatherbarrow, *Dostoevsky: The Brothers Karamazov* (1992); R. Matlaw, *The Brothers Karamazov: Novelistic Techniques* (1967); W. G. Moss, *Russia in the Age of Alexander II, Tolstoy and Dostoevsky* (2002); D. O. Thompson, *The Brothers Karamazov and the Poetics of Memory* (1991); V. V. Zenkovsky, "Dostoevsky's religious and philosophical views" (1962).

CHAPTER EIGHT

The evolution of artistic faith in White's *Riders in the Chariot*[1]

P atrick White said he wanted to write a novel about "saints" – those who ride invisibly in the Chariot of faith as "apostles of truth" (Malouf, 2007, p. 13). At the centre of *Riders in the Chariot*, Himmelfarb the Jew expresses his frustration at being unable to visualise the riders, the hidden *zaddikim*. The problem of seeing or recognition was also formulated by Kierkegaard as he speculated in *Fear and Trembling* on the possibility of what strange "movements of infinity" might lie concealed within the ordinary man in the street, such as the pipe-smoking cheesemonger as he "vegetated in the dusk":

> Today nobody will stop at faith; they all go further. It would perhaps be rash to inquire where to, but surely a mark of urbanity and good breeding on my part to assume that in fact everyone does indeed have faith, otherwise it would be odd to talk of going further. (Kierkegaard, 1985, p. 42)

Kierkegaard felt he himself did not have faith, but that the Hegelians (the objects of his satire) who believed they were "going further" by means of a dialectic of compromise, had in fact not yet attained

---

1   A version of this chapter was first published as "The evolution of artistic faith in Patrick White's *Riders in the Chariot*" in *Ariel*, 40 (2009), pp. 47–68.

188 THE ART OF PERSONALITY

this state of half-knowledge. The world of ethics and reasoning is not that of faith and spirituality, which is both ordinary and inscrutable. Like Kierkegaard's cheesemonger, White's Mrs Godbold knows "the grey hours when the world evolves", and "the wheels of her Chariot are solid gold" (White, 1961, p. 73); and Mary Hare, in her mystical union with nature, sees in the colours of sunset the "swingeing trace-chains of light" when the wheels "plough the fields of tranquil sky" (*ibid*, p. 25). White's ambitious tapestry of imagery is founded on the evocation of such moments of dusky or smoky indirect communication, as his riders recreate through their interweaving yet distinct lives the story of the Crucifixion against the backdrop of a broad canvas ranging from Eden to apocalypse. In this context, the Chariot deity that revolves between heaven and earth becomes the governing aegis not only of the riders but also of the novelist, as he puts his trust in the meaningful relationship of his disparate materials – a relationship that will have the power to evoke a sense of the ethereal.

As with most literary fictions which have an allegorical flavour, there has always been debate about the degree to which White's vision evolves organically from his artistic materials or how much it is predetermined and superimposed from without. White was himself suspicious of schematic interpretations of his work, presumably owing to the dangers of reductionism; though his writing with its wealth of systematic theological, poetic and metaphysical references does understandably invite such interpretations and gives them legitimacy. Whatever interpretation the four riders invite, they also inevitably embody aspects of the artistic struggle for realisation, and gradually link up into a coherent picture as the novel itself progresses. They all live on the fringes of social acceptability, yet each has a specific contribution to make to the spirituality of the social fabric: Mary Hare with her enhanced observation of natural process; Himmelfarb with his analytical powers; Mrs Godbold with her endurance and practicality; Alf Dubbo with his ability to mingle emotional colours into harmonious pattern. This sketchmap of artistic characteristics is White's starting-point for a deeper investigation. As the different insights of the characters develop and interweave, in response to contact with the Chariot, they synthesise into a more comprehensive vision of artistic activity which could be termed "artistic faith".

This evolutionary viewpoint, espoused by creative writers since the time of Coleridge, falls in line with both modern psychoanalytic thinking and with those philosophers of aesthetics who place the capacity to relax "palpable design" (as Keats termed it)

THE EVOLUTION OF ARTISTIC FAITH IN PATRICK WHITE   189

at the heart of creativity. Susanne Langer, for example, following in the tradition of Whitehead, Russell and Cassirer, distinguishes between "discursive" and "presentational" forms, and emphasises the untranslateability of the art-symbol, whose essential meaning or "underlying idea" is bound up in its particular form and cannot be explained away by academic interpretation: "To understand the idea in a work of art is more like having a new experience than like entertaining a new proposition" (Langer, 1942, p. 263). The genuinely creative artist employs his medium to engage in a process of exploration and discovery under the aegis of this governing "idea", when the links in the art-symbol seem to be constructed not by authorial control but by internal necessity, and the work takes on a life of its own. As Leonard Bernstein writes: "Form is but an empty word, a shell, without this gift of inevitability" (Bernstein, 1969, p. 30). The tension between egocentric and creative value systems, familiar in theories of poetics from the Renaissance onwards, preoccupies White continuously. According to Langer, the "elements" of an art-symbol (sounds, colours, characters) gain their spiritual significance from their relationship to a "whole" (Langer, 1953, p. 57): that is, from their harmony and ordering. Further, she writes, the artist is impelled by a sense of "moral obligation towards the Idea", which she treats as a Platonic Idea guiding his manipulations of the medium (*ibid.*, p. 121). The idea controls the creative artist, rather than the other way round – hence the sense of inevitability. What kind of spirituality informs artistic sensuality – indeed, what is an artist? The nature of the artist as a generic entity is a latent preoccupation in all White's novels, and in *The Vivisector*'s portrait of an individual artist it becomes the overt subject of the narrative.

Any investigation of White's "underlying idea" of the artist entails treating the novel as an art-symbol, in the sense of a container for meaning rather than a didactic treatise. A creative work always *shows* more than it *says*. In *Riders*, the writer himself is a quester or rider in the Chariot of his own work, struggling to objectively view the total picture by means of his own subjectivity. The novelist's role, like that of the Dubbo the fourth rider, is one that evolves by means of observation, noting the interaction of differing qualities and trying to extract their essence. While technically a supervisor, he is emotionally an instrument of his own work and its destiny. The writer's mentality develops alongside his faith in the life of his own work, which gradually gathers credibility as these distinct strands of being become integrated into a focused single vision characterised by its ability to encompass "the Whole"

190   THE ART OF PERSONALITY

(in the Jungian sense, which White adopts). As he writes in *The Vivisector*: "Mightn't the Whole have been formally contained from the beginning in this square-legged, scrubbed-down, honest-to-God, but lacerated table?" (White, 1973, p. 370). The lacerations are the various elements of the art-symbol which reveal the creative mind in action – a pattern formed by usage, "honest to God".

The limits of imagination and intellect

The story starts in Coleridge's Xanadu, that sumptuous monument to human imagination and artisanship which nonetheless never realised what Coleridge called the "self-circling energies of Reason" (his later term for faith). Its man-made vision, an indulgent "pleasure dome", is embedded in a riot of natural process which appears to add to its glory, whilst subtly undermining its stability. We are drawn into Xanadu when we relinquish the "flickering eyes" of our everyday vision (White, 1961, p. 12) and follow Mary Hare, a "speckled and dappled" creature of nature, as she tunnels her way through the undergrowth to "watch her vision form", which she always sees "as if for the first time" (p. 18). It is a house – and a mentality – inherited from her father. But like that of Kubla Khan, Norbert Hare's vision is destined to crack, indeed must crack if those "caverns measureless to man" are ever to be revealed, and men to be rescued from "the rubble of their own ideas" (p. 345). All the same it is a nest of visionaries by comparison with the house-of-bricks minds of Mrs Flack and Mrs Jolley, whose sensation-seeking is conveyed luridly by the "monstera deliciosa" squirming triffidly outside their window (p. 462). They are squeamish about such big old houses and their inhabitants: "And Them, laying upstairs, in Irish linen. Dreaming" (p. 255). White is explicit about the Romantic origins of his philosophical quest: Xanadu, however faulty, is the rich and fertile soil of all creative work.

Norbert Hare is one of those whose dreams are buried in his own rubble. But he does have sufficient imagination to suspect that there are "moments of illumination" that indicate a "splendour beyond himself", and that his daughter has contact with such moments. In the episode when he is drowned in his own well, Mary holds out a "pole" to him; she is herself an instrument of the Chariot, "a fearful beam of the ruddy, champing light, reflected back at her own silly, uncertain father" (p. 25); where "fearful" has its ambiguous sense of both being afraid and of inducing fear. Although her intention is "merciful", the directness of her beam-like approach blinds

THE EVOLUTION OF ARTISTIC FAITH IN PATRICK WHITE 191

and terrifies him; it is another representation of those "emotions whirling, spokes of whitest light smashing" between them (p. 61). In this sense she kills his preconceived notion of the beautiful, his own narcissistic creation; but in doing so she is responding to his own desire to transcend himself, for his eyes are searching beyond his "native grey raggedy scrub of cynicism" and are occasionally "appeased" not by Xanadu but only by his sense of something beyond, on the horizon, unattainable (p. 16). This something is experienced by him as ugly, like Mary herself, a foreign otherness, "ugly as a foetus ripped out too soon" (p. 61). Norbert in his weakness is unable to tolerate the ugliness of the unknown, hence fails in his artistic aspirations. Mary as artist succeeds where he failed, although her talent is engendered by his.

Mary appears happier than her father owing to her Blakeian innocence. She is sensitive to the hidden spiritual beauties of natural form and can "recognise the Hand in every veined leaf" (p. 67) and feel "the little soft feathers of the wheels" of the Chariot furrowing cloudlike through the sky (p. 344). Why then, we wonder, does she import the forces of philistinism into her life in the form of Mrs Jolley? It is traditional in poetic modes of writing for the source of inspiration (figured here by the Chariot) to have its false counterpart in the narcissistic self-imprisonment that Mary terms the "chain of evil" (p. 343). As Blake writes, "If the doors of perception were cleansed every thing would appear to man as it is, infinite. For man has closed himself up, till he sees all things thro narrow chinks of his cavern" (Blake, 1974, p. 154). Mrs Jolley is one of those with enclosed perception, not so much unartistic as anti-artistic; she has "a blue eye that would see just so far and no further" (White, 1961, p 47), a caricature of the sky. With her eyes "blue for mothers" and her pink birthday cakes "for a bad girl" she is a caricature of the wise and homely Peg who served Mary with motherliness as a child, and who is superseded by Mrs Godbold who nurses her when she has pneumonia. The arch-fiend Mrs Flack says her son Blue "has eyes which will see what I want to know" (p. 254). The pseudo-artist projects his own misconceptions and is not open to revelations beyond his own control. When confronted by a manifestation of Chariot-lit "joy" between two people, joyless Flack and Jolley are simply "baffled", because it is beyond their comprehension (p. 247). Their badness takes the anti-artistic form of blurred vision, a substitution for the spiritual realities to which art can penetrate.

Yet there is also a sense in which Mary and Mrs Jolley are partners in crime – not literally, but in terms of feelings of guilt.

192   THE ART OF PERSONALITY

Mary feels she has "killed" her father with her beam of vision – the "crime of seeing" (p. 39) – and Mrs Jolley feels she killed her husband while holding his cup of tea. The pair do not simply contrast; they interdigitate, in a way that stimulates the story's development. Mary terms their relationship "trial by Jolley" (p. 68). Paradoxically, she brings in the housekeeper to begin to destroy the house: to put her in touch with the idea of guilt and innate sinfulness. Without the intimacy of their collision, founded on a recognition that "evil is also good" and anyway "who is to decide what is bad?" (p. 88), there would be no story. Xanadu would crumble gently into the soil as in Mary's idealised escapist desire to "sink into it and the grass will grow out of me" (p. 172). Like many a Romantic she would like to fade far away into the forest dim. But there would be no cracking, no conflagration, no piercing the walls of the cavern. Despite her insistence that "my experience will remain", there would be decay but no revelation. Her self-enclosed dreaming needs to reach out to piebald humanity to become truly artistic. The spiritual education of all the riders is co-extensive with the cracking of Xanadu, through to the point at which it is replaced by ordinary houses for ordinary people to live in: not the values of Jolley claustrophilia, but the daily life inspired by the Godbold heritage, open to the sky – a new heaven and a new earth. White's integrated artistic vision is built out of the ruins of the old Romanticism, its fertile bedrock.

The strange, antagonistic companionship with Mrs Jolley opens up the house of memories for Mary Hare and provides the dynamism for reviewing her buried past history as an ugly, unloved child. This relationship is the precursor to her discovery of Himmelfarb in the garden and consequently, to her finding a love-object in the human not merely the animal world. The crisis of Mrs Jolley killing the snake whose "confidence" she never quite won (p. 92) sends Mary out to the Plum Tree, nature's church, where she encounters the Jew – who ironically describes himself as a "snake" (p. 116). He emerges as if he were indeed a natural, snake-like emanation of the Edenic garden: "And he came out from under the branches" (p. 98). The plum tree's white blossom brings colour back to the sky; the sun hangs on its branches like a premonition of the jacaranda in the crucifixion scene. It is one of those fluid moments, reminiscent of Wordsworth's "spots of time", that White describes as "islands" of reciprocal recognition and understanding in the midst of everyday bustle. These "epiphanies" as they have been termed (Beatson, 1976; Edgecombe, 1989) are marked by the interpenetration of ethereal Chariot imagery with earthly forms – melting moments in

THE EVOLUTION OF ARTISTIC FAITH IN PATRICK WHITE   193

the sky, a watery state of "confusion and solution", the tracery of undergrowth, a "hatching" of light and shadow that causes familiar material forms to disappear. In such a "tent" of semi-materiality Mary Hare and the Jew "go to hell" together, and back. Trial by Jolley has strengthened Mary's capacity to contain evil within her compass of vision; she is ready to serve humanity.

White's narration of the holocaust (one of the earliest fictional recordings) has a documentary quality that makes it read like a novel within a novel, marked halfway by a brief pause to remind us of the existence of protagonist and listener. From it, on a more metaphysical plane, two significant figures emerge who are instrumental in guiding Mordecai in the direction of confronting his identity. On the female side there is the enigmatic Reha, whose conversation is purely practical, of jelly and shopkeepers, yet who may or may not have an unspeaking inward perception. Certainly she is conscious of the fact that there is an "end" and it is nigh. However Mordecai cannot live up to her desire for him to be a Messiah-figure. Her silent faith is in this sense misplaced, and he betrays it, as imaged by their dead dog awaiting him on the threshold of their violated home, after he has run away. Reha reappears in various forms – most hauntingly the Lady from Czernowitz, epitome of the "dark women" of his race whose mysterious music originated, one supposes, in the "strange inexpressible words" that flowed "out of the mouth" of his mother (p. 107), the origin of artistic attentiveness. By the time he arrives in Australia Mordecai has decided that "the intellect has failed us" (p. 221). He takes a job drilling holes at the Brighta factory in order to discipline his arrogance, lest his mind "take its own authority for granted" (p. 337). Reha has helped to rescue him from the sterility of his "niggling intellect" with its "masks of words" (marking White's own suspicions about verbal expression – he believed art and music were more reliably authentic). Reha is partnered in Mordecai's mind by a male promoter of truth in the form of the dyer, who likewise appears a humble character at first, yet turns out to be another hand of God, like Shakespeare's "dyer's hand", running the Chariot blood-colours through the history of the people, and leading to his communion with Dubbo. These aspects intermingle "in the moment of perception" when "all the inklings were married together: the dyer's image was with him for always, like his new wife, or his own fate. Now he was committed ... or must deny his own purpose, as well as the existence of the race" (p. 143).

At the moment when Reha appears at her most perceptive, with her hair-thicket echoing the spokes of the Chariot, shining with an

194   THE ART OF PERSONALITY

inner light (p. 151), Mordecai is pathetically scribbling on a piece of paper, attempting to draw the Chariot in non-verbal terms, yet without the technical or imaginative capacity. Reha implicitly shows him that he is no artist – at least, not yet. As he says to Mary, "it is not clear how we are to use our knowledge, what link we provide in the chain of events" (p. 337). He is waiting to be used as a link in some greater picture, just as White, as author, is depending on the links that tie his complex narrative together to make themselves clear as he progresses. He too is relying on the sensuous, musical and pictorial qualities of symbolism to touch his story into life – brushed by the Chariot-wheels.

Double vision

Mordecai's story is a reminder of the pitfalls of the controlling authorial intellect which hampers poetic inspiration. The pseudo-artistic vision is gloriously satirised in the Brighta Bicycle Lamp Factory at Barranugli. Brighta is White's everyday hell: a benevolent institution with regular holidays, wage-packets, efficient secretaries and rhythmical breaks for the infernal pleasures of "smoke-o". Its barren ugly garden of earthly delights, Bosch-like, is modelled on Milton's Pandemonium (also one of the original sources for Coleridge's Xanadu), a "temple" of light and music from whose "arched roof"

> Pendent by subtle magic many a row
> Of starry lamps and blazing cressets fed
> With naphtha and asphaltus yielded light
> As from a sky. (*Paradise Lost*, I: 727–730)

The casually dropped phrase "as from a sky" is the source of Jolley-blue, the world of imitation mother-values that is espoused with a certain pathos by both Mrs Jolley and Shirl Rosetree in her comic but desperate search for social belonging to cover the wound of her internal lostness. What are people – real living people – if they cannot be Jews? she wonders, and comes up with the formula that they are "methos" (Methodists). "That is what people are, it seems" – meaning, that is a way of being that should guarantee survival.

Brighta is on one level a caricature of the Chariot with its lightful revelations, and Rosetree's efficiency a caricature of the artist's virtuosity. Yet (as with Mary and Mrs Jolley) this is not a purely antithetical contrast. The factory turns out to be a place where individual identities can emerge from the crowd and as at Xanadu, "islands" of fruitful communication can form unexpectedly, even absurdly. There are hints of the heavenly spheres in Dubbo's earthly revolutions of "sweeping ... swept and swept ... an occupation to be endured" (p. 223). The Chariot of artistic inspiration works through music and movement, as well as colour and imagery. Dubbo, the dauber who glories in oilpaints, is a revival of the dyer from Mordecai's previous life (just as Reha reappears in the form of Ruth). His mechanical sweeping is what brings him closer to the Jew, who is analogously drilling and drilling, in expiation of his own sins – not those of the world, as he does eventually come to realise. White pursues the implications of his own descriptive language with its sensuous word-clusters, until connections begin to form. He has already located Himmelfarb's need to connect with a non-intellectual mode of seeing, through his scribble-drawing of the Chariot. Alf Dubbo can create images that are capable of "seeing" his ongoing inner anguish, just as Mary Hare has absorbed his story into her imaginative house of memories. This is confirmed, comically, by the foreman's diagnosis that Himmelfarb "needs a mate", which is then prophetically fulfilled by his "meeting the silence" of the abo in the midst of the noise of the factory. At the same time the drill echoes the vibrating of the voices of the dark women inside him, a type of music. When the black's sweeping comes "level with the Jew's drill" there is "a certain warmth of presence" (p. 229). There is an engagement of wheels. The picture of artistic activity is enriched by the emotional links sparked by their disparate, apparently opposing, talents: Mordecai's intellectual faith will learn to harmonise with Dubbo's repudiation of his religious upbringing, creating between them something more authentic than either, in terms of artistic insight.

Later it is the sweeping cycle-movement that also links Dubbo with Mrs Godbold and her ironing "in long, sad, steamy sweeps, singing as she did", her own mode of worship (p. 257). Her "skill in passing the iron over the long strips of fresh, fuming, glistening sheets" echoes the Chariot-language of strips of gleaming light and circling repetitive movement. This is the way she fulfils her personal mission, which was set in motion after she failed to save her brother as a child being crushed by the wheels of the haywain, the cruel or deadly Chariot of fate: "as the wheel of minutes ground ... as the wheel of the cart trundled, lurched" (p. 267). So she learns the limits of her personal strength, realising that she cannot of her own will "hold off the weight of the

196 THE ART OF PERSONALITY

entire world". This traumatic episode is necessary to establish her faith, which then shines through in her personal solidity as "white maid", "white pillar", "white tower", its means of expression her "white ironing board". She becomes a vehicle for the Chariot's light: like a work of art herself, her white sculptural being takes shape, with its spiritual connotations – the wheels of solid gold. When the desperate Mrs Chalmers-Robinson begs Ruth for a "peep" into her tower of inner strength she finds it hard to accept that "If I was to tell, it doesn't follow that you would see. Everybody sees different. You must only see it for yourself" (p. 299). "'Tell, Ruth, tell!' begged the mistress." From the flatness of the fens, which are echoed in her bone structure and visage, emerges Ruth's scaffolding of internal harmony like Ely Cathedral itself. Ruth's encounter with Dubbo reinforces her own inner identity, and enables her to emotionally detach herself from the "weaker side" of herself that had found its false vocation in supporting her useless husband Tom. When Tom dies, so does "Mrs Godbold's self". Ultimately her own children will be in a position to profit from her experience and to make better, more equal, marriages of reciprocal give and take; they become a model for a new artistry of living.

Thus the cyclings that occur in the cycle-lamp factory are not merely mechanical but also spiritual encounters, Chariot-tinged. Mrs Godbold's ironing, and the similar movement of washing, resulting from the gashing of the drill and the blood pouring in the washroom at Brighta ("strangely, fascinatingly beautiful"), is what brings all three riders together: "so the golden chains continued to unwind, the golden circles to revolve" (p. 247). Reha is relived in the form of Ruth, from whose statuesque form emanates the final message Himmelfarb has to take on board: namely that when all the faith-colours run together on the banks of the last river, and it is finished, "it is the same" (p. 500). Artistic vision, we learn from the novel, is essentially comprehensive, though it may be flawed by dogma as a result of the artist's personal imperfections. The picture of the artist that develops as the novel progresses increases in complexity as the author appreciates the psychological and spiritual tensions generated by his characters' interaction. The links made not only between characters but in overall symbolic structure reflect back into the psyche of the novelist, if we continue to regard his writing as exploratory rather than preconceived, as indeed White always insisted himself. The idea of the artist lodges not in any one character but in their interweaving into "the Whole" of the art-symbol.

Integration and recognition

Alf Dubbo's history is the last to be narrated, since his job is to gather the threads of the narrative together into the fabric of the novel, integrating the vision of the writer. His name derives not only from his colour-daubing but also from the doubling of his parental figures. His ancestors are referred to metaphorically as a mixture of Irish descent and the "Great Snake" of the aboriginal dreamtime (also known as the "rainbow snake"); they are white and black, English and colonial. There is also a sense in which his biological and his foster-parents represent different aspects of the same couple. On the one hand there is his whore-mother with her client; on the other, the sexually unfulfilled parson-father whose platonic "sister" is obsessed by the "strength and loveliness" of some imaginary dead previous husband. Mrs Pask introduces Alf to the sensuality of oilpaints yet is horrified by what he does with them – producing vermilion foetuses that will later reappear in the form of aboriginal whorls and dreamtime markings in his painting of the Deposition. Calderon points out that she has merely "uncovered his imagination". In effect this is what he does himself when he reveals the sad, soft-hearted "white worm" at the core of his being, the vestigial shadow of his sexuality. Alf has a "piebald soul" (p. 415) and needs to find some way of integrating these double parents within himself if he is to fulfil his artistic mission. His mind is like not one but "two fish, since the white people his guardians had dropped another in" (p. 393). His seduction by his father becomes a type of initiation rite, driving him out of the parental home. As with Ruth Goldbold, a moment of trauma launches him into life. His vocation, he discovers, is to wander the banks of the archetypal river which is the "lifestream of all outcasts, goats and aboriginals" (p. 351), investigating the rubbish dump where the townsfolk keep their "true selves", using his talent to explore the hidden reaches of humanity. He is sent by his destiny to live with maternal whores, through whom he learns about those other, original (aboriginal) parents whose "metho love" flickers with "livid jags" of passion, like lightning, as they "danced together on the squeaky bed" (p. 361). The pun on "metho" with its purple flames highlights the contrast with Mrs Rosetree who believes that being a "metho" is the way to become safe and respectable. She seeks refuge in an institutional badge and in consequence becomes a lost soul; whereas what is (in appearance) the same word signifies for the nascent artist the colour-play of an inner "fire".

198   THE ART OF PERSONALITY

At Mrs Khalil's, Dubbo is their "pet abo" (a play on sound). The warmth of this alternative family sponsors another link in the artistic chain of being: his semi-mystical communion with Ruth Godbold. Ruth is searching for her renegade husband Tom, but finds Dubbo; and their pathways are redirected. Dubbo is drunkenly singing an absurd travesty of a song of praise:

And Brighta Lamps,
To see with,
To see see see,
And be with ... (p. 315)

It is an invocation to the imitation Chariot – or is it the real one, in earthly disguise? In its light, lying on the floor, with sidelong gaze, Dubbo discovers a new angle on things. He holds his arm across his face "to see better" and says "Now I think I see ... I will get it all in time". The two riders participate reciprocally in one of those dreamier moments of abstraction – "not exactly watching, for they each had their thoughts" (p. 320). It is another island of contemplation in the midst of the "commotion of life", an artistic dream where confused emotions can take symbolic shape. In the mind of Mrs Godbold, "watching the scaffolding of music as it was erected", Dubbo's drunken chant conjures the cathedral of her childhood in the Fens, where the same phrase "scaffolding of sound" had created a golden ladder heavenwards "as if to reach the window of a fire" (p. 264). The same imagery recurs later, linking Chariot and cathedral, when Mary imagines the Jew's face on its pillow-pillar of fire being the source of a "canopy of golden stalactites" (p. 471). For Dubbo, at Mrs Khalil's, the scene is now set for the time when his "secret self" will be "singing at last". His nascent creativity is drawn out by the bright human pageantry before his eyes.

Meanwhile, back at Brighta, Dubbo has put out an unconscious invitation to intimacy in the form of the Bible left open in the washroom at the passage with Ezekiel and the Chariot. As part of his artistic development he needs to remake, or repair, his internal contact with his pastor father, and he intuits Himmelfarb's pastor-like ability to read the sacred book. Himmelfarb (heaven-touched) and Calderon (cauldron) are complementary father-figures; they constitute a type of marriage of heaven and hell in Dubbo's mind – and as Blake made clear, both elements are required for artistic vision. The communion is mutual: now it is Himmelfarb's turn to discover a voice that is "utterly his own", as he reads aloud to

THE EVOLUTION OF ARTISTIC FAITH IN PATRICK WHITE   199

the musical accompaniment of tap and cistern. Reciprocally, this link puts Dubbo back in touch with his formal education. Dubbo claims to read the Bible "not for any of *his* reasons" (his father's) but because "you can see it all" (p. 349). Nonetheless beneath this specious distinction he seems to suspect a way in which he has "betrayed" the pastor by renouncing his upbringing; and at the same time, a way of atoning or making reparation for it by means of contact with the Jew. It is not of course the normal contact of a relationship, but an engaging of Chariot-wheels, a brushing of feathers. Indeed one of Alf's characteristics is an emotional detachment that goes with his sense of artistic vocation; when he appears to smile, it is not a spontaneous expression of joy as with Mrs Godbold, but a trick of light "concentrated on the planes of his excellent teeth" (p. 351). He has by now renounced the hypocritical "agreeable voice" in which he had told Mrs Pask he would like to paint Jesus Christ, and is discovering instead the deeper blood-identification which will lead to his imprinting a "little dirty trumpet" on the pillow – his soul's voice or signature. His tubercular disease becomes his personal receptor of the "jarring emotions" of those he brushes against on street corners, river banks, factory floors. The emotions then emerge in colour through his finger-tips, in artistic response. The "jewellery of wounds" flows equally from "blood or paint" (p. 487).

Yet another duality, between Himmelfarb and Rosetree, again hides a deeper congruence within its contrast, and leads us to the denouement – the mock crucifixion. From the moment of their first encounter the rider and his alter-ego are touched into unwilling recognition. It begins with the transaction at the employment office, when Himmelfarb is directed by a minor character – comically unconscious of the truth he is enunciating – to enrol under the "kinda continental" management of the factory – "made for you personally" (p. 222). Himmelfarb is Haim/Harry's name-echo and core of identity, the dark voice from his own aboriginal roots that has found employment within his own version of Xanadu – the factory. Acknowledging this voice and face is dangerous, no longer because of the holocaust without but because of the holocaust within. His "rosy" daughter understands this, with her fascination with saints and roses, and so does his wife – but she prefers to shut out the knowledge through her ruthless jolley-materialism. The crucifixion scene is felt by many to be an example of authorial enforcement rather than of artistic faith in the story's evolution. If we consider its wider context, however, this picture of the self-sacrificing or missionary qualities of the artist becomes more complex. As throughout the novel, the qualities of an individual are modified by those of other characters and play their part in a definition of artistic faith that is still in process – hence the governing metaphor of the Chariot with its continually turning wheels. Thus the artistic nature of Himmelfarb himself has similarities with White's earlier Christlike hero Voss, whom he described as "megalomanic" (White, 1988, p. 104). He appears to be an example of artistic hubris. Yet in *Riders* he is not alone but one of a pair, and this affects the emotional balance and hence the meaning. It is not the difference between Mordecai and Haim that gives the final holocaust its aura of transcendence, but rather, their fusion. It is intellectually absurd, but artistically inspired. Himmelfarb's fate is the expression of Rosetree's inner state when faced with a demand to commit himself to his own identity.

The prelude to the mock crucifixion is when Rosetree sees Himmelfarb's two eyes framed but "set at discrepant angles". He then sees how they fuse together, like beams or spokes, to make more than their sum: "all the lines of vision that could be traced from the discrepant eyes, fell into focus ... to make the one great archetypal face" (p. 424). It is "disturbing, exhilarating, frightening" – is it anger or joy? It is perhaps a mixture of all these that leads Harry/Haim to see himself as he is – as "Himmelfarb", touched by rosy-fingered heaven – and then to begin to write "Mordecai" (the word of death) in the steaminess of the bathroom mirror. The mirror takes over from the hatchway as frame for his self-recognition. It is a form of painting, a self-portrait. Like rosy strings of sunset clouds, "the least vein in his terrible eyeballs was fully revealed to him" (p. 503). The burnt-out childhood of the archetypal scapegoat smokes heavenward in the two-faced, one-faced Jew, in empathy with what has happened to his alter-ego in his own factory – his own mental world. Seeing through the glass darkly, steamily, smokily, is the prelude to seeing face to face. His own scribble-painting picks up Mordecai's earlier attempt to draw the Chariot, under Reha's observation; and vindicates his death as a type of symbolic poetry. Rosetree's meeting in the mirror is analogous to the meeting of Himmelfarb with his father Moshe in the "acetylene nebula" of his semi-conscious state as he drifts into death on Mrs Godbold's kitchen table, finally achieving the heart attack that releases his spirit.

At the end of the death scene, Mrs Godbold observes that "He was, you might say, overlooked" (p. 501). It is perhaps a riskily over-cerebral pun on White's part, given that the writer is close to establishing his own overview of his materials. But the sensuous

THE EVOLUTION OF ARTISTIC FAITH IN PATRICK WHITE 201

links work – leading forwards into the mirror-scene with Rosetree, and backwards to the eyes in the hatchway, then to Dubbo watching the deposition scene through the window of the shed. A small movement confirms the transference of emotion: when young Maude Godbold thinks she "sees a face" by the fire's dying purple light, and we then realise it is Dubbo's (p. 485). These events are framed as on a canvas, like the Table that contains the Whole – chairs, children, cows and asses, poets and prophets – in its chain of being. Dubbo's watching reminds us faintly of Flackeian voyeurism – of which the artist probably always has some tinge, rather as the war correspondent is always looking for a subject, even to the extent of stealing a scene. There is a resonance here with centuries of religious painting in which a self-portrait of the painter, however small and insignificant, is included at the foot of the Cross. Himmelfarb is of course unconscious of Dubbo watching through the window. His identification with him as a Chariot-rider, however, has been expressed throughout in terms of both flowing river and mechanical circling movements. Now on the banks of the interminable and ultimate river, "he who had drilled holes, could not stop now for souls, whatever the will, whatever the love", a musical expression of how his strictly Jewish identity, when acknowledged rather than denied, has eventually led him to greater universality (p. 491).

As the threads of the artistic tapestry are pulled together, Mary Hare feels the "fluttering bones" of Himmelfarb's Chariot-wheels against her cheek and is "translated. Her animal body became the least part of her, as breathing thoughts turned to being" (p. 485). Her blind tunnelling through the undergrowth around Xanadu is superseded, because now, "direction had at last chosen her". In her individual way, like the others, she embodies artistic inspiration. At the end, she knows about the fire before she sees it, just as "when placed right at the core of her great house, she would sense mist climbing up out of the gullies" (p. 472); she intuits the vaporous message of Coleridge's chasms and their heralding a new state of being. This state has the archetypal quality of the type of death that underlies classical tragic form – the commitment to a transformation which Kierkegaard would term a leap of faith. The "spokes burnt black" of her wicker hat show her empathy with Himmelfarb's condition, a conflagration caused by the Chariot, at the same time marking the cracks in the fabric of Xanadu that release her spirit from fleshly confines. What literally happens to her after this is left deliberately unknown, but her message is received by Dubbo as through painting he reinstates her in her

202   THE ART OF PERSONALITY

natural habitat, a "ring-tailed possum in a dreamtime womb". The collapse of Xanadu in effect allows culture and artisanship to merge back into their aboriginal unconscious roots with its dreamtime "whorls" of wind, animals and water, the banks of the river "reversing the relationship between permanence and motion" (p. 514). The whorls and whirling of primitive primary colours are held within a Chariot whose shape is only half-visualised, for the painter realises it does not need to be realistically depicted. But the riders, he knows, must emphatically exist as paintable earthly presences. They provide something for us to identify with, and it is their inter-relationship that gives structure to the picture as a whole.

It is in line with this that Mrs Godbold and her children remain to carry on the story, their earthiness and solidity comprising those "straight white shafts" that halt "the face of darkness" and "see further" than others. They see further than both the brick-box of philistine respectability and the grand ruin of imagination's pleasure-dome. The beautiful ending of the novel echoes that of *Paradise Lost* when, with the conflagration of Eden in the background, the "hast'ning angel" leads Adam and Eve down the hill with "the world all before them". The art of living transcends even that of dying; and Mrs Godbold supersedes Mary Hare who initially guided our eyes into the imaginary thicket:

> Now she could approach her work of living as an artist after an interval will approach and judge his work of art ... She would lower eyes to avoid the dazzle and walk on, breathing heavy, for it was a stiff pull up the hill, to the shed in which she continued to live (p. 551).

The pull up the hill is the final revolution of the Chariot-wheels that crushed her brother. Like Mother Courage she carries on with the cart and the world on her back. She has learned to "avoid the dazzle" and so can "go further" than the relativist Hegelians, despised by Kierkegaard, without being swallowed by the impact of knowledge.

White referred to "the cast of contradictory characters of which I am composed" (White, 1988, p. 20); and in *Riders*, we can see how the tensions set up by these contradictions, with their sensuous immersion in artistic process, are combined into a greater "Whole" which ultimately defines the novelist's credo. The four main characters illustrate various facets of the artist: Mary Hare's absorption in natural process shapes her search for an object of devotion which will transform her being; Himmelfarb's cerebral

THE EVOLUTION OF ARTISTIC FAITH IN PATRICK WHITE   203

intellectualism is discarded when he realises it was a futile attempt to deny his identity; Dubbo's detached egocentricity facilitates his dabbling in the colours of the ancient unconscious; Ruth Godbold gathers her materials (both flesh and linen) into formal harmony on a table-top, an artistic frame for experience. They are all servants rather than originators of the Chariot's impulsion, as artists always feel about their inspiration. They are all "elements" in the total fabric of the work, and serve its "underlying idea". They have their individual guilts and talents. But only in the creative tension of their conjunction do they have communicative power, the back-breaking power to suspend disbelief and pull the reader up the hill. The artistic mind is one that can encompass and reflect this wholeness – the integration of disparate and disjunctive elements into an organically evolving art-symbol. The Chariot itself, which started as an authorial technical device, gradually gains authority as an integrating force as it touches the novel's elements into life and its form acquires inevitability. In accordance with "learning from experience" in the psychoanalytic sense (Bion, 1962), the author's mind is made by its own creation. Identifying with this process, and with the riders' varying artistry, the reader is empathically drawn along in the Chariot of the work in its quest for the integrity of artistic faith.

CHAPTER NINE

On psychoanalytic autobiography[1]

My longstanding interest in psychoanalytic autobiography became more substantial as a result of teaching for several years a module on Narratives of the Self for a course in Psychoanalytic Studies. The close correspondences with various aspects of psychoanalytic method suggested to me that it might be of interest to therapists to survey some of the general characteristics of psychoanalytic autobiography, garnered mainly from the sayings of those who have written their own or who have made a special study of autobiographical writings.

The last century saw an upsurge of interest in autobiography or "life-writing" – the art of narrating the self – that was no doubt influenced by the advent of psychoanalysis, since when there evolved a category of autobiography which sees itself as deliberately psychoanalytic, and a companion category of literary criticism of autobiographies from an overtly psychoanalytic point of view. No modern autobiography can have been written without somehow measuring itself in relation to psychoanalysis, implicitly or explicitly. Bion defined psychoanalysis as a means of introducing the patient to himself; and autobiography is another of those means. In this chapter therefore I would like to consider the

---

1   A version of this chapter was first published in *Psychodynamic Practice*, 18 (2012), pp. 397–412.

nature of autobiography as a particular mode of writing which, like psychoanalysis, attempts to answer the question posed so simply and eloquently by King Lear: "Who is it that can tell me who I am?" (*King Lear*, I. iv. 238).

Sometimes a distinction is made between "autobiography" and "memoir"; however I shall use the terms interchangeably, since in any case people define them differently. Virginia Woolf complained that standard biographies and memoirs related only external events and omitted "the person to whom things happened" (Woolf, 2002, p. 79). G. B. Shaw said that "Things have not happened to me ... it is I who have happened to them" (cited in Finney, 1985, p. 13). Dr Boswell said rather wistfully of his good friend Samuel Johnson that if all their friends had diligently joined their memories together, Dr Johnson "might have been almost entirely preserved" (cited in Anderson, 2001, p. 34). In fact it was the intimacy of his personal, subjective record that gave eternal life to his subject; his *Life of Dr Johnson* is autobiography as much as biography.

I shall not be looking at the kind of autobiography where the main interest lies in the author having lived through major historical events or known important people, nor at the kind that attempts to record all the facts or events in a person's life, as if a complete accumulation of facts might amount to a truthful picture of mind or character. Nor is it necessary to confine one's definition to auto-biographies which explicitly label themselves as psychoanalytic – especially since these tend to be bound to specific psychoanalytic theories or popular interpretations of them and of what psycho-analysis is about (childhood trauma, repression, etc).

Rather, I propose to adopt, as a definition for psychoanalytic autobiography, writing that interests itself in the essence of a personality over a period of time, using time itself as a structural co-ordinate, and using the vivid depiction of external events, people and places, as its medium or means to an end – namely, that of interior observation. This is in line with definitions of autobiography such as that of B. Mandel: "The autobiographical consciousness is that which thinks about itself present, past and future" (in Olney, p. 49). This is a self-analytic journey of discovery, and its writers often consciously view themselves as involved in a process of actively remaking their present lives. As the poet Edwin Muir put it: "I must take stock of my own life, and though that is in appearance an investigation of the past, I know it is important for the future: because of the change that it must bring about" (cited in Finney, p. 199). And closely scrutinising one's life is liable to change it. For as Bion says: "In an analytic situation there is the analyst, a patient

ON PSYCHOANALYTIC AUTOBIOGRAPHY 207

and a third party who is watching – always" (Bion, 2005a, p. 19); and "the thing itself is altered by being observed" (1991, p. 216). The change is an integral feature of the additional dimension.

Affinities

Autobiographers characteristically observe their present activity of remembering at the same time as their past life in memory; it is part of the same story. Montaigne, with intentional paradoxicality, called this kind of autobiographical contemplation "the greatest act": "Have you known how to meditate and manage your life, you have performed the greatest act of all … I have no more made my book than my book has made me" (Montaigne, 1908, p. 469). If the writing is successful – sufficiently artistic – it takes on a life beyond the author's knowledge and intentions, that reflects back on himself, and on others through empathy. Precisely because of this sense of personal discovery, such a work inspires the reader to know better not just the writer, but themselves.

Autobiography as a genre is underpinned by a network of philosophical and metaphysical associations to such questions as the nature of memory, of truth, of values, of consciousness, of being and becoming, of reality itself, etc., all of which have their relevance to psychoanalysis. It is also, inevitably, much concerned with childhood, with the family and internal family, and with the principles of personality development. And there is in autobiography an implied intimate relationship with the reader – a special invitation to identify, with a transference quality, as if the reader's empathy were necessary to its fulfilment. This sense of a strong tie with an outsider or "other", stronger than in other genres, has been called a "memoir-making force" (Larson, 2007, p. 164).

James Gammill has recorded a conversation with Melanie Klein in which she pointed out to him the following passage from Proust's *Le Temps Retrouvé* (1927): "I would ask of them neither to praise nor to denigrate me, but only to indicate whether the words they read in themselves correspond to that which I have written" (cited by Gammill, 2012, p. 40). Proust defines here the kind of empathy he requires in a reader, and Mrs Klein implies she is asking for the same type of objective self-scrutiny. It is typical of the active response that the autobiographer imagines in his reader, a genuine "correspondence" of words, somewhat analogous to Meltzer's (1983) description of the analyst's countertransference and the dream which is evoked in his own mind.

208   THE ART OF PERSONALITY

There are many affinities therefore between psychoanalysis and autobiography. Some have even considered autobiography to be the first mode of psychoanalysis, starting perhaps with St Augustine's *Confessions* which have been described as the first deliberate "manifesto of the inner world" (Brown, 1967, p. 205), set in motion by the author's mourning processes following the death of his mother, in classic psychoanalytic fashion. There is a sense of course in which all art forms are autobiographical – and not just the literary forms; this goes back presumably to some pre-historical point at which the individual became differentiated from the group and recognised intuitively that there is such a thing as an individual consciousness, when man became self-aware. This is the "self-reflexive consciousness" of which Coleridge spoke – implying a perspective beyond the self, as when Meltzer writes that commonsense "cannot conceive of a realm of mind that is beyond self, as Freud has taught us to do with his discovery of the concreteness of the superego" (1973, p. 150). The earliest long narrative ever transcribed – Homer's *Odyssey* – can be taken as a type of veiled and dreamlike autobiography (as James Joyce recognised when he wrote his own *Ulysses*). For it is wellknown that the boundary between fiction and autobiography is a fluid one. Christopher Isherwood said all his novels were "a kind of fictional autobiography... autobiography is always fiction" (cited by Finney, p. 90).

The search for truthful forms

Autobiography can take almost any form, from fiction and history through to philosophy and even scientific theory. Valéry said that "there is no theory that is not a fragment, carefully prepared, of some autobiography" (1958, p. 58). Freud wrote a literal autobiography but found it uninteresting, and said his real autobiography was to be found in *The Interpretation of Dreams*. He wrote: "This book has a further subjective significance for me personally – a significance which I only grasped after I had completed it" (1900, p. xxvi). Jung too wrote his *Memories, Dreams, Reflections*; and Muir confirmed that "No autobiography can confine itself to conscious life ... sleep is a mode of experience, and dreams a part of reality" (1980, p. 49). Take, for example, a dream recounted by Joan Baez about her father – or two fathers:

> Last night I had a dream about him. I dreamed he was sitting next to himself in a theater. One of him was as he is now, and the other

was the man of thirty years ago. I kept trying to get him to look at himself and say hello. Both faces smiled very understandingly, but neither would turn to greet the other.

I don't think he's ever understood me very well … (Baez, 1977, p. 265.)

The fathers that cannot look at one another – that do not join across time despite watching the same play – embody the gap in communication with the daughter.

The premise for anyone writing a psychoanalytic autobiography is that any individual mind, however ordinary, is of enduring value if it is engaged in the process of searching for the truth about itself, and if this self can be artistically brought to life. As Hegel said, "consciousness of self is the birthplace of truth" (cited in Gusdorf, 1980, p. 38). Bion says simply, in the preface to his autobiography *The Long Week-End*:

In this book my intention has been to be truthful. It is an exalted ambition; after many years of experience I know that the most I can claim is to be "relatively" truthful. … By "truth" I mean "aesthetic truth" and "psychoanalytic truth"; this last I consider to be a "grade" of scientific truth. (Bion, 1982, p. 8)

These words echo Rousseau's flagship declaration for the Romantic movement:

I have begun on a work which is without precedent, whose accomplishment will have no imitator. I propose to set before my fellow-mortals a man in all the truth of nature; and this man shall be myself … I should like to make my soul transparent to the reader's eye. (Rousseau, 1782, p. 1)

Rousseau's ideal may be regarded as naïve by the modern or postmodern cynical eye which knows there is no such thing as "transparency". Yet Bion (who regarded the Romantics as the first psychoanalysts) tackles this sort of cynicism and defeats it through a more careful and precise formulation. He insists on retaining truth (in its multiple vertices) as an aspiration for psychoanalytic autobiography, however difficult of attainment.

Joseph Conrad too, in his *Personal Record,* wrote of the "asceticism of sentiment" in which "leaves [of a novel] must follow upon each other as leagues used to follow in the days gone by, on and on to the appointed end … Truth itself" (Conrad, 2008, p. 223). Being a novelist, telling tales of the sea, his real autobiography

210   THE ART OF PERSONALITY

lay in his novels, truth-driven like a ship on the waves. His course may be set by the compass, but once launched, his story is not self-controlled – it unfolds, with leaves like leagues; it has inevitability, like Coleridge's *Ancient Mariner*. The autobiographer, it has been often said, is not so much writing about himself, as "writing himself".

This does not mean he can invent his own persona. As Conrad said himself, "Imagination, not invention, is the supreme master of art as of life" (*ibid*, p. 228); or Bion, likewise, in the context of describing observation processes, advises: "Concentrate on what you imagine – speculative imagination, speculative reason" (Bion, 2005a, p. 17). Invention has no necessary connection with truth. Psychoanalytic autobiography is in the service of imagination: even if it may appear to be "all lies" (as Shaw maintained), these have to point to some psychic truth. This has to be *perceived* by the author, not invented by his omnipotent self. He expects the book to deliver his self-knowledge – to *himself.*

It has been said that autobiography is a unique genre in that "all the portraits of other people contribute to the central selfportrait" (Finney, p. 81). Finney cites E. M. Forster on the "word-masses" which are the novelist's "characters" and which, in sum, "roughly describe himself" (the author). Perhaps indeed, as Forster's remark suggests, autobiography is not so unique in this – the same may be said of many fictional narratives or dramas. The point is that the self-portrait, in whatever genre, must be accurately observed, not embroidered or idealised. Bion warns that he is not writing about the real people and communities that form the fabric of his story:

> I write about "me" ... This book is about the relationships of one man and *not* about the people, communities, groups whose names are mentioned. If I could have resorted to abstractions I would have done so. Such a procedure, without any preparation, would leave the reader grappling with meaningless manipulations of jargon.
>   (Bion, 1982, p. 8).

He describes his narrative as "the formulation of phenomena as close as possible to noumena". The "phenomena" are the people, places, events that form the context of his life. They are vividly evoked (otherwise they do not catch the reader's imagination), but the purpose of their existence in the narrative is to map some principle or mental pattern within the author's own mind – the "noumenal" pattern. St Beuve wrote: "Memoirs look to an essence beyond existence, and in manifesting they serve to create it" (cited in Gusdorf, p. 47) – this is the existential side of autobiography.

Dealing with the same existentialist penumbra, Kierkegaard insists that in his many pseudonymous works "there is not a single word which is mine" and his role is merely to take on the "civil responsibility" for the utterances of these fictional authors: "That is I am impersonally or personally in the third person a *souffleur* [prompter] who has poetically produced the authors" (Kierkegaard, 1992, pp. 625-26). On the one hand, this is a metaphysical stance familiar in theories of poetry, as when Keats describes the poet as one who "has no identity" because he has dispersed his own amongst his characters (Keats, 1970, p. 157). The poet is the detached observer of an intimate conflictual dialogue which is both his (experienced "on the pulses" as Keats would say) and not his. (Kierkegaard does in fact describe this collaboration between two parts of his author-self in terms of masculine and feminine.) On the other hand, we sense that he can tolerate the internal investigation only when veiling his own identity in the guise of Constantius, Climacus or de Silentio, "peeping out through the loopholes" (to borrow Keats's phrase [1970, p. 268]). The works constitute a "covert autobiography" (Sprinker, 1992, p. 330).

In *Repetition*, Kierkegaard claims that the character Regina, whose existence he finds tormenting because it brings home to him his own lack of faith in love, is "not a reality but a reflection of the movements within him and their exciting cause" (cited in Sprinker, p. 330). The "movement" is the psychoanalytic one of loss and the struggle to regain (or to repair), just as Bion's movement is to metabolise his self-accusation of cowardice by re-encountering the ghosts that haunt his mind. Yet none of these works would achieve their "abstract" goal of internal patterning without being rooted in *mimesis*, the successful representation of external realities, of life as it is lived. The more effectively writing reminds us of "a life", the deeper and more abstract can be its meaning. And if philosophy can be written autobiographically, then so can (and perhaps should) psychoanalytic papers. According to Meltzer, every "honest" psychoanalytic paper is autobiographical and therefore "aspires to being a work of art" (1983, p. 165); herein lies its originality. If it is not autobiographical, perhaps it is not truly psychoanalytic either. Such papers should not be (Bion complained) "a pain to read" (1980, p. 127).

212   THE ART OF PERSONALITY

Taking responsibility for one's "self"

All these authors are trying to direct the reader's attention away from the voyeuristic attitude of unearthing the secrets of someone else's life (the attitude of pronouncing judgement), to the analytic one of learning *how someone else thinks* – which cannot be done without parallel self-analysis on the part of the reader. D. H. Lawrence famously advised to "Never trust the artist. Trust the tale" (1971, p. 8); he meant, there is a difference between the writer's intentions, and the teller as embodied in the tale. One is liable to project a preconceived image of the self; the other will (if well written) construct an identity for the self organically, from within the body of the work. (Coleridge's famous distinction between "mechanical" and "organic" modes of composition is apt here.) The "truth" lies in the tale itself, for both author and reader, and its meaning cannot be superimposed by either the reader or the conscious, deliberating self of the author. Kierkegaard's defensiveness may be seen in the light of an attempt to protect the wider significance of his tale, which he does not wish to be restricted to transient time, place and personality; for "my personal actuality is a constraint that the pseudonymous authors in pathos-filled wilfulness might wish removed, the sooner the better, or made as insignificant as possible" (Kierkegaard, 1992, p. 627). Too much literalness means there is not space for enough feminine hidden meaning. The reader must take responsibility for empathy ("pathos") rather than dismissing it as merely the writer's attempt to relieve himself of uncomfortable and indigestible feelings.

The writer himself of course can use existentialism and psychoanalytic abstractions to *avoid* his own self-analysis. The ways in which "knowing about" psychoanalytic theory can replace "knowing" (in Bion's terms) is familiar in psychoanalysis. Yeats wrote a deliberately symbolic autobiography, changing characters into archetypes and making a virtue of them being "reborn as an idea, something intended, complete" (cited in Olney, 1980, p. 262). They become allegorical signs or labels – "something intended" – rather than real symbols, which are organic and evolutive. Olney writes: "Yeats could always plead a weak factual memory coupled with a strong creative forgetfulness" (p. 262). But it doesn't ring true. This deliberate abstracting reads as vanity rather than self-analysis. It contrasts completely with the vigour of his poetry with its urgency and hawklike self-scrutiny. So there is a category one might call fake psychoanalytic autobiography; and perhaps some

ON PSYCHOANALYTIC AUTOBIOGRAPHY   213

of the fashionable efflorescence of accounts of abused childhoods also fall into this category. Psychoanalysis is not in essence about trauma and abuse, nor about using archetypes as beautiful masks to cover over what Yeats so vividly terms the "rag and bone shop of the heart" (a genuine poetic symbol). "Myself must I remake", he truly wrote in that same poem ("An acre of grass") – a maxim for all psychoanalytic autobiography. The therapeutic task is neither to wipe clean nor to blame external circumstance, but to "uncover the resistances that oppose this extension of [the patient's] knowledge about himself" (Freud, 1919, p. 159); or as the ancient classical dictum puts it, to "know thyself".

Keats's famous reinterpretation of the world as a "vale of soul-making" rather than a vale of tears, is a fable about how a "spark of identity", come from God, is schooled by its encounter with a "world of circumstances" into a fully fledged soul (1970, pp. 249–151). Others write of the "consciousness of self" that remains constant and at the core of other emotional events that occur around it. In two evocative passages cited by Norman Holland in his book *The I*, we have firstly the poet G. M. Hopkins writing of "my selfbeing, my consciousness and feeling of my self, that taste of myself, of *I* and *me* alone and in all things which is more distinctive than the taste of ale or alum, more distinctive than the smell of walnut leaf or camphor, and is incommunicable by any means to another man" (cited in Holland, 1985, p. ix). This revives his childhood question, "what must it be to be someone else?" Then a passage from Tolstoy compares his consciousness in childhood and in old age:

> I am conscious of myself in exactly the same way now, at eighty-one, as I was conscious of myself, my "I", at five or six years of age. Consciousness is immovable. Due to this alone there is the movement which we call "time". If time *moves on*, there must be something that stands still. The consciousness of my "I" stands still.
>   (cited in Holland, 1985, p. ix)

While Hopkins' self-consciousness arouses in him an awareness of otherness, Tolstoy's makes him aware of "the movement which we call 'time'." We know from Heraclitus that it is impossible to step into the same river twice, so when time enterst he picture, even if consciousness is "standing still", it is clear that the self is not a simple but a dramatic entity. Virginia Woolf used this tension to give aesthetic shape to her narrative when she spoke of "making the two people, I now, I then, come out in contrast" (Woolf, 2002, p. 87).

214   THE ART OF PERSONALITY

Autobiography, writes Gusdorf, "requires a man to take a distance with regard to himself, in order to reconstitute himself in the focus of his special unity and identity across time" (1992, p. 35). This entails an opportunity for internal reality to triumph – on the lines of "Death, thou shalt die". Time becomes redeemable (rather than "unredeemable" as in T. S. Eliot's *Burnt Norton*) when a link is made between two aspects of the self, entering the river at different moments – makes time redeemable; there is a second chance to relive that past moment, even if "only" internally. Thus Shakespeare's Richard II, after relinquishing his "hollow crown", and imprisoned in the cell where he will shortly meet his death, meditates on time: "I wasted time, and now doth time waste me" (V. v. 49). His words are a measure of his new self-knowledge and in that sense they redeem the time he previously wasted through hollow narcissism. Redeeming time can also germinate those life-shoots which were never really experienced on the pulses or given a chance to flourish, as when Jung writes: "Many aspects of life which should also have been experienced lie in the lumber-room amongst dusty memories, glowing coals under grey ashes" (Jung, 2001, p. 106).

Spots of time

It is in this context, of attempting to redeem time, that autobiography is often felt to be therapeutic for the writer. "One sheds one's sicknesses in books", said D. H. Lawrence, "in order to be master of them" (cited in Finney, p. 162). Pascal wrote in his *Pensées* (1670) that "man's unhappiness arises from one thing alone: that he cannot remain quietly in his room" (Pascal, 2005, p. 38). And a modern autobiographer, Thomas Larson, writes: "I learned that anyone who could narrate his condition and its development within his family could be freed from that condition [of imprisonment]. The way out of the cell … came for me through writing memoir" (Larson, 2007, p. 183). Through autobiography, the cell or claustrum may be converted into a room for thoughts, *pensées*. There is a difference between transformation and evacuation however – as in Clive James's justification: "Sick of being a prisoner of my childhood, I want to put it behind me … the mainspring of a confessional urge is guilt" (James, 1980, p. 1). The "evacuative" sort of autobiography is not truly self-analytic.

Marion Milner's interest in psychoanalysis was preceded by *A Life of One's Own* (1934) in which she conveys her experiments in

ON PSYCHOANALYTIC AUTOBIOGRAPHY   215

self-awareness, and describes how writing things down enhanced the quality of her self-observation:

> Instead of trying to force myself into doing what I imagined I ought to do I began to inquire into what I was doing. I little knew what the apparently simple act of trying to be aware of my own experience would involve me in ... Particularly was I struck by the effect of writing things down. It was as if I were trying to catch something and the written word provided a net which for a moment entangled a shadowy form which was other than the meaning of the words ... This effort to describe made me more observant of the small movements of the mind. (Milner, 1986; pp. 23, 71)

She also describes "wide" and "narrow" forms of attention. The "shadowy form" is the deep grammar of the emergent symbol, reminiscent of Kierkegaard's male and female functions of the author. The idea of the observation "net" is used similarly by Bion: when he writes that an artist could say: "'I'll show you' and would put a line on a piece of paper around that idea" (Bion, 2005a, p. 18) he is perhaps recalling Matisse's definition of drawing as "putting a line round an idea". The importance accorded to observation is key to modern psychoanalytic teaching, as it has always been to art and science. Milner differs from Bion in divorcing observation from truth in the ethical sense: saying that rather than "endlessly pursuing the soul's salvation" she was trying to "lose it" and instead to "achieve the play attitude" (p. 90). However her super-ego-ish view of the soul's "salvation" really refers to deference to authority (indoctrination) rather than to truth – to being good, rather than goodness. Although the "play attitude" has its place, and is popularly equated with creativity, narrating one's own story (or part of it) is by most autobiographers viewed as an exacting and probably painful process, but one that demands to be heard and to find its readers.

Autobiographical writing is not *merely* playful; and nor is it *necessarily* therapeutic – and indeed, the same can be said of psychoanalysis. Both require the condition that Bion (1970) termed "patience", a continual oscillation between paranoid-schizoid and depressive orientations (Ps<–>D). "Truth" does not necessarily effect a cure for existing ills, and may indeed stir up latent conflicts. Virginia Woolf committed suicide shortly after writing *Sketch of the Past*, the last and most original of her autobiographical pieces, begun in 1939 when war was looming. "Shall I ever finish?" she wrote; "The battle is at its crisis and comes closer to this house daily" (Woolf, 2002, p.

216   THE ART OF PERSONALITY

109). The *Sketch* is complex in structure, partly owing to the pressure of the present (the war), and partly owing to the semi-comic context in which she sidesteps into personal memoir in order to relieve the tedium of writing a standard, literal biography of Roger Fry – periodically throwing both manuscripts in the waste bin. Her biography of Fry represents the type of lifewriting modelled by her ponderously intellectual father, who morbidly buried any vital psychic spark in the "mausoleum book" that he established in memory of his dead wife, demanding that his children worship it. Virginia Woolf's own story and identity is inserted between the leaves of a more conventional type of writing, just as her life as a writer evolved against the restrictions represented by her father and Victorian society's respectable male-dominated viewpoint. This contrast between the satirist and the visionary in her seems to force into being some extraordinary passages, such as the baby's-eye view of lying in her cot in the nursery at St Ives while the yellow blind swishes in the wind like the waves outside:

> If life has a base that it stands upon, if it is a bowl that one fills and fills and fills – then my bowl without a doubt stands upon this memory. It is of lying half asleep, half awake, in bed in the nursery at St Ives. It is of hearing the waves breaking, one, two, one, two, and sending a splash of water over the beach; and then breaking, one, two, one, two, behind a yellow blind. It is of hearing the blind draw its little acorn across the floor as the wind blew the blind out. It is of lying and hearing this splash and seeing this light, and feeling, it is almost impossible that I should be here; of feeling the purest ecstasy I can conceive. (p. 78)

Her "bowl of life" stands upon the base of this particular memory. Such memories comprise what she calls "moments of being", slotted into the routine of everyday life and unconsciously inspiring it with meaning.

Martha Harris, using the example of a teenage boy fishing, writes of how certain ordinary but subliminal moments lead from recreation to re-creation: "privately he may notice the leaf falling into the water, or the shadow in the rock pool, and these recollections may refresh him for all his life, though he does not speak of them" (Harris, 2007, p. 175). They are the dormant shoots beneath Shakespeare's *Winter's Tale* with its wordplay on "recreation" (III. i. 239). William Blake gives a similar description of how the daughters of Beulah (Imagination) feed the sleepers with thoughts (*Milton*, I. 49). Not consciously but unconsciously, our

ON PSYCHOANALYTIC AUTOBIOGRAPHY 217

autobiography is writing itself all the time through its moments of contact with internal objects, attained through external moments of being. Wordsworth in *The Prelude* calls such moments "spots of time" (XII. 208). *The Prelude* was subtitled "Growth of an individual mind", and all these spots of time follow on from the picture of "the babe that gathers passion from his mother's eye", upholding the entire narrative structure. Another such moment – complementary in terms of lifespan – may be found in D.H. Lawrence's poem "Sorrow" in which the slow death of his mother finds metaphoric life in wisps of ascending cigarette-smoke.

As Frank McCourt told his students in the classrooms of New York:

> Every moment of your life, you're writing. Even in your dreams you're writing ... Dreaming, wishing, planning: it's all writing, but the difference between you and the man on the street is that you are looking at it, realising the significance of the insignificant, getting it on paper ... ruthless in observation. You are your material.
> (McCourt, 2005, pp. 244, 246)

Life-changing moments may appear insignificant to the external eye, but they bring a new knowledge which is ethical in nature and which is intimately connected with suddenly, or finally, *seeing it:* "ruthless in observation" as McCourt puts it. The impact of unvarnished truth comes with a sense of loss of freedom – you do not get the truth, it gets you – as in Meltzer's description of the "cruelty" of symbol-formation which he compares to trapping birds (cited in Williams, 2010, p. 83).

An example of the impact on the observer is George Orwell's account of "A Hanging in Burma", which goes well beyond standard journalism:

> It was about forty yards to the gallows. I watched the bare brown back of the prisoner marching in front of me. He walked clumsily with his bound arms, but quite steadily, with that bobbing gait of the Indian who never straightens his knees. At each step his muscles slid neatly into place, the lock of hair on his scalp danced up and down, his feet printed themselves on the wet gravel. And once, in spite of the men who gripped him by each shoulder, he stepped slightly aside to avoid a puddle on the path.
>
> It is curious, but till that moment I had never realised what it means to destroy a healthy, conscious man. When I saw the prisoner step aside to avoid the puddle, I saw the mystery, the unspeakable wrongness, of cutting a life short when it is in full tide. (Orwell, 1970, p. 68.)

218   THE ART OF PERSONALITY

The implications of the condemned man whose self-respect led him to avoid the "puddle", with the slightest of movements, despite the tyrannical grip of his destiny, constituted a moment of revelation that went to the heart of the "mystery" of life itself. For the observer it is a moment of execution of his previous complacency, the ignorance from which he had been shielded.

Adrian Stokes wrote an autobiography founded on the Kleinian dichotomy between paranoid-schizoid and depressive positions. Unlike most autobiographies, the main "characters" in his story are not people but landscape or architectural features. He associated the Hyde Park of his childhood with paranoid-schizoid confusions of a depressed and dilapidated internal mother's body. He wanted everything to be visually "put right", and had an innate preconception of a restored, harmonious landscape which became real on his first journey to Italy, experiencing the journey through the tunnel of Mont Cénis as a kind of rebirth (by contrast with the "obscene hole" under the Serpentine lake in the Park). Before he actually got there however, his preconception found a home in a single word "mensa" that he learned in Latin lessons with a teacher whom he liked:

> I knew one word the first day – mensa, a table – and how to decline it. I was fascinated, deeply stirred …Not that I have any gift for languages, yet I possess the image of this declension of the word "mensa" on the first day of Latin, taught by a Miss Brown whom I liked. Of the table, for the table, by the table, each expressed by one simple word. The genitive case was the possessiveness of a simple love…
>
> The mensa table… was a revolution in my life, an image the "feel" of which corresponds with a simple table prepared for an al fresco meal, the family mid-day meal under a fig-tree… with one word I possessed in embryo the Virgilian scene; a robust and gracious mother-earth. (Stokes, 1997, p. 84).

The word itself, introduced by a humble mother-figure, was his Mont Cénis tunnel to the aesthetic fulfilment that he craved. It was for him a Wordsworthian "spot of time" or Woolfian "moment of being".

Moments of being can also be literary or cultural, in so far as a genuine life-identification is made; as in McCourt's account of first reading *Hamlet*: "I was so moved by the play because so much of it was about me and my gloomy life … I wished I could have attached a note to let Hamlet know who I was and how my

ON PSYCHOANALYTIC AUTOBIOGRAPHY   219

suffering was real and not just in a play." (McCourt, 2005, p. 36.) The power of identification to collapse time and to conflate levels of reality is characteristic of autobiography as it is of the dreams and associations on which psychoanalysis is based. Only the "suspension of disbelief" (as Coleridge called it) enables imagination to operate such that psychic reality becomes dominant.

Weaving the memories

If noting "moments of being" is how the autobiographer gathers his material, the next challenge is to weave them into a narrative, a graph whose co-ordinates reach across time and between people – external figures who are also internal figures or "abstractions". Every autobiographer has their own method of doing this, but there can be few successful autobiographies in which the voice of the child does not predominate – both as a child, and as child-within-the-adult. The child's voice is what we want to hear. As Larson put it (in relation to McCourt): "To hear the voice of the child is to trust the tale *and* the teller" (Larson, 2007, p. 48).

Here is a brief extract from one of John Mortimer's two biographies: this is from the "poetic" one, written as a play, *A Voyage Round my Father*:

> IRIS: How's your Mum and Dad?
> BOY: Quarrelling.
> IRIS: I never see them quarrel.
> BOY: It's life … they come back from parties, and they quarrel.
> IRIS: I shouldn't like that.
> BOY: Perhaps they're not my parents anyway … (Mortimer, 1990, p. 28).

The boy, endeavouring to appear sophisticated, believes it is not fashionable to come from an unbroken home. The scene is set in the Garden, a world of light and colour which has become lost to the father owing to his blindness, yet which he insists on controlling *as if* he could see. The dramatic life of plants in the Garden contrasts with the unreality of the emotion in the divorce law-courts where he works as if he were an actor; and the play's texture hinges on the tragic-comic interplay between these two contrasting worlds. For him the Garden is real life and the courts a somewhat addictive game of chess. Yet his fierce protectiveness of the Garden values amounts to a type of tyranny over his family and over those whose "normal" vision clashes with his own. His wife and son appear obedient to all his whims, which causes friction in the son's own marriage later on. His wife complains, "You get more like him every day." Only at the end of the play, when the father admits "I'm always angry when I'm dying", does it become clear that it is love, not submission to tyranny, that has motivated their toleration of the eccentric blind man. After his death the son, free at last, moves to the front of the darkened stage, considering all the things he is "meant to feel" – "growing up, the end of dependence, the step into the sunlight when no one is taller than you and you're in no one else's shadow" – and says: "I know what I felt. Lonely" (p. 90). At that point the back of the stage becomes brilliantly lit with projections of the garden in full flower – signifying introjective identification through mourning, with the father's blindness understood and the inner world rejuvenated.

The happy childhood has its own shadows. Richard Herring in his comic autobiographical theatre sketch *The Headmaster's Son* founds his irony on the fact that he came from a happy home and had nothing to complain about – except, of course, being the headmaster's son. Perhaps we should assume that few people have an un-abused childhood, and they always need to remake it in some way or another. Are there any parents who don't get it wrong – "wrong from beginning to end" in Lewis Carroll's immortal words? (condemning Alice's recital of "You are old, Father William"). When the child is the focal orientation (the five-year-old consciousness noted by Tolstoy), all the other characters fall into place, in their role as siblings, part-objects, or as variants on the male-female role of the combined object.

Key to this is the nature of memory and remembering. Those who have studied this phenomenon (eg Ricoeur, 2004; Olney, 1980) conclude that memory as "retrieval" (or "recall") is distinct from reconstructive, creative memory. They may co-exist in a narrative, but the second is the genuinely psychoanalytic factor, rather than the retrieval of early trauma. Bion in *Attention and Interpretation* (1970) distinguishes between literal memory and "remembering". Memory, like desire or invention, is a function of the self with its preconceptions; whereas re-membering (with its pun on "putting together", reconstituting, repairing) is the true psychoanalytic activity, brought into being through the transference dialogue between two minds. Even though, as Melanie Klein reminded her students, "it's not all transference" – there should always be an awareness of the life events behind the transference.

One psychoanalyst calls this special type of narrative "joining the dots". Gilead Nachmani writes of how he came to psychoanalysis from a family background of storytelling; his curiosity was aroused by noticing how stories changed as they were retold, and this led him to focus on his own "story":

> For most of my life I have had a love of storytelling and narration. I grew up in a home where my parents and maternal grandparents were great storytellers. They had lived them and then told them. I began to notice how the stories changed over and questioned the changes.
>
> I think that one of the most fundamental reasons for becoming an analyst was to learn my story and at least be able to tell it to me. Some people come to see us without stories, and others with incomplete or distorted stories. We listen, and question, trying to make connections between people, motives, affects: we try to connect the dots. When we do so, we imply that there may be another story of explanation. Our questions suggest that splitting defences may be diminished. We take beta elements into our alpha reveries, and transform them into K+, L+, H+, possibilities. Coherence, and cohesiveness may ensue ... Engaging in these dialogues emerging from reveries is what I love to do. (Personal communication, 2009).

These reverie-dialogues, according to Bion (whose language Nachmani is using) operate under the third eye of an abstract "observing" force; for in his view there are always three vertices in a psychoanalytic situation. Bion writes: "In an analytic situation there is the analyst, a patient, and a third party who is watching – always" (2005a, p. 19). Since Bion, in fact, psychoanalysis might be seen as autobiography of both partners in tandem, under the supervision of a third eye or "O" that maintains its orientation in a truthful direction; Meltzer calls it a "conversation between internal objects". This goes back to the nature of autobiography as a kind of fiction, which paradoxically, is more truthful than fact in the everyday sense of documentable events. It entails the kind of "distance" which "reconstitutes self" (Gusdorf). If it is "playful" it is strenuously so, not narcissistically indulgent. It is the kind of fiction which is imaginative rather than inventive. There is no end but death to Yeats's "Myself must I remake", since life entails a continual reconstruction of identity.

Both psychoanalysis and autobiography therefore are a venture, possibly a dangerous one, into the kind of fiction that is stranger than fact, where the condition of being "Alone on a wide, wide sea"

222   THE ART OF PERSONALITY

(Coleridge) is only alleviated, potentially, by the companionship of
the unknown reader. Every autobiographer is in the position of
Shakespeare's Prospero at the end of *The Tempest:*

> Gentle breath of yours my sails
> Must fill, or else my project fails. (V. i. 11–12)

CHAPTER TEN

The infant and the infinite: on psychoanalytic faith[1]

The nature of faith and its relation to belief, trust, doubt, and despair, is one of the oldest themes in existence, though relatively new in the language of psychoanalysis outside that of Jung (1938), owing to Freud's suspicion of religion in the post-Darwinian climate of his age. In this paper I would like to explore the meaning of "psychoanalytic faith" as a real, not illusory, psychological factor operating within the intimacy of the consulting room, as distinct from a body of dogma that regulates what may be believed by "the faithful" of psychoanalytic and religious churches. The philosopher William James, contemporaneous with Freud, pointing out that it was necessary to separate personal religion from institutional religion, found in his study *The Varieties of Religious Experience* (1902) that people's personal religions are as various as their personalities. One could locate faith as the means by which the individual infant – the protagonist of the psychoanalytic session – encounters the infinite, that is, the unbounded and unknown potentialities of its psychic development.

This is a movement designated by Bion in Platonic-religious terminology as "oneness with O" or "at-one-ment" (a characteristic

---

1   A version of this chapter was first published in *Psychodynamic Practice*, 21 (2015), pp. 112–125..

pun which he was nonetheless not the first to use, as he pointed out himself): the "One" being godhead or the Platonic Form or Idea of the good or beautiful. Bion introduced the term "faith" in *Attention and Interpretation* (1970), though the idea was already implicit in Melanie Klein's "theological" picture of object relations, as Meltzer has described it, in the form of the infant's trusting dependence on the object. Meltzer writes:

> In general, it could be said that psychoanalysts followed Freud's lead in adopting a somewhat cynical attitude towards religion and its history. It is perhaps a tenable view that man has always invented gods, and naturally invented ones that suited him, being no better than himself but more powerful. But that view supposes that religions are invented by adults, rather than evolving in the minds of infants, later to be mythologised. The vision implicit in Melanie Klein's discoveries about infantile mental life is that mental life is essentially religious, and that the growth of the mind is somehow inextricably tied up with the evolution of the relationship between the self and its internal objects. Consequently, death of the mind is entailed by these objects being expelled, dethroned, invaded, corrupted, or fragmented. (Meltzer, 2005, p. xvi)

My starting point therefore is that, as in religion faith only has meaning in terms of a relationship to God, so in psychoanalysis it only has meaning in terms of the relationship with internal objects. What I mean by psychoanalytic faith is the religious aspect of the mentality that governs the actual psychoanalytic process, through the orientation of the individual minds that partake in it. Certainly this is the way in which Bion and Meltzer envisage the operation of faith, even when they are not specifically referring to that term: psychoanalysis depends on faith in the process, not faith in the personal qualities of the analyst or indeed of the patient. Not all psychoanalytic commentators would agree with this fundamental premise; some confuse it with belief; others use the concept as if synonymous with adamant optimism or dogged determination, in relation to the self and improved ego-strength, in a context of freedom of will and "creative illusion". This tends to reinforce the notion of faith as irrational, divorced from the world of facts and reason.

Those who consider faith to be a useful developmental concept observe that its function is to negotiate our relationship to the unknown – the future shape of the personality. It comes into play when the mind is on the threshold of an enlargement of vision, which is accompanied by an upheaval in established beliefs. Faith is a type of knowing, not a type of believing; as Bion says, "I only believe when there is no fact available" (1991, p. 295). Faith is the most mysterious way of knowing that we know about, accessible only through not-knowing or at times un-knowing – the ultimate in negative capability. Unlike belief, which Bion points out is destroyed by facts (1991, p. 180), faith works constantly in tandem with doubt, and the faith–doubt orientations are part of a single fluctuating movement. The "extended psyche" (to borrow Freud's term) has intimations of the infinite, without *knowing* it in any ordinary sense. Faith is to do with existing in the face of this awareness, not with avoidance. Only when development gets stuck, for narcissistic or masochistic reasons, does the infant's projective worldview become a tyrannical one that "believes in" authority or submission and consequently requires illusion as an antidote, a comforter. In ongoing developoment, the "K-system" is extended by the "O-system" (Bion, 1970, p. 35). An "act of faith" may indeed strengthen the infant ego, or it may shatter it. This is the danger of any "catastrophic change" that disturbs the status quo; but key to the destructive or creative potential is the link between ego and object, infant and infinity. "Tolerance of doubt and tolerance of a sense of infinity" are the linking factors in the growth of knowledge (Bion, 1962a, p. 94). This is not "late Bion" – just Bion.

Bion has been accused by some of inaccurately using the Platonic–Kantian tradition in philosophy. However, as C. M. Woodhouse (1982) pointed out, this tradition has retained its vitality precisely because it may be constantly reinterpreted whilst at the same time preserving its essential spirit and form, namely, the potential to move between worlds – the real and ideal, the experiential and the innate. Roger Money-Kyrle in his 1968 paper on "Cognitive development" divides both philosophers and psychoanalysts into "nominalists" or "realists, followers of Plato" (Money-Kyrle, 2015, p. 211), and both Bion and Meltzer are avowedly among the latter. For the realist-idealists, the realm of internal objects and ideas is seen as a place which has a nonsensu-ous reality in the mind, and is not merely a figure of speech. For some – the nominalists – the internal world is a "metaphor only" as Bion puts it (1991, p. 418); for others, it is a reality that regulates our contact with and knowledge of the external world, as mapped by Money-Kyrle in *Man's Picture of His World* (1961). Both internal and external reality exist and are not merely postulated, imagined or believed in; both therefore need to be observed and to become known, which is a scientific ("knowing") activity. Religion, science,

226 THE ART OF PERSONALITY

and art are, according to Bion, three "vertices" of knowledge which need to be held in a creative tension (see Williams, 2005a). Indeed in Bion's terms, owing to its fundamental part in these linkages, faith could be considered a special feature of "learning from experience", at the heart of the entire process.

As developed in *Attention and Interpretation*, an "act of faith" is seen as "peculiar to scientific procedure" (Bion, 1970, p. 34), by which he means the "discipline" of eschewing memory and desire that allows faith to operate, in whatever field of investigation. The "artist's O" becomes "apprehensible when it has been transformed into a work of art" (a symbol). Carefully, in order to stress the emotional element of fear, he uses the verb "apprehend" rather than "comprehend", as does Meltzer in *The Apprehension of Beauty* (1988). Based on this emotionally complex attitude, he advocates an analogous state for psychoanalysts:

> It may be wondered what state of mind is welcome if desires and memories are not. A term that would express approximately what I need to express is "faith" – faith that there is an ultimate reality and truth – the unknown, unknowable, "formless infinite". (Bion, 1970, p. 31)

In Bion's vivid metaphor, psychoanalysis is engaged in the hunt for "that ferocious animal, absolute Truth" – a quarry which is of course never encountered, we only glimpse its coat (the "stripes on the coat of the tiger" [1991, p. 112]), in conformity with the neoPlatonic view that noumenal truth enters the world of phenomena in pieces, cloaked to suit human comprehension. The important feature is that the human mind recognises that the stripes derive from an infinite source of knowledge, an O-system rather than a K-system; they are simply "aspects of the 'evolved' O" (p. 31). The term "infinite" (used by Bion and the poets) is not the same as "undifferentiated". Milton's "formless infinite" contains an infinite variety of forms, like Michelangelo's stone, from which the artist's attention (and skill) extracts a finite realisation.

Thus the psychoanalyst's O, like the artist's, is already a transformation won from the formless infinite and set to work in a specific symbol-making setting. Symbol-formation is an innate human tendency, part of the Kantian a priori equipment. Bion sees the "self" as an entity comprising both the psychic and the physical, as vividly illustrated in his story in the Memoir (1991) of how mental life begins with the meeting of sperm and ovum, and is keen on merging the caesura between conscious and unconscious, as in

THE INFANT AND THE INFINITE: PSYCHOANALYTIC FAITH   227

the Grid, replacing it with a series of logical steps toward abstraction. Mental life begins simultaneously with bodily existence, and dialogue within the psyche occurs instantaneously with differentiation within the soma, at some infinitely primitive level. Indeed Klein's "unconscious phantasy" is by definition differentiated and applies to all mental movements however primitive or sophisticated. All symbols are the product of unconscious fantasy. The problem lies in detecting the differentiations, namely, in developing the capacity for attention that enables the symbol to take shape in the transference situation, something both more intuitive and more accurate than interpretation in the classical sense.

There is a fundamental divergence between the post-Freudian religious discussions that continue to focus on the "future of an illusion", and the post-Kleinian picture of the infant self developing in association with the potentially infinite development of its internal objects, that is, through contact with reality. (I use "post-Kleinian" not in the political or institutional sense but in the sense which prompted Meltzer to claim Mrs Klein as the first post-Kleinian: that is, as the implicit originator of an evolving picture founded in her clinical discoveries.) Nonetheless Freud's original paternalistic view of religion is still commonly held as fulfilling a perverse need for a punitive superego that then stimulates rebellion or the need for consolation; and the popular maternalistic view of a comforting earth-mother who masochistically retires into non-entity in order to allow the infant free rein is perhaps an equally pessimistic idea of internal deity.

These almost caricatural male and female objects do not correspond with philosophic or poetic views of faith such as James's when he writes of "the impulse to take life strivingly [that] is indestructible in the race" and through whose "maximal stimulating power ... the infinite perspective opens out" (cited in Carlson, 1997, p. 380). The infinite perspective is what establishes a space for unlimited, unfolding possibilities in internal object relations. There is no fixed goal in view; instead, the infant self identifies with an evolving O through a continual series of infinitesimal points of contact. Beliefs, which (as James emphasises) are also an important dynamic in the "strivings" of human personality, can thereby lose the fixed quality of opinion or dogma, and can change and develop according to the realities of experience.

In the analytic situation, in the post-Kleinian view, the infant or analysand needs ultimately to "identify with the evolution of O" not with the parent or analyst as a person. Bion concludes *Attention and Interpretation* with the words:

228 THE ART OF PERSONALITY

> What is to be sought is an activity that is both the restoration of god (the Mother) and the evolution of god (the formless, infinite, ineffable, non-existent) which can be found only in the state in which there is NO memory, desire, understanding". (Bion, 1970,
> p. 129)

Thus in psychoanalytic terms, the leap of faith results in the internalisation of the evolutionary aspect of the object. It involves overcoming envy of the "growth-stimulating objects" and entails an advance in the structure of the personality, so is never just an acquired piece of information that can be selected and stored by the self (subject) without any help from the object. Reparation (restored internal deity, introjection, incarnation) is not enough. It is not just the mental food which is required but also the digestive *function* of the object (as Money-Kyrle points out), that is, the capacity to think – restoration and evolution together. In a series of mediations, the object itself has to be more than "god the Mother" – it has to be in touch with the ineffable, evolutionary O, the source of object-ness, in order to ensure its own participation in a developmental process rather than a fixed moral or doctrinal system.

In this picture of personality development, faith is not an optional extra in the armoury of the psyche. It is essential to truth-seeking. The alternative to "F-faith", writes Meltzer, is "F-fiend": to succumb to lies, invented by the ego, the narcissistic infant-self, ending in "being" a lie: "Truth requires submission under the vertex of L, K and if possible F, where the value is creating rather than destroying" (Meltzer, 1978, p. 107). The great poets, such as Shakespeare and Homer, according to Bion, could "penetrate a state of mind that did not yet exist – ours" (1987, p. 232). They could intuit mental events through a capacity for deep symbolisation that he equates with an act of faith. "An "act of faith" has as its background something that is unconscious and unknown because it has not happened." (Bion, 1970, p. 35). Faith operates in the area of the not-yet-existing: heralding the future not of political or social events, but of mental events that are yet to be realised, whether in cultural or individual terms, instants away or centuries. Later, they come true – that is, they are experienced, by one or another mind. This type of imagination – supremely, the poetic imagination – was defined by Kierkegaard as "the medium of infinitisation", in other words, the basis for a movement of faith, which can only occur when the self has arrived at one of those developmental nodes at which a future shape or existence is sensed. At such points of catastrophic change, Bion suggests the personality is faced with

THE INFANT AND THE INFINITE: PSYCHOANALYTIC FAITH   229

three possible alternatives: the "commensal" route of non-reactive coexistence, the "parasitic" or destructive one, or the "symbiotic" (fruitful) conjunction (1970, p. 78).

Alastair Hannay, Kierkegaard translator and scholar, asks: "May the relation to religion be discussed profitably in terms of some alternative theology, one which will allow the Kierkegaardian insights to throw light on and enrich our grasp of human being?" (Hannay, 1998, p. 348). To which we may answer: yes, psychoanalysis could be seen as such an alternative theology. Meltzer admired Kierkegaard; and although there do not seem to be any specific references to him in Bion's writings, Bion's picture of mental growth through the transference process has been compared by David Walters (2009) to that of Kierkegaard. Kierkegaard, the founder of existentialist philosophy and an acute psychologist, took faith as his underlying, formative theme, the basis for being-and-becoming. He used a series of pseudonyms to free his arguments from his own persona and to enable different internal points of view to find a voice in the discussion. Like Bion, who says that "O" or the "thing-in-itself" is best described as "passionate love" (1994, p. 183), Kierkegaard saw faith as a passion, on a par with love, fear, awe, etc. Like Bion, who warned that "knowledge 'about' something may be the outcome of a defence against the consequences of an "act of faith"'" (1970, p. 35), he knew that passionate commitment is something which human nature always tries to resist. We seek refuge in classification, he says: "One does not love, does not have faith, does not act; but one knows what erotic love is, what faith is" (Kierkegaard, 1992, p. 344). Knowing about is an alternative to learning from internal objects, which entails an emotional plunge into the unknown. Kierkegaard's lifelong analysis of the nature of faith was set in motion by questioning his own motives in renouncing his engagement to a girl named Regine. This led him to conclude that he himself did not have faith: "If I had had faith I would have stayed with Regine" (1996, p. 158). He came up with many rational, even noble, excuses for avoiding marriage, but knew it was really a failure of faith.

Kierkegaard takes faith to be meaningful only on a personal level, not a cultural or social one. Faith concerns the "project of the selfhood", namely the individual's quest for identity – the quest to "become himself", which he recognises to be a task instinctively avoided, observing that people naturally prefer to cloak themselves in some fictional or substitute identity. One's true identity cannot be "chosen" but rather is "given", and is only fulfilled through passionate experience. Kierkegaard writes:

230   THE ART OF PERSONALITY

> Every movement of infinity occurs with passion, and no reflection
> can bring about a movement. That's the perpetual leap in life
> which explains the movement. ... In passion, the existing subject
> is infinitised in the eternity of imagination and yet is also most
> definitely himself. (Kierkegaard, 1985, p. 71n)

This "infinitising" movement takes place in "the eternity of imagination" (in Blakeian terms), and is the equivalent of Bion's "alignment with O". For Kierkegaard, as with others in the neoPlatonic
tradition, faith is envisaged as enabling a synthesis of finite and
infinite. Thus it is not good enough to renounce worldly desires and
relationships, however virtuous this may appear; this is an incomplete spiritual movement. The finite mind cannot dematerialise;
rather, through faith the infinite is incorporated in earthly form,
in a transformation. Coleridge (1972), in the same tradition, distinguishes an imaginative symbol, which allows the eternal to shine
through the temporal, from a mechanical sign or allegory which
is a manmade container for information. Kierkegaard explains
further that when the "subject", or person, is "infinitised", he does
not merely know himself in a theoretical way, but actually *becomes*
himself – an existential transformation, as in Bion's definition of the
function of a psychoanalysis. "Reflection" and "pathos", according to Kierkegaard, represent two contrary ways of coming to
knowledge, analogous to Bion's "knowing about" versus "learning
from experience", K- and O-systems. (He is scathing about Hegel
as representing the former.) No amount of "reflection" or dialecti-
cal argument can substitute for what is essentially a movement of
"pathos", felt on the pulses.

In psychoanalysis, a correct interpretation may be incorrectly
delivered, as for example when used as a projective defence, and
thus is not "correct" in Money-Kyrle's sense of being founded on
the analyst's unconscious perception of their own inner world.
Indeed a total reliance on reflection, free from any taint of the
mystical or intuitive (Money-Kyrle's "valid intuition"), is liable to
result in "infinite resignation", satirised by Kierkegaard as a form of
moral complacency, self-satisfying but stultifying. To resign oneself
to loss (or loss of contact), pretending that one values only the infinite not the earthly, is actually an evasion of passion. Kierkegaard
distinguished necessary suffering from "religious masochism"
and made it quite clear that it is an error to believe that sorrow is
more "meritorious" than joy (journal note, cited in Kodalle, 1998,
p. 409). Movements of faith, he said, are accompanied by moments
of "lightheartedness and humour": in Bion's terms, by the fleeting

THE INFANT AND THE INFINITE: PSYCHOANALYTIC FAITH   231

experience of "security", a sense of aesthetic harmony, gained after a sustained period of "patience" (1970, p. 124). In contrast to the assumptions of religious or doctrinal fundamentalism, faith does not lead to death but to life, which is harder to tolerate.

To the existing personality, of course, faith is an "absurd" movement, though Kierkegaard is careful to make a distinction between the absurd and "nonsense". The "absurd" is the way to advance the "project of the selfhood", which progresses in a series of small but radical transitions (like Bion's catastrophic change), rather than through argument and dialectic. Indeed, like Bion's LHK, Kierkegaard's definition of "existence" is a capacity to hold emotional elements in "tension", as distinct from arguing for one at the expense of another. Tolerating this tension leads to a "leap" which is the antithetical alternative to the "will" – the psychic tool of the narcissistic infantile ego. The leap occurs in the gap between old and new knowledge, which makes a space for what Bion calls "psyche-lodgement" (*Memoir*, 1991, p. 265), a place where memory and desire are not. When an individual comes to the boundary between his own existence and his potential future existence, Kierkegaard says, he "has come to the border of the wondrous" (as in Meltzer's "amazement"), a boundary which implies religious "atonement" (as in Bion) and results in "repetition" on a higher plane of existence (see Green, 1998, p. 273). Kierkegaard's "repetition" is in Kleinian terms a type of infinitised reparation in the face of the depressive position. That is, it is not "beyond" the depressive position, but a particular facet of the infant's dependence, accepting the reality of an imminent sea-change, and incorporating some of the object's infinitising or developmental pull.

Cutting the link of faith leads to the objects' deprivation and impotence (omnipotence), unable to help the infant self. So when the tension of L, H, K is found intolerable and the leap to catastrophic change is not made, there is a temptation to minus L, H, K – that is, to inventing lies about the self and its relation to internal objects which at their extreme may lead to despair. It is despair, not doubt, that is the antithesis to faith. Despair is defined by Kierkegaard as "wanting to be rid of oneself"; it betrays itself in those who claim to want to "be themselves" but "exclude the thought of being established by a "power"", and who are thus not real but "pseudo-selves" (Hannay, 1998, pp. 343-344). Pseudo-selves are those whose identity is defined solely in relation to others in society and have no sense that their identity is established by an internal power or godlike object. They are "outward-looking" not "inward-looking"; they are "not clarified" (here Kierkegaard's language again echoes closely that of William Blake). And psychology tells us that we may be different people at different moments – faithful or despairing, existing or non-existing, being ourselves or pretending to be someone else.

The parallels are clear between the poetic-religious-philosophical views of faith, and the Bion–Meltzer post-Kleinian model of the mind. Meltzer adopted Bion's linkage of L, H, K in his (1988) formulation of "aesthetic conflict", in which the infant's simultaneous love and hate of its ambiguous mother with her inscrutable inner world is resolved through an awakening of the desire for knowledge. This may take a constructive scientific or artistic form, or both; or alternatively, the pain of not-knowing may be perverted into a fantasy of intrusive manipulation of the object's interior. In the doubt–faith oscillation, as in Bion's Ps<–>D, we see the infant's aesthetic conflict as founded on its love-hate reaction to the beauty of its mother's face, a dazzling sun immediately qualified by flitting clouds. The tension between love and hate gives birth to curiosity about the mother's internal world, the source of all further investigations both internal and external, and the basis for the establishment of a sense of reality. This search for knowledge leads to developmental catastrophic change as aspects of truth are ingested by the self in a perpetual process of becoming.

It is also clear that there is a major distinction between the post-Kleinian, Platonic orientation of Bion and Meltzer (which is aligned with that of the poet-philosophers) and the Freudian-instinctual orientation of those who regard the desire for knowledge as an autonomous instinct that simply gets "mixed up" with love and hate (Britton, 1998, p. 3), rather than springing of necessity from the emotional tension between infant and mother, with implications for fantasies about the worlds that the mother represents. Indeed the (essentially) post-Freudian view forgets the Kleinian emphasis on the mother's internal world as the primary object of the infant's curiosity – the infant's first intimations of O and its first cognitive steps being founded on the part-object relationships of the feeding experience (see Money-Kyrle, 1978). The essential feature of the Kleinian tradition is the fact of the infant mind's dependence on internal objects for all real knowledge and all real personality development. Bion and Meltzer, following the poet-philosophers, insist that this type of developmental dependence relies on the capacity for faith. Meltzer says that Bion's idea of faith is not like the child swimming for the first time without water wings, confident of Daddy's support, but is more like "floating free in shark-infested waters" (1978, vol. 3, p. 99). This is the required "leap" of

THE INFANT AND THE INFINITE: PSYCHOANALYTIC FAITH   233

faith. But it does also acknowledge the role of "Daddy's support" as the ethics of existing knowledge are superseded and refined in a continuing evolutionary process.

The language of psychoanalytic theory is notoriously poor when it comes to evoking experiences of "pathos" as distinct from "recollection": that is, emotionality rather than interpretation. For this reason I would like to offer a couple of poetic examples to illustrate through analogy what faith looks and feels like. Poets have often expressed their faith in poetry in terms of a commitment not just to a specific muse or inspiring figure, but to the muse's operation in a particular poem. Their metaphors offer a template for other relationships which require faith. The possibility of an act of faith occurs in response to an emotional disturbance – such as love, beauty, mortality. When faith is allowed to operate, the poet him- or herself is placed in a position of being used as a mediator, a vehicle for conveying the poem's knowledge. As Rimbaud said: "It is wrong to say "I think"; rather, I am thought." Poets are required by their muse to express some special, idiosyncratic yet universal knowledge, first felt on their own pulses and then captured for other readers to identify with. The "apprehension" of an aesthetic object or poem initiates a movement out of the existing self, experienced as a sense of service to a power beyond itself – in psychoanalysis, to the internal object. This movement of abnegating self and taking on service to the other is a perennial theme of poetry.

The poet Emily Dickinson described herself as a "loaded gun" who, in writing poetry or rather this particular poem, felt she was carried away by a master-force, her "owner":

> My Life had stood – a Loaded Gun
> In Corners – till a Day
> The Owner passed – identified –
> And carried me away –
>
> And now We roam in Sovereign Woods –
> And now We hunt the Doe –
> And every time I speak for Him
> The Mountains straight reply –
>
> (poem no. 764 in Dickinson, 1999)

The crux of the matter is the word "identified", whose double sense implies both that the poet has been recognised by the "owner" (the internal or love-object), and that she has become one with the originator or the experience that ensues: "I" becomes "We". In this

234   THE ART OF PERSONALITY

way, the Gun of her life is transformed into the poems which speak out – "every time I speak for Him" – and elicit a response from the world, the Mountains.

My second example is an extract from "Faith and Love", a poem by Roland Harris (who was an analysand of Bion's in the 1960s). The poem was written in the 1940s in response to reading the theologian-psychologist Thomas Aquinas. It begins:

> The three substitutes
> In love for faith
> Are memory, hope
> And sudden death.
> 　　　　(Harris, R., 1970)

Memory, hope and death are non-passionate substitutes that escape from turbulence by too easily relinquishing the aesthetic or love object. Aquinas said that "for those with faith, no explanation is necessary. For those without, no explanation is possible." Explanation belongs to the realm of memory and desire, of "knowing about" not of learning from experience. Contact with the disturbing new idea or aesthetic object may be avoided with the excuse that it is unattainable; avoidance may take the form of replacing faith with some more comfortable emotion or even result in extinction of the idea. As Bion points out, it is not only bodies that may be killed, but also ideas: "A foetal idea may kill or be killed – and that is not a metaphor only" (1991, p. 418). He means that a metaphor may actually contain a foetal idea, in line with the neoPlatonic view that a new idea can only be contained in a symbol; but the mind may or may not be prepared to receive it, to make that link with the infinite. And the drama of noticing and containing "foetal ideas" is something that occurs in the consulting room, through the transference communication between the internal objects of both analyst and analysand. (As is well recognised these days, it is the communication rather than the verbalisation that is important and that makes the psychoanalytic symbol.)

Using a metaphor very similar to Emily Dickinson's, Harris continues:

> Out of the waste of sky
> 　　invincible arrows
> 　　of beauty and danger,
> 　　when the strong Stranger
> 　　bends me, and trains his eye!

THE INFANT AND THE INFINITE: PSYCHOANALYTIC FAITH   235

The bow, like the gun, is not used by the poet – it *is* the poet. The poet himself is used by a "Stranger", a visitor from the realms of the unknown. In psychoanalytic terms the Stranger is the internal object, the mother-father figure whose knowledge arrives in advance of the self, creating anxiety and turbulence. Faith in the essential benevolence of this object is required for the personality to "bend" to the oncoming catastrophic change, whose shape, as always, is unknown. There is a natural recoil against the infinitising aspect of the object which changes the existing shape and structure of the self. Harris continues to describe the parts of the personality that dare not commit themselves to faith and that therefore counsel against passionate experience:

> The voices crying
> > "Beware beware
> > A false happiness
> > Is sadder than despair" –
> > Have the intense
> > Substitute for experience.

Fearful of being let down, the cautious mind seeks an alternative, a "substitute for experience" – memory, hope, desire, prudence. How can one distinguish between the real thing and its various substitutes – which may feel equally "intense" or be even more satisfying?

This is surely the central dilemma of the psychoanalytic consulting room: the choice between comfortable familiarity and the painful reality of the unknown experience that is trying to make an entrance into the space created by the turbulent proximity of two minds (Bion, 1987). The problem which faces psychoanalysts, as it has always faced religious priests, is to avoid parasitic dependence on the faith of past pioneers, and instead to free the operation of faith in their patients, which itself depends on the operation of faith in their own minds and practice. Martha Harris warned against rigidifying the memory of those who were faithful pioneers, by turning them instead into dogmatic guardians of the Faith:

> The dependent group structure so often manifests itself in the reliance upon a crystallised selection of the theories of Freud (the original Messiah), sometimes pitted against a similar extrapolation from Melanie Klein (a latter day saint). Bion is unlikely to escape the same fate. (Harris, M., 1978, p. 32)

Psychoanalysis, if we have any faith in the process, should teach us self-scrutiny not doctrinal allegiance, which is an illusory way to preserve psychoanalytic knowledge, and essentially non-analytic in its possessiveness and idolatry. The danger is that the group guardians, by concentrating on dialectic rather than pathos, rules rather than "discipline" (in Bion's sense), are liable to lose touch with the poetic spirit of the pioneers.

But neither is psychoanalysis a "love story" in which faith is defined as aiming to restore the power of infant "illusion" (Kristeva, 1987). In terms of the analyst's personal emotions, Bion emphasises (as did Freud) the need to seek a neutral or objective perspective beyond individual love or hate: a major difficulty in maintaining the therapeutic transference relationship being the struggle to be "disciplined", to "remain analysts" rather than succumbing to either love or hate, to refrain from omnipotently trying to "be helpful" (1991, p. 665), as distinct from enabling "pain-talk" (1991, p. 434). Pain-talk, of course, is not masochism but the kind of suffering associated with "patience". Hence the "experience of sadness" originating in that relationship (Bion, 2005b, p. 64) – the depressive position that does not need to be overcome or gone beyond, but simply to be undergone. Bion regarded this as the gaining of "wisdom", as distinct from being so "well educated" that we are unable to be wise (*ibid.*, p. 66). To relinquish infantile omnipotence and allow internal objects to do the thinking requires faith in a process which relies on the "transference from internal objects" to enable the analyst to "seem to perform functions for the patient that are essential to the development of their thinking" (Meltzer, cited in Williams, 2010, p. 79). To be wise is to retain faith in the process rather than in the personal capacities of the analyst: to "respond analytically rather than parentally" (Meltzer, 1983, p. 9). This is dependent on the analyst's tolerance of negative capability – Keats's term now generally used as the best depiction of the analytic stance. What the infant needs is not illusion but infinity; and the psychoanalytic process is the aesthetic object that can combine both "god the mother" and the "ineffable", and be a metaphorical container for states of mind yet unknown.

In conclusion: to have faith in someone means to have faith in the quality of their internal objects. To have faith in the psychoanalytic process means to have faith in the possibility of a "conversation between the internal objects" (Meltzer) of two minds. The transference–countertransference relationship takes place in a space which is beyond either of the individual minds but shaped by their turbulent encounter. Faith in the process is faith in the "infinite" unfolding of this encounter.

REFERENCES

Abraham, K. (1913). *Dreams and Myths: A Study in Race Psychology.* Trans. W. A. White. New York: Journal of Nervous and Mental Disease Publishing Company.

Anderson, L. (2001). *The New Critical Idiom: Autobiography.* London: Routledge.

Baez, J. (1977). My father. In R. Lyons (Ed.), *Autobiography: A Reader for Writers* (pp. 261–269). New York: Oxford University Press.

Bamforth, I. (2000). Kafka's uncle: scenes from a world of trust infected by suspicion. *Medical Humanities* 26: 85-91. http://mh.bmj.com/content/26/2/85.full.

Barker, J. (1994). *The Brontes.* London: Weidenfeld & Nicolson.

Beatson, P. (1976). *The Eye in the Mandala: Patrick White: a Vision of Man and God.* London: Paul Elek.

Bernstein, L. (1969). *The Joy of Music.* London: Panther.

Bion, W. R. (1962a). *Learning from Experience.* London: Heinemann.

Bion, W. R. (1962b). A theory of thinking. Reprinted in *Second Thoughts,* pp. 110-119. London: Heinemann, 1967.

Bion, W. R. (1967). *Second Thoughts.* London: Heinemann.

Bion, W. R. (1970). *Attention and Interpretation.* London: Tavistock.

Bion, W. R. (1973–74). *Brazilian Lectures.* 2 vols. Rio de Janeiro: Imago.

Bion, W. R. (1980). *Bion in New York and Sao Paulo.* Perthshire: Clunie Press.

Bion, W. R. (1982). *The Long Week-End.* Abingdon: Fleetwood Press.

Bion, W. R. (1987). Emotional turbulence (1976). In: *Clinical Seminars and Four Papers* (pp. 223–233). Abingdon: Fleetwood Press.

238 REFERENCES

Bion, W. R. (1991). *A Memoir of the Future*. Single-volume edition. London: Karnac.

Bion, W. R. (1994). *A Memoir of the Future*. Single-volume edition. London: Karnac.

Bion, W. R. (2005a). *The Tavistock Seminars*. Ed. F. Bion. London: Karnac.

Bion, W. R. (2005b). *Italian Seminars*. Ed. F. Bion. Trans. P. Slotkin. London: Karnac.

Blake, W. (1974). *Complete Writings*, ed. G. Keynes. Oxford: Oxford University Press.

Bollack, J. (2006). *Prometheus Bound*: drama and enactment. In: D. Cairns & V. Liapis (Eds.), *Dionysalexandros: Essays on Aeschylus and his Fellow Tragedians in Honour of Alexander F. Garrie* (pp. 79–90). Swansea: Classical Press of Wales.

Breger, L. (1989). *Dostoevsky: The Author as Psychoanalyst*. New York: New York University Press.

Britton, R. (1998). *Belief and Imagination: Explorations in Psychoanalysis*. London: Routledge.

Bronte, C. (1972 [1850]). Biographical Notice of Ellis and Acton Bell; Preface to *Wuthering Heights* In: W. J. Sale, Jr (Ed.), *Emily Bronte: Wuthering Heights* (pp. 3–12). New York: Norton.

Bronte, E. (1941). *The Complete Poems of Emily Bronte*, ed. C. W. Hatfield. New York: Columbia University Press.

Bronte, E. (1972 [1847]). *Wuthering Heights*, ed. W. J. Sale, Jr. New York: Norton.

Brown, P. (1967). *Augustine of Hippo*. London: Faber.

Burian, P. (1997). Myth into muthos: the shaping of tragic plots. In: P. Easterling (Ed.), *The Cambridge Companion to Greek Tragedy* (pp. 228–83). Cambridge: Cambridge University Press.

Byron, G. G. (1973). *Lord Byron: Selected Letters and Journals*, ed. L. A. Marchand. Cambridge, Mass.: Harvard University Press.

Campbell, J. (1949). *The Hero with a Thousand Faces*. New York: Pantheon.

Carlson, T. (1997). James and the Kantian tradition. In: R. A. Putnam (Ed.), *The Cambridge Companion to William James*, pp. 363–384. Cambridge: Cambridge University Press.

Carroll, L. (1865). *Alice in Wonderland*. London: Macmillan. Republished online by Forgotten Books (2008).

Cassirer, E. (1946). *Language and Myth*. Trans. S. Langer. New York: Harper.

Cecil, D. (1970 [1934]). *Early Victorian Novelists*. London: Fontana.

Chizhevsky, D. (1962). The theme of the double in Dostoevsky. In: R. Wellek (Ed.), *Dostoevsky: Twentieth Century Views* (pp. 112–119). Englewood Cliffs, NJ: Prentice-Hall.

Coleridge, S. T. (1836). On the Prometheus of Aeschylus. In: H. N. Coleridge (Ed.), *Literary Remains (Volume 2)*, pp. 323–60. London: Pickering.

Coleridge, S. T. (1972 [1816]). *Lay Sermons*, ed. R. J. White. London: Routledge.

REFERENCES   239

Coleridge, S. T. (1997 [1816]). *Biographia Literaria*, ed. N. Leask. London: Dent.

Conrad, J. (2008 [1912]). *The Mirror of the Sea and A Personal Record*. Ed. K. Carabine. London: Wordsworth.

Danta, C. (2001). *Literature Suspends Death: Sacrifice and Storytelling in Kierkegaard, Kafka*. London: Bloomsbury.

Davie, J. (Trans.) (1998). *Euripides: Electra and Other Plays*. London: Penguin.

Davies, S. (1998). *Emily Bronte*. Plymouth: Northcote House.

Davies, S. (2002). *The Professor, Agnes Grey* and *Wuthering Heights*. In: H. Glen (Ed.), *The Cambridge Companion to the Brontes*. Cambridge: Cambridge University Press.

Dickinson, E. (1999). *Poems*, ed. R. W. Franklin. Cambridge, Mass: Harvard University Press.

Dodds, E. R. (1951). *The Greeks and the Irrational*. Berkeley: University of California Press.

Dostoevsky, F. (1976 [1880]). *The Brothers Karamazov*, ed. R. E. Matlaw. Trans. C. Garnett, rev. R. E. Matlaw. New York: Norton.

Dostoevsky, F. (1993 [1864]). *Notes from Underground*. Trans. R. Pevear & L. Volokhonsky. London: Vintage.

Dostoevsky, F. (1994 [1875]). *An Accidental Family*. Trans. R. Freeborn. London: Penguin.

Easterling, P. (2008). Introduction. *Electra and Other Plays*, ed. D. Raeburn. London: Penguin.

Easterling, P. E. (1997). A show for Dionysus. In: P. E. Easterling (Ed.), *The Cambridge Companion to Greek Tragedy* (pp. 36–53). Cambridge University Press.

Edgecombe, R. S. (1989). *Vision and Style in Patrick White*. Tuscaloosa: University of Alabama Press.

Eliot, T. S. (1944). *Four Quartets*. London: Faber.

Farr, D., & Gardarsson, G. O. (2006). *Metamorphosis: An Adaptation*. London: Oberon.

Finney, B. (1985). *The Inner I*. London: Faber.

Forster, E. M. (1927). *Aspects of the Novel*. London: Edward Arnold.

Frank, J. (1995). *Dostoevsky: The Miraculous Years: 1865–1871*. Princeton, NJ: Princeton University Press.

Freeborn, R. (1994). Introduction. *Dostoevsky: An Accidental Family*. London: Penguin.

Freeborn, R. (2003). *Dostoevsky: Life and Times*. London: Haus.

Freeden, I. (2002). A troll in the consulting room. *British Journal of Psychotherapy* 19 (2), pp. 189–202.

Freud, S. (1900). *The Interpretation of Dreams*. Standard Edition, 4.

Freud, S. (1919). Lines of advance in psychoanalytic therapy. *Standard Edition*, 17: 159–168.

Freud, S. (1928). Dostoevsky and parricide. *Standard Edition*, 22: 177–194.

Freud, S. (1932). The acquisition and control of fire. *Standard Edition*, 22: 183–194.

240 REFERENCES

Gammill, J. (2012). The role of Martha Harris from the beginning of the GERPEN. In: M. H. Williams (Ed.), *Enabling and Inspiring: A Tribute to Martha Harris* (pp. 39–43). London: Harris Meltzer Trust.

Gaskell, E. (1971 [1857]). *The Life of Charlotte Bronte*, ed. W. Gerin. London: Dent.

Gérin, W. (1978). *Emily Bronte*. Oxford University Press.

Gezari, J. (Ed.) (1992). *Emily Jane Bronte: the Complete Poems*. London: Penguin.

Goodridge, J. F. (1964). *Emily Bronte: Wuthering Heights*. London: Edward Arnold.

Gray, R. (1973). *Franz Kafka*. Cambridge University Press.

Green, R. M. (1998). "Developing" *Fear and Trembling*. In: A. Hannay (Ed.), *The Cambridge Companion to Kierkegaard*, pp. 257-281. Cambridge: Cambridge University Press.

Greenberg, M. (1971). *The Terror of Art: Kafka and Modern Literature*. New York: Basic Books.

Grolnick, S. A. (1984). Play, myth, theater, and psychoanalysis. *Psychoanalytic Review, 71* (2): 247–265.

Gusdorf, G. (1980). Conditions and limits of autobiography. In J. Olney (Ed.), *Autobiography: essays theoretical and critical* (pp. 28–48). Princeton: Princeton University Press.

Hall, E. (1997a). The sociology of Greek tragedy. In: P. E. Easterling (Ed.), *The Cambridge Companion to Greek Tragedy* (pp. 93–126). Cambridge: Cambridge University Press.

Hall, E. (1997b). Introduction to *Euripides: Medea and Other Plays*. Oxford: Oxford University Press.

Hall, E. (1999). Introduction. *Euripides: Bacchae and Other Plays*. Oxford: Oxford University Press.

Hannay, A. (1998). Kierkegaard and the variety of despair. In: A. Hannay (Ed.), *The Cambridge Companion to Kierkegaard,* pp. 329-249. Cambridge: Cambridge University Press.

Harris, M. (1978). The individual in the group: on learning to work with the psychoanalytic method. Reprinted in: M. H. Williams (Ed.), *The Tavistock Model: Papers on Child Development and Psychoanalytic Training by Martha Harris and Esther Bick*, pp. 25-44.

Harris, M. (2007 [1969]). *Your Teenager*. London: Harris Meltzer Trust.

Harris, M. (2011 [1975]). *Thinking about Infants and Young Children*. London: Harris Meltzer Trust.

Harris, R. J. (1970). *Selected Poems*. Perthshire: Clunie Press.

Hatfield, C. W. (Ed.) (1941). *The Complete Poems of Emily Jane Bronte*. New York: Columbia University Press.

Herring, R. (2009). *The Headmaster's Son*. West End Centre, Aldershot: theatre performance.

Hewitt, H. V. (2002). *Patrick White: Painter Manque*. Melbourne: Miegunyah Press.

Holland, N. (1985). *The I*. New Haven, CT & London: Yale University Press.

Hughes, T. (Trans.) (1999). *Aeschylus: The Oresteia*. London: Faber.

REFERENCES   241

Ibsen, H. (1966). *Peer Gynt*. Transl. P. Watts. London: Penguin.
Ibsen, H. (1981). *Four Major Plays: A Doll's House; Ghosts; Hedda Gabler; The Master Builder*. Trans. J. McFarlane & J. Arup. Oxford: Oxford Universit Press.
Ibsen, H. (1988). *An Enemy of the People; The Wild Duck; Rosmersholm*. Trans. J. McFarlane. Oxford: Oxford University Press.
Ibsen, H. (1996). *Brand*. A version for the stage by G. Hill. London: Penguin.
Ibsen, H. (2006). *Three Major Plays: Peer Gynt; Rosmersholm; When We Dead Awaken*. Trans. D. Rudkin. London: Oberon.
James, C. (1980). *Unreliable Memoirs*. London: Picador.
James, W. (1902). *The Varieties of Religious Experience*. New York, NY: Longmans, Green.
Janouch, G. (1969). *Conversations with Kafka: notes and reminiscences*. New York: New Directions.
Joseph, F. (1995). Dostoevsky: The Miraculous Years. Princeton: Princeton University Press.
Jung, C. G. (1913). The theory of psychoanalysis. *Psychoanalytic Review*, 1: 1–40.
Jung, C. G. (1938). Psychology and Religion. *Collected Works (Volume 11)*, ed. G. Adler and R. F. Hull. Princeton University Press.
Jung, C. G. (1969 [1930]) The stages of life. *Collected Works (Volume 8)*, ed. G. Adler and R. F. Hull. Princeton University Press.
Jung, C. G. (2001 [1933]). *Modern Man in Search of a Soul*. London: Routledge.
Jung, C. G. and Kerenyi, C. (1951). *The Science of Mythology*. London: Routledge.
Kafka, F. (1953). *Letters to Milena*. Transl. T. & J. Stern. London: Secker & Warburg.
Kafka, F. (1961). *Metamorphosis and Other Stories*. Trans. W. Muir & E. Muir. Harmondsworth: Penguin.
Kafka, F. (1977). *Letters to Friends, Family and Editors*. Transl. R. and C. Winston. New York: Schocken Books.
Kafka, F. (1988). *The Diaries of Franz Kafka*. 2 vols. Trans. J. Kresh (vol. 1), M. Greenberg (vol. 2). New York: Schocken Books.
Kafka, F. (1990). *Letters to Friends, Family and Editors*. Ed. R. Winston. New York: Schocken Books.
Kafka, F. (2009). *The Metamorphosis, A Hunger Artist, In the Penal Colony, and Other Stories*. Trans. I. Johnston. Arlington, Virginia: Richer Resources.
Keats (1970). *Selected Letters*, ed. R. Gittings. Oxford University Press.
Kierkegaard, S. (1985). *Fear and Trembling*. Trans. A. Hannay. Harmondsworth: Penguin.
Kierkegaard, S. (1992 [1843 in Danish]). *Either/Or*. Trans. A. Hannay. London: Penguin. 1992.
Kierkegaard, S. (1996). *Papers and Journals: A Selection (1834-1855)*, ed. A. Hannay. London: Penguin.
Kierkegaard, S. (2009). *Concluding Unscientific Postscript*. Ed. A. Hannay. Cambridge University Press.
Kitto, H. D. F. (1939). *Greek Tragedy*. London: Methuen.

242 REFERENCES

Klein, M. (1932). *The Psychoanalysis of Children*. London: Hogarth.
Kodalle, K. M. (1998). The utilitarian self and the "useless" passion of faith. In: A. Hannay (Ed.), *The Cambridge Companion to Kierkegaard*, pp. 397–410. Cambridge: Cambridge University Press.
Langer, S. (1942). *Philosophy in a New Key*. Cambridge, Mass: Harvard University Press.
Langer, S. (1946). Introduction to E. Cassirer, *Language and Myth*. New York: Harper.
Langer, S. (1953). *Feeling and Form: A Theory of Art*. London: Routledge.
Larson, T. (2007). *The Memoir and the Memoirist*. Swallow Press: Ohio: Swallow Press.
Lawrence, D. H. (1990 [1923]. *Studies in Classic American Literature*. London: Penguin.
Leatherbarrow, W. J. (1981). *Fedor Dostoevsky*. Boston, Mass: Twayne.
Leatherbarrow, W. J. (1992). *Dostoevsky: The Brothers Karamazov*. Cambridge: Cambridge University Press.
Lloyd-Jones, H. (1970). (Ed.) *The Libation Bearers by Aeschylus*. Englewood Cliffs, NJ: Prentice-Hall.
Malouf, D. (2007). Castle Hill Lear: Patrick White Reappraised. *Times Literary Supplement*, January 5 (pp. 12–13).
Mandel, B. J. (1980). Full of life now. In J. Olney (Ed.), *Autobiography, Essays Theoretical and Critical* (pp. 49-72). Princeton UP.
Matlaw, R. (1967). *The Brothers Karamazov: Novelistic Techniques*. The Hague: Mouton.
Matlaw, R. E. (1976). On translating *The Brothers Karamazov* In: R. E. Matlaw (Ed.), *The Brothers Karamazov* (pp. 736–745). New York: Norton.
McCourt, F. (2005). *Teacher Man*. London: Harper.
McFarlane, J. (1988). Introduction to *An Enemy of the People; The Wild Duck; Rosmersholm*, pp. ix–xxv. Oxford: Oxford University Press.
Meltzer, D. (1970 [1967]). *The Psychoanalytical Process*. Perthshire: Clunie Press.
Meltzer, D. (1973). *Sexual States of Mind*. Perthshire: Clunie Press.
Meltzer, D. (1978). *The Kleinian Development*. Perthshire: Clunie Press.
Meltzer, D. (1983). *Dream Life*. Perthshire: Clunie Press.
Meltzer, D. (1992). *The Claustrum*. Perthshire: Clunie Press.
Meltzer, D. (2005). Introduction to M. H. Williams, *The Vale of Soulmaking* (pp. xi–xix). London: Karnac.
Meltzer, D., & Williams, M. H. (1988). *The Apprehension of Beauty*. Perthshire: Clunie Press.
Miller, J. H. (1963). *The Disappearance of God*. Cambridge, Mass: Harvard University Press.
Miller, J. H. (1982). *Fiction and Repetition*. Oxford: Blackwell.
Miller, R. F. (1992). *The Brothers Karamazov: Worlds of the Novel*. Boston, Mass: Twayne.
Mills, S. (2006). *Euripides: Bacchae*. London: Duckworth.
Milner, M. [as Joanna Field]. (1986 [1934]). *A Life of One's Own*. Rpt. London: Virago.

REFERENCES 243

Milton, J. (1958). *Prose Writings*. London: Dent.

Milton, J. (1966). *Milton: Poetical Works*, ed. D. Bush. Oxford: Oxford University Press.

Mitchell, S. A. (1998). From ghosts to ancestors: the psychoanalytic vision of Hans Loewald. *International Journal of Relational Perspectives*, 8 (6): 825–855.

Money-Kyrle, R. (1961). *Man's Picture of His World*. London: Duckworth.

Money-Kyrle, R. (2015). *Man's Picture of His World and Three Papers*, ed. M. H. Williams. London: Harris Meltzer Trust.

Montaigne, M. *Essays* (1908 [1603]). (Vol. 3). Trans. J. Florio. London: Richards.

Morley, P. (1972). *The Mystery of Unity: Theme and Technique in the Novels of Patrick White*. Montreal: McGill University Press.

Mortimer, J. (1990). *A Voyage Round my Father*. Harmondsworth: Penguin.

Morwood, J. (Trans.) (1997). *Euripides: Medea and Other Plays*, ed. E. Hall. Oxford University Press.

Morwood, J. (Trans.) (1999). *Euripides: Bacchae and Other Plays*, ed. E. Hall. Oxford University Press.

Moss, W. G. (2002). *Russia in the Age of Alexander II, Tolstoy and Dostoevsky*. London: Anthem Press.

Muir, E. (1980). *An Autobiography*. London: Hogarth Press.

Murray, N. (2004). *Kafka*. NJ: Yale University Press.

Nachmani, G. (2009). Personal communication.

O'Gorman, E., & Zajko, V. (Eds.) (2013). *Classical Myth and Psychoanalysis*. Oxford: Oxford University Press.

Olney, J. (1980). Some versions of memory/ some versions of *bios*: the ontology of autobiography. In J. Olney (Ed.) *Autobiography, essays theoretical and critical* (pp. 236-67). Princeton UP.

Orwell, G. (1970 [1931[). A Hanging in Burma. In S. Orwell and I. Angus (Eds.), *Collected Essays, Journalism and Letters of George Orwell*, vol. 1 (pp. 66–71). Harmondsworth: Penguin.

Padel, R. (1982). *In and Out of the Mind: Greek Images of the Tragic Self*. Princeton UP.

Pascal, B. (2005 [1670]). *Pensées*. Trans. R. Ariew. Indianapolis: Hackett.

Perlina, N. (1985). *Varieties of Poetic Utterance: Quotation in* The Brothers Karamazov. Lanham: University Press of America.

Pick, J. (Ed.). (1953). *The Hopkins Reader*. London: Oxford University Press.

Raeburn, D. (Ed.). (2008). *Sophocles: Electra and Other Plays*. London: Penguin.

Ricoeur, P. (2004). *Memory, History, Forgetting*. Trans. K. Blamey and D. Pellauer. Chicago: University of Chicago Press.

Robert, M. (1982). *Franz Kafka's Loneliness*. Trans. R. Manheim. London: Faber.

Robertson, R. (2002). *Kafka: A Very Short Introduction*. Oxford University Press.

Rousseau, J. (1782). *Confessions*. Trans. W. Conyngham Mallory. *Talebooks.com*.

Russell, F. (1998). *Northrop Frye on Myth*. New York: Garland, 1998.

REFERENCES

Rutherford, R. (1996). Introduction to *Euripides: Medea and Other Plays*. London: Penguin.

Rutherford, R. (1998). Introduction to *Euripides: Electra and Other Plays*. London: Penguin.

Rutherford, R. (2005). Introduction to *Euripides: The Bacchae and Other Plays*. London: Penguin.

Schorer, M. (1972). Fiction and the Analogical Matrix. In: W. J. Sale, Jr. (Ed.), *Wuthering Heights* (pp. 371–376). New York: Norton.

Schultz, W. (2000). *Cassirer and Langer on Myth: An Introduction*. London: Routledge.

Shelley, P. B. (1977). *Shelley's Poetry and Prose*, ed. D. H. Reiman & S. B. Powers. New York: Norton.

Sommerstein, A. (2000). *Greek Drama and Dramatists*. London: Routledge.

Sommerstein, A. (Ed.) (2009). *The Persians and Other Plays*. London: Penguin.

Sommerstein, A. (2010). *Aeschylean Tragedy*. London: Duckworth.

Sprinker, M. (1992). Fictions of the self: the end of autobiography. In Olney, J. (Ed.), *Autobiography, essays theoretical and critical* (pp. 321-42). Princeton: Princeton University Press.

Steven, L. (1989). *Dissociation and Wholeness in Patrick White's Fiction*. Waterloo, Ontario: Wilfrid Laurier University Press.

Stokes, A. (1997 [1947]). *Inside Out*. Reprinted in D. Carrier (Ed.), *England and its Aesthetes* (pp. 69–118). Amsterdam: Overseas Publishers Association.

Sutherland, S. R. (1977). *Atheism and the Rejection of God: Contemporary Philosophy and* The Brothers Karamazov. Oxford: Blackwell.

Thompson, D. O. (1991). *The Brothers Karamazov and the Poetics of Memory*. Cambridge: Cambridge University Press.

Thorlby, A. (1972). *A Student's Guide to Kafka*. London: Heinemann.

Valéry, P. (1938). *The Art of Poetry*. Princeton: Princeton University Press.

Van Ghent, D. (1961). *The English Novel: Form and Function*. New York: Harper Torchbooks.

Vellacott, P. (1961). (Ed.) *Aeschylus: Prometheus Bound and Other Plays*. London: Penguin.

Vellacott, P. (1963). Introduction. *Euripides: Medea. Hecabe. Electra. Heracles*. Harmondsworth: Penguin.

Vellacott, P. (1969). Introduction. *Aeschylus: The Oresteian Trilogy*. Harmondsworth: Penguin.

Vernant, J. P. & Vidal-Naquet, P. (1988). *Myth and Tragedy in Ancient Greece*. Trans. J. Lloyd. New York: Zone Books.

Vogler, T. (1968). Story and History in *Wuthering Heights*. In: T. Vogler (Ed.), *Wuthering Heights: Twentieth Century Interpretations* (pp. 28–43). Englewood Cliffs, NJ: Prentice Hall.

Walters, D. (2009). Transference and countertransference as existential themes in the psychoanalytic theory of W. R. Bion. *Psychodynamic Practice* 15: 161-172.

White, P. (1961). *Riders in the Chariot*. London: Eyre and Spottiswoode.

White, P. (1973). *The Vivisector*, Harmondsworth: Penguin.

White, P. (1988). *Flaws in the Glass*. London: Vintage.

Williams, M. H. (1987). *A Strange Way of Killing: The Poetic Structure of* Wuthering Heights. Perthshire: Clunie Press.

Williams, M. H. (1994). A man of achievement: Sophocles' Oedipus plays. *British Journal of Psychotherapy* 11 (2): 232–241.

Williams, M. H. (2005a). The three vertices: science, art and religion. *British Journal of Psychotherapy* 21: 429-441.

Williams, M. H. (2005b). *The Vale of Soulmaking: The Post-Kleinian Model of the Mind*. London: Karnac.

Williams, M. H. (2008). The hieroglyphics of Catherine: Emily Bronte and the musical matrix. In: S. Hagan & J. Wells (Eds.), *The Brontes in the World of the Arts* (pp. 81–100). Aldershot: Ashgate.

Williams, M. H. (2009). The evolution of artistic faith in Patrick White's *Riders in the Chariot*. *Ariel, 40 (4)*: 47–68.

Williams, M. H. (2010). *The Aesthetic Development: The Poetic Spirit of Psychoanalysis*. London: Karnac.

Williams, M. H. (2012). On psychoanalytic autobiography. *Psychodynamic Practice*, 18 (4), pp. 397–412.

Williams, M. H. (2013). Playing with fire: Prometheus and the mythological consciousness. In: V. Zajko & E. O'Gorman (Eds.), *Classical Myth and Psychoanalysis* (pp. 233–250). Oxford: Oxford University Press.

Williams, M. H. (2014). Louise Bourgeois and the witches: the complexity of the feminine in the art of Louise Bourgeois. In: R. L. Andreassen & L. H. Willumsen (Eds.), *Steilneset Memorial: Art, Architecture, History*, pp. 21– 29. Stamsund, Norway: Orkana.

Williams, M. H. (2015). The infant and the infinite: on psychoanalytic faith. *Psychodynamic Practice* 21 (2), pp. 112–125.

Williams, M. H. (2017). The oedipal wound in two stories by Kafka. *Psychodynamic Practice* 23 (2), pp. 120–132.

Winnington-Ingram, R. P. (1983). *Studies in Aeschylus*. Cambridge University Press.

Woodhouse, C. M. (1982). How Plato won the west. In: M. Holroyd (Ed.)., *Essays by Divers Hands*, vol. 42, pp. 121–142. London: Royal Society of Literature.

Woolf, V. (2002 [1940]). Sketch of the Past. In J. Schulkind (Ed.), *Moments of Being* (pp. 78–160). London: Pimlico.

Yeats, W.B. (1936). Introduction to *Oxford Book of Modern Verse, 1892–1935*. Oxford University Press.

Zajko, V. (2009). Mutilated towards alignment. In: R. Rees (Ed.), *Ted Hughes and the Classics* (pp. 100–119). Oxford University Press.

Zajko, V., & Leonard, M. (Eds.) (2006). *Laughing with Medusa: Classical Myth and Feminist Thought*. Oxford: Oxford University Press.

Zenkovsky, V. V. (1962). Dostoevsky's religious and philosophical views. In: R. Wellek (Ed.), *Dostoevsky: Twentieth Century Views* (pp. 130–145). Englewood Cliffs, NJ: Prentice Hall.

INDEX

Abraham, K. 3, 4, 5, 17
adolescence 66, 84, 88, 111, 122, 146,
    167
    and the artist xii, 112–114, 153
    confusion 21
    and the group 115, 117, 127, 141
    and sexuality 12, 55
    turbulence 71, 160, 171
Aeschylus 6ff, 19, 21, 22ff, 42
    Choephori 19, 22–25
    evolution and fate 11, 16
    Prometheus Bound 7–17
    revenge, nature of 25
aesthetic conflict xi, 65, 84, 104, 131,
    132, 181, 232, 233
    and catastrophic change 181
    deflected/retreat from 45, 113,
    117, 157, 165, 176
aesthetic object 233, 234
    psychoanalytic process as 236
    see also internal object
aesthetic structure x–xi, xii, 45, 52,
    71, 209, 213, 218, 231,
    of personality ix, xi
    in philosophy 1, 71, 188

and post-Kleinian model 2
    and symbol-formation x, 1
alter-ego 5, 31, 60, 89, 135, 139,
    142, 156, 160, 172, 177, 199
analyst, qualities of 17, 206, 209,
    221, 224, 226, 230, 235, 236
analyst-figure, in literature xii, 14,
    17, 63, 68, 89, 99, 119, 126,
    148, 153, 207, 221, 226
    caricatured 123, 170
Aristotle x, xii, 5, 38, 42
art-symbol xi, 2, 43, 71, 189, 190,
    196, 203
    see also symbol-formation
autobiography xii, 122, 124, 134,
    205ff
basic assumptions (Bion) 23, 39,
    103, 106, 112, 114, 148, 158,
    235
Bernstein, L. 189
Bion, W. R. 7, 16, 20, 38, 65, 114,
    119, 147, 205, 206, 226, 228,
    230, 234, 235
    alpha- and beta- elements 83,
    128

248 INDEX

autobiography 210, 211
endoskeleton *vs.* exoskeleton
   63, 88, 100, 158
faith 224–225
the Grid 3, 4
knowing *vs.* knowing about 8,
   11, 101, 203, 212, 229, 232,
   236
lies *vs.* truth 100, 209
memory 220, 228
pain vs. suffering 9, 68, 82
"O" 16, 70, 185, 221, 223,
   225–227, 230, 232
Ps<–>D 215, 232
psyche-lodgement 88, 101, 231
three vertices (art, science,
   religion) 109, 126, 209
   see also basic assumptions;
catastrophic change
Blake, W. 124, 132, 191, 198, 216,
   230, 232
Bollack, J. 12, 14, 15
Boswell, J. 206
Bourgeois, L. 43, 55
Brecht, B. 21
Britton, R. 232
Bronte, C. 70, 75
Bronte, E., and music 65–86
   and Byron 66
   on memory 69
   and Platonic Idea 70
Byron, G. G. 66–69, 71, 81
Campbell, J. 4
Carroll, L. 220
Cassirer, E. 2, 4, 17, 189
catastrophic change (Bion) x, xii,
   14, 16, 38, 60, 65, 68, 89, 97, 111,
   131, 153, 180, 181, 225, 228,
   231, 235
Cecil, D. 72
claustrum (Meltzer) x, 63, 65, 116,
   123, 145, 153, 158, 214
Coleridge, S. T. 5, 6, 7, 70, 85, 188,
   190, 194, 201, 208, 210, 212,
   219, 222
combined object 38, 62, 97, 109
confusion of identity 21, 24, 71,

121, 162, 169, 171, 193, 218
Conrad, J. 209, 210
container–contained (Bion) xi
creativity ix, 1, 2, 6, 11, 13, 15, 16,
   57, 71, 76, 203, 220
   and destruction/wounding 55,
      79, 88, 90, 97, 147, 150, 189
   as evolving O 16
   and faith 85, 188
   and internal objects 112
   parodied 53, 143, 182
   vs. play 175, 215
   represented by baby 73, 78, 92,
      225
   and repression 102, 146
   and three vertices 108–109, 226
   see also inspiration
curiosity/K-link xi, 11, 53, 58, 76,
   84, 105, 178, 182, 221, 232
   intrusive 62, 64, 170
Davies, S. 72, 84
death and life forces/instincts 13,
   16, 53, 67, 97, 156, 168
   see also creativity
depressive position 143, 172, 215,
   218, 231, 236
Dickinson, E. 233–234
Dodds, E. R. 55
Dostoevsky, F. 155–186
   An Accidental Family 20, 167
   The Brothers Karamazov 156,
      159ff
   devil's advocate 167, 184
   The Idiot 156
   internalisation 185
   Notes from Underground 94,
      157ff
   psychology caricatured 169,
      175ff, 183
   sadomasochism in 182
   splitting and integration 156,
      158–159, 162, 166
   teaching methods 172–175
dreams/fantasy 22, 24, 55ff, 66, 78,
   119, 169, 192, 198, 219
   aboriginal 197, 202
   countertransference 63, 199, 207

creative 69, 71, 127, 129, 132, 178

disturbing 22, 27, 61, 63, 83, 112, 113, 116, 145, 171

forensic 125

as internal characters 7, 11, 12, 59, 68, 149, 167

narratives 56, 78, 82, 89ff, 111, 122, 134, 197, 208, 217

theory of 3–5, 17, 89

education, of the personality xii, 73, 74, 84, 88, 102, 155ff, 184, 192, 199

false 121, 140, 160, 163, 174, 179

Eliot, T. S. 214

envy 119, 125, 228

aspirational 84, 167

Euripides xi, 20, 32ff

The Bacchae 55–64

Electra 32–38

Medea 43–55

as psychologist 28, 46, 59, 62

religious language 61

on women and patriarchy 50, 63

faith, in internal objects 85, 132, 155, 164, 168, 180, 195, 201

artistic-poetic 130, 188, 200

lack of 87, 99, 100, 108, 109, 161, 166, 168, 169, 211

psychoanalytic 223ff

fantasy/phantasy, role of 5, 17, 20, 23, 63, 114, 120, 132, 133, 150, 227, 232

of parental intercourse 20, 34, 95, 181

unconscious (Klein) 227

see also dreams

Finney, B. 206, 208, 210, 214

Forster, E. M. 69, 156, 184, 210

Freud, S. 6, 42, 87, 108, 125, 208, 223, 224, 227, 232, 235, 236

dream theory 5, 89

extended knowledge 213, 225

two principles 13, 156, 232

Gammill, J. 207

Gaskell, E. 74, 75

Gerin, W. 74

Goodridge, J. F. 72

Greenberg, M. 108

Gusdorf, G. 209, 211, 214, 221

Hall, E. 17, 20, 52

Hannay, A. 229, 231

Harris, M. 2, 216, 235

Harris, R. J. 234–235

Herring, R. 220

Holland, N. 213

Hopkins, G. M. 213

Ibsen, H. XII, 111ff

adolescent group 115, 117, 127, 141

artist and muse 112, 144, 149

Brand 112–114

life-lie 112, 132, 133, 137, 142, 143, 144

The Master Builder 144–146

mother, internal 113, 128, 132

Peer Gynt

trolldom 117, 131

When We Dead Awaken 147–153

The Wild Duck 132–144

Idea, Platonic/underlying 1, 2–3, 5, 7, 67, 68, 70, 74, 83, 85, 156, 189, 203, 225, 234

in art-symbol 196, 215

of beauty 97

and classical Necessity 11

vs. idealisation 113, 144, 150, 156

parodied 173

and psyche-lodgement 88

identity x, 20, 35, 48, 59, 60, 63, 71, 87, 93, 123, 133, 173, 193, 203, 213 , 229

false or lost 101, 231

"no identity" (Keats) 211

infant ego/child parts xi, 5, 8, 9, 16, 24, 42, 93, 121, 132, 159, 223, 224, 225, 227

and aesthetic conflict 232

narcissistic/omnipotent 228, 231, 236

somatic demands 91

250 INDEX

inner world xi, 12, 30, 32, 90, 108, 111, 140, 156, 208, 220, 225, 230, 232
inspiration 17, 69, 70, 114, 167, 184, 191, 194. 195, 203
    caricatured 140–141
    muse figure xi, 38, 69, 80, 112, 144ff, 233
    see also creativity, internal object
internalisation/ introjection 68, 76, 83, 89, 164, 168, 170, 179, 180
    extreme/ possessive 58, 127
    of functions 228
    and mourning 185, 208, 220
internal object xi, 4, 69, 112, 117, 123, 130, 132, 139, 164, 169, 176, 183, 217, 221, 224, 225, 233, 235
    combined 38, 62, 97, 109
    developing/ evolutionary 227, 228
    educational 229, 231
    vs. instincts 43
    intrusion into 25, 32, 61, 63, 232
    transference from 236
    tyrannical 24, 49, 63, 161
    see also aesthetic object; creativity; inspiration, muse
James, C. 214
James, W. 223, 227
Janouch, G. 87 ff
Joyce, J. 208
Jung, C. 2, 3, 4, 13, 19, 42, 190, 208, 214, 223
Kafka, F. xi,
    A Country Doctor 97–101
    father, conflict with 87, 93
    The Great Wall of China 103
    infant's somatic experience 93–96, 101, 104
    Investigations of a Dog 103–109
    language and society 100, 102
    The Metamorphosis 90–97
    music and religion in 104, 109

and psychoanalysis 87, 98, 99, 108
A Report to an Academy 101–103
the wound 88, 92, 95, 98
on writing 89, 93
Keats, J. x, 7, 10, 16, 17, 38, 90, 99, 105, 138, 151, 158, 188, 211, 213, 236
Kerenyi, C. 3, 13
Kierkegaard, S. 82, 85, 87, 88, 187, 188, 201, 202, 211, 212, 215, 228–231
Kitto, H. D. F. 32, 58
Klein, M. x, 2, 6, 42, 149, 207, 218, 220, 224, 227, 231, 232, 235
Langer, S. 1, 2, 3, 4, 5, 17, 71, 74, 78, 86, 189
Larson, T. 207, 214, 219
Lawrence, D. H. 212, 214, 217
LHK (love, hate, knowledge) x, 84, 93, 143, 165, 231, 229, 232
    negative of 117
    see also aesthetic conflict
Lloyd-Jones, H. 24
Mandel, B. 206
masochism/ sadomasochism 27, 66, 68, 80, 86, 171, 172, 177, 182, 225, 227, 230
    vs. pain-talk 236
Matisse, H. 215
McCourt, F. 217, 218, 219
McFarlane, J. 111
Meltzer, D. 4, 8, 24, 208, 211, 217, 224, 225, 226, 227, 229, 231
    aesthetic conflict 65, 232
    claustrum 63, 145
    dreams and religion 2, 8
    symbol-formation 217, 228
    transference–countertransference 207, 221, 236
memory, function of 14, 71, 83, 95, 102, 104, 114, 117, 162, 192, 206, 220, 228
    in autobiography 207, 214, 220–222
    dead or useless 69, 142, 148, 216

as education 159, 180, 184
weaving of 79, 120, 219
Miller, J. H. 72
Mills, S. 55
Milner, M. 214, 215
Milton, J. ix, 5, 7, 10, 49, 66, 70, 75, 81, 151, 155, 167, 194, 226
Money-Kyrle, R. 2, 20, 67, 181, 225, 228, 230, 232
Montaigne, M. 207
Moore, T. 66, 71
Mortimer, J. 219
Muir, E. 206, 208
Munch, E. 133
music, function of 33, 65ff, 94–97, 104, 107, 108, 193–195, 198, 201
and "O" / Platonic Idea 70, 74, 78, 83
myth 1ff, 19, 43, 45, 60, 64, 160
and psychoanalysis 1–6
and religion 6, 38, 58, 224
Nachmani, G. 221
narcissism/omnipotence x, xi, 6, 15, 55, 59, 86, 117, 140, 151, 176, 191, 214, 225, 228, 231
see also tyranny, internal
object relations xi, 3, 4, 17, 69, 112, 130, 181, 185, 202, 217, 224, 225, 227, 231, 236
conversations of (Meltzer) 221
vs. egotism/narcissism 6, 68, 117, 124, 161, 167
part-objects 53, 220, 232
see also internal object
observation ix, 148, 188, 189, 206, 209, 210, 215, 217
"third eye" (Bion) 206, 221
see also analyst, qualities of
Odyssey of Homer 208
Oedipus/oedipal conflicts x, 4, 15, 19, 34, 37, 87, 88, 95, 159, 183, 245
and catastrophic change/ K-link 6, 38, 43
parodied 123
perverse 31

Olney, J. 212, 220
omnipotence see narcissism/omnipotence
Orwell, G. 217
Oxford Dictionary of Music 74
Padel, R. 9
pain, depressive/ developmental 8, 9, 10, 13, 14, 15, 88, 143, 172, 236
of not-knowing 232, 235
as suffering 9, 68, 82
of writing 215
paranoid-schizoid 215, 218, 232
parents, fantasy of 19, 20, 26, 30, 33, 44, 77, 91, 95, 97, 99, 105, 120, 143, 145, 159, 164, 181, 197, 219
patriarchy 39, 47, 48, 50, 51, 55, 56, 103
perversity xi, 31, 45, 48, 52, 62, 67, 144, 171, 177, 227
reversal of 65ff
phantasy, unconscious see dreams/ fantasy
Plato/Socrates x, 2, 4, 5, 17, 25, 35, 70, 85, 99, 151, 189, 197, 223, 224, 225, 230, 232, 234
realist-idealists vs. nominalists (Money-Kyrle) 225
post-Kleinian model x, 2, 227, 232
preconception 2, 16, 89, 138, 183, 218, 220
projective identification 22, 27, 31, 62, 67, 100, 117, 138, 161, 176, 230
psyche-lodgement (Bion) 88, 91, 101, 102, 196, 231
Psychoanalytic Association of Biella vii, 63
puberty 12, 79, 111, 132, 133, 136, 137, 143, 144, 160, 171, 174
religion 2, 57, 68, 72, 85, 87, 97, 99, 103, 106, 108, 123, 155, 161, 168, 224, 230
fundamentalist 106, 124, 231
and psychoanalysis 223, 227, 229, 232, 235

252 INDEX

three vertices 104, 109, 225-226
Ricoeur, P. 220
Rousseau, J. 3, 122, 209
Schorer, M. 74
self-analysis xii, 2, 10, 65, 85, 87,
124, 156, 171, 206, 212, 221,
229
see also self-knowledge
self-knowledge 2, 5, 43, 90, 121,
177, 181, 210, 214
vs. external/ intellectual 101,
106, 174, 182
see also Bion, knowing *vs.*
knowing about; curiosity/
K-link
Sella, S. M. vii
sexuality, types of 20, 23, 51, 53, 58,
136, 138, 140, 177, 197
see also parents, fantasy of
Shakespeare, W. 7, 11, 38, 41, 60, 63,
66, 70, 96, 102, 125, 145, 181,
193, 214, 216, 222, 228
Shaw, G. B. 206, 210
Shelley, P. B. 7, 9, 11, 12, 15, 17, 75
somatic experience 8, 73, 91, 92,
101, 104, 136, 171, 172
Sophocles 21, 24, 33, 34, 35, 36, 41,
42
Antigone 27
Electra 25-32
Oedipus Tyrannus xi, 19, 30, 38,
43
Stokes, A. 149, 218
superego 12, 42, 43, 93, 113, 135,
145, 147, 168, 176, 208, 215,
227
symbol-formation 1, 20, 76, 81, 83,
123, 189, 217, 226, 230, 235
see also art-symbol
thinking/thought 2, 8, 20, 39, 66,

85, 119, 128, 176, 188, 236
growth of 8, 16, 17
vs. unthinking 83, 95, 112, 115,
142, 180
Tolstoy, L. 213, 220
transference 126, 146, 171, 207, 220,
227, 229, 236
countertransference 63, 199,
207, 234
truth, psychic xii, 13–14, 37, 65, 76,
103, 105, 109, 111, 114, 155,
172, 187, 208, 217
aesthetic and psychoanalytic
209, 221, 226, 228
vs. external/factual 15, 121,
134, 142, 153, 183, 206, 212,
221
vs. lies 13, 100, 112, 209, 116,
123, 133, 144, 165, 182
tyranny, internal 7, 8, 10, 19, 24, 61,
63, 67, 85, 124, 151, 218, 219,
225
vs. love 220
see also claustrum; narciss-
ism/omnipotence
unknown, the 45, 66, 78, 103, 106,
191, 223, 224, 226, 228, 235,
236
caricatured 123
vs. knowing about 229
and Platonic ideas 70
Valéry, P. 208
Van Ghent, D. 73
Vellacott, P. 6
Vernant, J. P. 6, 19, 42
Vogler, T. 73
Walters, D. 229
Woodhouse, C. M. 225
Woolf, V. 206, 213, 215–217
Yeats, W. B. 69, 212, 213, 221